WAIT TILL YOU HEAR THIS . . .

This book is dedicated to the loves of my life –
my wife, Norma, and my children, Ellen,
Marion, Jennifer, Elliott and Spencer,
my 'ma' Bella and Uncle Jim

Wait Till You Hear This . . .

The Life and Laughs of Andy Cameron

Andy Cameron with Norman Macdonald

MAINSTREAM
PUBLISHING

EDINBURGH AND LONDON

First published in Great Britain in 2004 by
MAINSTREAM PUBLISHING COMPANY (EDINBURGH) LTD
7 Albany Street
Edinburgh EH1 3UG

ISBN 1 84018 935 5

A catalogue record for this book is available from the British Library

Typeset in Alternate Gothic2 and Janson Text
Printed and bound in Great Britain by
Mackays of Chatham plc

CONTENTS

Chapter 1

THE BABY FROM THE BLITZ

THE TROOP TRAIN THUNDERED NORTH FROM LONDON TO GLASGOW CARRYING hundreds of soldiers home on leave. The Second World War was raging and the carriages were filled with battle-weary warriors and one gurgling wean with a thumb in its mouth wanting to be fed. That was me.

My father delved into his kit bag and fished out one of the three bottles of baby milk he had prepared before we headed off on the nine-hour train journey. The other soldiers in the carriage simply shook their heads and held their noses as it became apparent that the infant – one Andrew Graham Cameron – needed his nappy changing as well.

The carriage window was opened to let out the smell and some of the soldiers joined in, for them, the rather complicated manoeuvres of changing my nappy. None of your disposable nappies with stick-on fastenings in those days – terry-towelling squares and nappy liners held together by two big safety pins.

After that, it was back to sucking my thumb and falling asleep to the rhythmic motion of the steam train making its way along the tracks to Scotland.

The other guys on the train had given my father, Hugh, a bit of stick as he explained how he had ended up on a troop train with a baby less than a year old in tow. He was heading to Glasgow, taking me to be brought up by his mother, Bella Cameron, in a tenement in Rutherglen. The ribbing got even worse when my father got to the bit about my mother running off with another man in London while he was doing his bit to defeat Rommel on the desert sands of Egypt. Not exactly the stuff of commando comics, but there you go.

However, that's exactly what had happened. I was discovered crying my eyes out in a bombed-out building, in London during the Blitz. I've been told that, while my father was an ambulance driver in the Medical Corps serving under the blazing sun in Egypt, my mother, Pat, was carrying on a dalliance with some other guy back home and I was in the way. My understanding is that she had handed me over to an old lady who was looking after me.

Abandonment is a very strong word, but I definitely feel that I was abandoned when my mother fell for someone else and wanted a new life. I've never seen my mother since, apart from in old photographs and in all my years I never felt the urge to find her again. I have no idea if she is dead or alive.

I was nine months old when the place I was staying in was hit and I was found in the rubble of a bombed-out building. People heard me crying and that's how they found me. I was wrapped in a shawl with my birth certificate tucked inside.

The authorities traced my father to some Army camp in Egypt and he was given compassionate leave to come home and take me back to Rutherglen for his family to care for me.

More than 40 years later, I was watching the news when I saw a story about a baby who had survived in the rubble of a building which had collapsed after an earthquake. The baby survived because it wasn't aware it was in an earthquake. That's what probably happened to me – I was in a bombed-out building, but I just didn't know it at the time. And I was crying only because I was hungry.

I don't know the name of the old woman who was looking after me. All I remember being told is that I was being cared for by her and the house was bombed. I don't even know if that old lady was killed when the bomb hit the house. And neither do I know who found me in the rubble. I wish I did because they probably saved my life and I owe them big time.

So that's how I came to be on a troop train heading for Scotland being cradled by my father and surrounded by soldiers and a bag of my dirty nappies.

I don't know what must have been going through my father's mind on that journey, but by all accounts my mother and father had had a reasonable marriage to start with, after they tied the knot in London in 1939.

My father had left Glasgow in 1935 and headed for London looking for work and that's where he met and fell in love with my mother, Emily Patricia Woods. I was born on 13 October 1940. But within a year of his son being born, my dad had been called up to the Army, everything had turned pear-shaped and here he was heading to Glasgow with a nine-month-old baby for granny to look after.

During his Army training, my father had to have the index finger of his right hand amputated when it became poisoned after an accident. I used to wind up my kids by telling them their granddad doesn't have that finger. They would ask why and I would tell them because I've got it. Silly, but they would fall for it every time.

I suppose what happened with my mother is one of those skeletons people have in their family cupboards. While I was growing up, it was never spoken about and even when I was told, I never heard my granny say a bad word about my natural mother. People are people and they take different roads out of different situations they find themselves in. I'm not saying my mother took the easy road out of a situation where she had a baby, a husband off fighting in a foreign land and she had fallen in love with another man. I'm sure it was difficult for her, but she took the road which was best for her.

I was gone and that was it – finished. I was the unwanted luggage and my mother's solution was to have someone else look after me. It was the circumstances of war and I don't have any feelings towards her either way. I don't condone what she did, as there were plenty of women who did hang on and wait for their husbands to come home from the war. After all, nobody knew if their loved one was going to come back alive. My mother was just one of a million women who fell for someone else while their boyfriend or husband was away from home fighting.

In many ways, I'm neutral about what my mother did and I'm not bitter or hateful. Years later, my father explained to me what happened and that lots of other men found themselves in the same situation. The only time I was ever curious was when I was in my early 20s. I was visiting my father in London and I asked him to explain what had happened between him and my mother.

He told me the story and asked if I wanted to go and see her. He knew she had remarried, was living in the Whitechapel area of the city and had eight children with her new husband.

Although I had eight stepbrothers and sisters whom I have never met, I said I didn't want to see her. She was my biological mother, but I had no inclination to meet her and ask her why she did what she did. I already knew why, as my father had explained it to me. It was just one of those things. After all, my mother had never tried to contact me, so I didn't try to contact her.

Strangely, though, when I'm asked by people in the banks for my mother's maiden name, I always say Woods – my biological mother's maiden name. But the only mother I ever had was my granny, Bella – she was the best thing that ever happened to me. In fact, my mother probably did me a favour because I couldn't have had a better upbringing and childhood.

So there I was being carried up the tenement stairs in Rutherglen by my father to be introduced to my new mother and father in the shape of grandparents Bella and Old Andra Cameron. For those first seven years of my life, Bella and Andra were my mammy and daddy as far as I was concerned and that's what I called them. I never knew any different and in this case, ignorance was certainly bliss.

No doubt there was a roaring fire as warm as the welcome I got at my granny and granddad's on 6 Bouverie Street, Rutherglen, when my father and I arrived after our train journey from London.

Like thousands of other families in Glasgow in those days, life was a room and kitchen in a tenement flat. Through the close and up one flight of well-cleaned stairs – Bella saw to that – there was the Cameron residence. Walk into the lobby and you'd see the coal bunker and my Uncle Jim's bike leaning against the wall. In the kitchen, your eyes set upon the big black fireplace and grate, which was always shining, and in it, a blazing coal fire. There was the sink – or jawbox as it used to be called – with a brass handle for the cold-water tap and in the middle of the room a table where the family always gathered at meal times.

Old Andra and Bella's chairs were either side of the fire and there was a set-in bed (as in, a bed set into a recess) and a cot for me next to the bed. A gas lamp provided the light when it got dark. Through in the other room there was another set-in bed and a bed settee and a few bits and pieces of furniture.

The room window looked out onto Bouverie Street and the kitchen window looked onto the backcourt and behind that, the corporation cleansing yard. In the backcourt, there was the wash house, which played a major part in tenement life, and two greens. The bigger of the two was where the people living in the tenement took turns to hang out their washing on particular days of the week and the other, smaller, green was for the youngsters to play on.

The toilet was outside on the landing and was always immaculate. And it's no joke – yes, we did use newspapers cut into squares as toilet paper! In 1951, when electricity was being installed in the building, the tenants paid extra to have a light in the outside toilet. That was down to Bella, who cleaned John Paton's house – the contractor installing the electricity. She spoke to him and organised the deal. The flats in the tenement were privately rented and the factor was Speirs and Adam, in Abercromby Street, Glasgow.

My granny, Bella, was 48 years old and had plenty of practice bringing up a family when my father and I arrived on her doorstep. After she married Andrew Cameron in 1911, she had given birth to seven children – Alec, Leezie, my father Hugh, Andrew, Isa, Marion and Jim – and they all grew up in the room and kitchen which was to become my home. Sadly, one of her children, Leezie, died of diphtheria when she was only three.

When it came to names, ours was a strange family. Bella was my granny's name, but Old Andra never called her Bella because he never liked the name so he called her Molly. My father's name was Hugh, but everybody you speak to in Rutherglen knew him as Dougie. I've no idea why people called him Dougie. My Auntie Marion was always known as Big Aggie. Another was my father's second wife, Doris, who was only ever called Redhead by him. Obviously, she had a beautiful head of red hair. But it was like being in the CIA – everybody had a different name.

And there were Andrew Camerons everywhere you turned. When I was getting married to my second wife, Norma, she said there was no way any of our children were being called Andrew because there were that many of them in the family already. There was Old Andra my granddad, his son Andrew and my uncle who was eventually known as Baldy Andra, then there was Young Andra – that was me – and Ginger Andra, who was my Uncle Andrew's boy.

Undoubtedly, the most important person to me and the biggest influence in the early years of my life was Bella. Words can't begin to explain how much I loved her, and how much I owe her for what she did for me – but I'll try. She not only looked after me as a mother, she shaped my life. Everything I am is down to Bella.

Isabella Campbell was born in 1893 at 12 Bouverie Street, Rutherglen, and for the next 70 years she would live no further away than a few closes from her birthplace. She left school at 11 years old and was put to work by her father helping him to make wire baskets and machine guards.

Her father, Hugh Campbell, was a 'bad auld bugger' according to Bella. Working long hours feeding him the wire from huge balls, she would sometimes nod off, only to be woken by a rap on the knuckles with his wire cutters. This not only kept her awake, but made sure she had the fastest hands in Rutherglen, as I found out to my cost any time I was cheeky.

Despite leaving school at such an early age, Bella could write beautifully and could count quicker than any calculator – especially when it came to money. Bella had a hard life, an extremely hard life looking after her family in the worst of economic conditions and she worked like a Trojan to bring money into the house. For years, she cleaned four houses a day to earn a wage and before she left for her work, Bella made sure there was a fire on in the house for the rest of us to get up to.

She was a typical Glasgow housewife in those days and was always one for fair play, common sense and taking on your responsibilities. In a nutshell, if it was your turn to clean the stairs, you should clean the stairs. But if you were having a baby or were ill, she would take your turn because you would do the same for her.

With all that went on in her life, it must have flown by, and the fact that she looked after herself until she died in 1983 when she was 90 says so much for her character. Bella was so many different things rolled into one – the washer woman, the cleaner woman, the one that fixed things in the house and the one who would fix you if you didn't toe the line.

Bella taught you to have respect for yourself and other people. She hated bullies and would have stood up to Goliath if somebody was being wronged. She was also a great enthusiast for life and, like me, she was an optimist – a glass-half-full person. If something went wrong, Bella would say, 'Tomorrow's another day and we haven't died a winter yet.'

I loved Bella's socialism. It wasn't a socialism in terms of politics, but in the way she behaved and treated other people. She would say, 'I'm not any better than anybody else, but I'm just as good as anybody else.' She treated everybody as an equal and would have spoken to the Queen the same way as she spoke to the neighbours upstairs.

Bella never swore but her big phrase was, 'Away to buggery!' If anybody went near her washing when it was out drying in the back green, Bella would shout, 'Here you, get yourself to buggery!'

Although I was brought up in a Protestant family who were diehard Rangers FC supporters, Bella – who was also in the Eastern Star, the female equivalent of the Masons – wouldn't put up with any bigotry. Old Andra's youngest brother, Duncan, had married a Catholic girl from Cleland, in Lanarkshire, Catherine Kelly, and when he had a drink in him he used to sing 'The Sash'. Bella got a hold of him one day and warned, 'You're going to lose a good wife carrying on like that and it's not fair.'

One word led to another and before long the whole family were having their say. The upshot was that both my Uncle Duncan and Aunt Cathy joined the Salvation Army. They emigrated to Canada in 1951 and their daughter, Cathy, is now a major in the Salvation Army over there.

On another occasion, my granddad, Old Andra, decided he wasn't going to his son Alec's wedding because he was marrying his girlfriend Lizzie Maguire in the chapel. Old Andra was doing the big Presbyterian thing at the time. 'I'll no' be in any chapel. I'm not going to the wedding,' he declared. However, Bella had different ideas. 'Aye, you'll be going to the chapel,' she declared. 'He's your boy and it's his decision. You're going and that's the end of it.' Needless to say, Old Andra was at the wedding in the chapel.

Bella always said that her son, Alec, got himself a wife in a million. In those days, people said mixed marriages didn't work. But of course it works if the two people love each other and are right for each other. A Catholic marrying a Protestant was a big thing in those days, but thankfully it doesn't bother people so much nowadays.

When I sit and think about Bella, what I loved about her was the laughs we had together. Making her laugh was a joy because she loved laughing and loved to hear other people laughing. 'The best sound in the world is a wean laughing,' she used to say. And she could raise a laugh herself. There was a grocery van called Bobby's Biscuit Bus, which came round the streets of Rutherglen. Shortly after Britain joined the Common Market, Bella's in the van and asking for a pound of tomatoes. 'You'll have to get modern, Bella,' says Bobby. 'We're in the Common Market now and it's kilos.' Bella replies, 'All right then, give me a pound of kilos!'

But sometimes she had a temper on her as well. I remember we had dried egg during the war and one day Bella and Old Andra were having a real shouting match at the table when she got so angry she threw the dried egg at him and the powder went all over the rest of us. We just sat there, covered in yellow powder, gobsmacked at what had just gone on. Of course, I was a wee clype and when our Doctor Cairnduff came to see Old Andra, I had to tell him that Bella had thrown dried egg all over him.

After Doctor Cairnduff retired, a Dr McMillan took over and he was the father of Robbie Coltrane, who is now a successful TV and film actor. One day, Dr McMillan came to see Bella, who was suffering from bad knees, and told her she must be getting on and near the half-century. Bella says, 'Nothing like a half-century – I'm only 54!' Although Bella could count, a century meant nothing to her.

Everyone in the tenement knew Bella's kindness. Even when she was in her 80s she was helping folk. One of our neighbours upstairs was Aggie Forsyth, who was a year younger than Bella but couldn't really look after herself. Bella would crawl up the stairs with a cup of tea and a biscuit for Aggie and come down the stairs backwards, her legs were that bad.

Bella was a great template to set your life by and if you lived your life according to Bella's credo you wouldn't go far wrong. She was only 4 ft 11 in. and built like a whippet, but she had the heart of a lion. When people describe someone they admire as a diamond or a gem, I've got to say that Bella was the crown jewels. Even though she lived a long and full life, I was still devastated when she died. Bella may have gone, but a big part of her lives on with me.

My granddad, Old Andra, was blighted by ill health after breathing mustard gas in the trenches during the First World War. Although he lived until 1948, Bella always said he was killed in the war, but it took 30 years for him to die.

Jobs were hard to come by and it was even harder for the family that Andra's bad health meant he never held down a job for long periods. For years, he suffered terribly from the effects of the mustard gas on his lungs and chest. At times, he would be gasping for breath just walking up the stairs. When he wasn't able to work because of his ill health – and that was quite a lot – he would take me by the hand and say that we would go for a wee dauner. That's the first word I remember – dauner, a wee walk.

Out into the street we would go with our dog, Glen, at our heels, slowly walking past tenement closes and saying hello to the folks as we passed them by, sometimes even stopping for a few moments to hear the latest gossip. Our destination was always Jenny's Burn because that was as far as Old Andra could go before he was out of breath. There was a bridge over the burn and as well as watching the water pass by we would watch the world go by. Old Andra would sit me up on the bridge parapet, my legs hanging over the inside of the wall and he would warn me to be careful not to fall.

He may have had a bad chest, but that wouldn't stop him puffing away at his Woodbines. He could hardly breathe at times, but he couldn't do without his cigarettes. Our little sojourn would happen every day during the summer and with Glen the dog sitting at Old Andra's feet and me watching the comings and goings of the wagons out of the corporation cleansing yard across the road, passers-by would stop and chat, asking how Bella and the rest of the family were.

Old Andra liked a laugh as well and he used to say to me that for a while he worked in the British Rope Works, at Farm Cross, Rutherglen, but he got his books for skipping out. It took me years to realise it was a joke. And years later I'm still telling that joke to my own sons, Elliott and Spencer.

Old Andra's sister Jean – whom I always called Auntie Jean, although she was my father's aunt – would tell me about growing up with my granddad. There were eight of them in a single end. Three of the girls slept in a bed, which was UNDER the bed. Their father had built this contraption so that it slid out from under the bed at night for them to sleep in.

Auntie Jean told me this story once about Andra putting his hand up the chimney to get soot on his hand and rubbing the dirt onto the faces of his three sisters while they were still asleep. Andra would get up at 6 a.m. to head for the rope works and the three sisters wouldn't get up for another hour for their jobs at the chenille factory at the bottom of Cathcart Street, at the back of the Quarry Bar, in Rutherglen. This morning, though, the girls – Jean, Meg and Thea – slept in and rushed out the house without washing properly and walked into their work with black marks all over their faces. Aye, Old Andra liked a laugh right enough, but he caught a right load of abuse off the girls when they got home that night.

Not all my aunts and uncles – or brothers and sisters as I thought they were for the first few years of my life – were staying at home with Bella and Old Andra. My father, of course, went back to serve in the Army during the war before settling in London. Uncle Alec was also in the Army and my Aunt Isa was in the Land Army based at Barlair Farm, New Luce, near Stranraer. Although she would often be home on leave – much to my delight.

My Aunt Marion was still in the house, as were Uncles Andrew and Jim. Jim was the youngest – a Bevin Boy working down the pits – and would have been 16 when I appeared on the scene as a new 'wee brother' for him. Sadly, Uncle Jim and Uncle Andrew are the only two members of that fantastic family alive today. I still see them regularly.

There can be no doubt that, as the first grandchild, I was spoiled rotten by everyone in the house, especially by my Auntie Isa and Auntie Marion. Of all Bella's children, Isa was the character and a half. Being in the Land Army she had muscles like a man and could fight like one too. I can still see her in my mind flexing her muscles and telling me, 'Go on, feel how hard they are.'

When Isa came home it was great fun. There were sweets for treats after running an errand for her and she taught you valuable lessons about growing up and looking after yourself. Isa had a very good friend, Nicole – who, although being French, spoke perfect English – and the two of them eventually emigrated to New Zealand together in 1951. I was sad to see Auntie Isa go.

I just loved it when Auntie Isa came back from the Land Army on leave. She was another one who smoked like a lum. She would say, 'Go and get me ten Woodbines from Ogg's corner shop and get yourself a Mars Bar.' I loved going to Ogg's, and not just to get a Mars Bar. I was in love with Mr Ogg's daughter, Aileen, who was about the same age as me, but stayed at the other end of Rutherglen. The only time I would see her was when she was helping out her dad during school holidays. And getting a Mars Bar was a really big deal – especially for a kid in Bouverie Street, as nobody got one in our street. It was like being the Pied Piper of

Hamelin – all the children following you pleading 'gonnae gie's a bit?'.

Rhubarb Rock was another favourite of mine. It was cheaper than a Mars Bar, but just as enjoyable.

Isa and her brother Jim used to fight like cat and dog when she was home and they were always arguing. They had different views on things, as brothers and sisters do. If she got annoyed or Uncle Jim got the better of her in an argument she would sit in a chair facing him pretending to read a book with two fingers sticking up just to annoy him.

Auntie Isa was a great teacher about life and looking after yourself. Although I couldn't fight sleep, Auntie Isa taught me that I should always be ready to stand up for myself and never be bullied. I was always a wee bit scared of bullies when I was very young until Isa put me right one day. I had come up the stairs looking and feeling sorry for myself when Auntie Isa asked what was wrong.

'A bigger boy hit me,' I admitted.

'Why didn't you hit him back?' she asked.

'If I'd hit him back he would have murdered me,' I said shamefaced.

'Well, you'll have to make up your mind – it's either him or me who'll murder you,' she proclaimed. 'Get back down these stairs and hit him back.'

On the very basic point that a doing from the boy was much preferable to a doing from Auntie Isa, back down the stairs I went, found the boy who had hit me and gave him a right good punch. It was his turn for tears and he ran away. I knew then that what my Auntie Isa had always said was true – bullies are only bullies because people let them be bullies. If you hit them back you might get another doing, but the bully will know that he's always going to take a punch if he picks on you.

Isa was that kind of character who stood up for herself and wanted me to be able to do the same – an important lesson I carried through the rest of my life. And it wasn't just me Isa stood up for. She even went into battle for her father. One day, Old Andra comes into the house with a cut eye and blood pouring from his nose. 'Jesus Christ, Andra, is that you drunk and fell up the stairs?' asks Bella.

'Aye, that's right,' says Old Andra. But right at his back is one of our neighbours, Mrs Niven. 'He didn't fall up the stairs at all, Bella,' she says. 'That Bertie Anderson took a liberty and punched him.'

Well, Isa was out the chair, where she had been sitting reading a book, like a greyhound out the traps and headed out the door. I ran after her and caught up with her just in time to see her turning Bertie Anderson round, landing a stoatir of a punch on his jaw and knocking him out cold.

On the odd occasion, my granny and I would go down to New Luce and visit Isa on the farm. Everybody there had a good word for Isa and she was well liked. On one of those visits, I got the chance to go bareback riding on a horse. Well, it wasn't quite Tonto and the Lone Ranger, but since the only horse I'd seen up to then was a clothes-horse, it was a big adventure for me.

Isa was going to the village from the farm to pick something up and she had learned to ride the farm horse bareback. 'Do you want to come?' she asked. And before you could say Stetson and six-shooter, I was being lifted up onto the horse, sitting in front of Auntie Isa. It was a really big horse. Well, when you're wee, every horse is big.

Off we went, and I can still hear the clip-clop, clip-clop of the horse's hooves on the road as we made our way though the Badlands to Dodge City – OK, if the truth were known, New Luce village! Auntie Isa even tied the horse to a post before she lifted me down and got me a lemonade while she went about her business. On the way back, it was even better. 'Hold on tight to the horse's mane,' she said and gave the horse a kick with her legs and we were off on a trot. These New Luce injuns didn't stand a chance of escaping.

After Auntie Isa left on a ship from the Broomielaw in 1951, I never saw her again until 1977, when she came home to see her mother, Bella, before she passed away. A few years later, when I was appearing at the Pavilion in Glasgow, I got a phone call at the theatre from a friend of my Auntie Isa to tell me she had died in

New Zealand. They don't make them like Auntie Isa any more.

My Auntie Marion – better known as Big Aggie – has been a great friend and support to me all through my life. Although she was 20 years older than me, I had more of a brother–sister relationship with her. She married Joe Montgomery about a few years after I came to stay with my granny and granddad, but lived only a few closes along from us at the top of Bouverie Street. She was never far away and I was glad of that.

Uncle Joe was in the Navy, but always seemed to be at home on leave. Old Andra used to call him the Dry Land Sailor. 'Where's your boat tied up – Shawfield?' Andra would ask.

Before I went to primary school, I would sometimes be called into action as an unofficial bookie's runner and be sent to the quoiting green just off Bouverie Street with my Uncle Joe's bookie's line. Quoiting – where you throw an iron ring or quoit, aiming to drop it over a pin sticking out of a clay head 21 yards away – was a very popular pastime in Rutherglen and the Scottish Championships were held there. But the quoiting green hut was also where the illegal bookmaker Jock Ewing took his bets. Uncle Joe would send me round with his bookie's line and his nom-de-plume 'Wee Joe 45' written on the bottom. The bets were usually a tanner (two-and-a-half pence) double.

And I also got to take my turn as the bookie's lookout in case the police came round. Jock would give you a shilling for being lookout and it was always with great excitement and derring-do that you would watch for the law. However much I kept my eyes peeled, I don't think I ever saw a policeman and had to shout my warning.

The quoiting green was a favourite place for us kids in Bouverie Street, either playing football there, watching the quoiters or even playing with a smaller and lighter set of quoits for children.

As a child, I remember the great parties people had in their houses with everybody doing a turn by singing or telling stories. But my Auntie Marion was so shy she didn't like singing in front of people. You had to turn the gas light down so it was dark before she would sing. Even in the dark, she would turn and face the wall away from everyone else. The strange thing was that after she'd finished her song and you put the light back on, she would be facing her audience. She had turned round to face everyone during her performance.

I was four when my Uncle Andrew came home from the war, and he saw how spoiled I was. Everyone was in the kitchen when he made a show of giving me a silver sixpence, which was a lot of money in those days. People were saying how generous Andrew was giving me the money. But when I went through to the room he followed me in and said, 'Right son, give me the tanner back.' He had given me the money just for show and reckoned I had been getting enough from his brothers and sisters in the house. I still wind him up about that today.

The only song Uncle Andrew could sing at parties was 'When They Sound the Last All-Clear' and that was always met with the uncles saying, 'Right, get the tin helmets out and where's your gas mask?'

Uncle Jim was always immaculately dressed and had a great sense of justice. He waited until I was 15 and able to bring a wage into the house before he got married. He had been going out with Pearl for four years before he decided it was the right time to leave the house.

Uncle Jim was probably the biggest influence of my formative years and he was definitely a big brother figure to me. Jim's got a thrawn bit in him – if he thinks he's right you'll never convince him he's wrong. I'm like that and I take that from him. I always stick up for what I believe in and he always did that.

He was a great one for doing things right and doing them on time. Along with Bella, he was one for disciplining me when I did something wrong, although he never laid a hand on me. If Uncle Jim had a stern word with you and pointed his finger that was enough. Sometimes, a slap would have been far more preferable than one of Uncle Jim's lectures.

Jim was a very good football referee, but never made the senior grade because he needed glasses and they wouldn't let a top grade referee wear glasses. That was a great shame because he was superb.

When my Uncle Alec married Lizzie Maguire in 1942 he

became a Catholic. He was a big part of my life. I also thought Auntie Lizzie was a wee angel and she could bake better than anyone I'd ever known. When Bella would take me to visit them in their house in Flemington, Cambuslang, the smell of her baking was brilliant.

Uncle Alec was another one with a great sense of humour and was very quick-witted, always able to come back at you with a line of patter of his own. Auntie Lizzie's party piece was 'Phil the Fluter's Ball' and she would do an Irish jig at the same time as singing it. A few years back, I was reminiscing with her about the parties and her singing this song. Lizzie said she could never do that song again and I asked her why. 'Carpets,' she said. 'You can't dance on carpets!' She needed the linoleum to dance on to hear the sound of the feet going.

If I needed to be looked after overnight I would go to Uncle Alec and Auntie Lizzie to stay and I would go to mass in the morning with their three children – Elizabeth, Jim and Kay. They stayed in a row of miners' houses down a lane and I really enjoyed staying with them. I was a bit of a rascal, though, and got many a row for a prank I used to get up to when I would visit them with Bella. Auntie Lizzie had a holy water font on the inside of the doorpost. It was held in place loosely by a nail and I would twirl it round, sending the holy water showering all over the hallway. Years later, when I was an entertainer, Uncle Alec and Auntie Lizzie were great supporters and would come to all my shows at the Pavilion in Glasgow.

Of course, my father was in the Army during the Second World War and stayed in London after he was demobbed. I didn't really know who this guy Dougie people talked about was when I was really young. As I said, as far as I knew, Bella and Andra were my mother and father. I only got to know my father after he had remarried and I was about seven years old. But what a life I was having before I knew anything about real mothers, fathers and all that stuff.

My early memories are of sitting on Bella's knee in the wash house and her singing 'Shoo Shuggy O'er the Glen', 'Mammy's Pet' and 'Daddy's Wee Hen' and songs like that. I also remember the air raid sirens going off and everyone rushing down to the wash house in case the tenement got bombed. These Germans must have been right good aimers if they were going to drop a bomb from a plane and hit the tenement and miss the wash house!

I was told that one time the siren went, Old Andra was messing about in a drawer when he should have been heading for the wash house. 'What the hell are you looking for?' asked Bella. 'I'm not going down there without my false teeth,' he replied. To which Bella retorted, 'Listen you, get down these stairs. It's bombs they're dropping not hot pies!'

During the summer, Bella would be in the wash house by 5 a.m. lighting the fire to heat the boiler. I used to go down to help her turn the mangle to wring the water out of the clothes before she would put the washing out on the line. One day, however, I needed more than a washing myself. I would have been about three years old and Isa and Marion had bought me a romper suit. It was a boiling hot summer's day – so hot the tar on the street was melting. Foolishly, Isa and Marion had let me sit on the pavement outside the tenement close and I started to play with the melting tar.

It wasn't long before me and the romper suit were as black as the Earl of Hell's waistcoat and when Bella came up the street from her work I shouted, 'Mammy!' And Bella asks, 'Who are you?' I was so black with the tar she didn't recognise me. What a roasting she gave Isa and Marion for letting me get into such a state. Bella had to rub me with margarine to get the tar off me and as I sat in the jawbox you could hear my screams three streets away.

Now, I wasn't born this ugly. I went through a lot of pain trying to jump the wash-house dyke and scraping my face on the wall when I missed to get like this. Jumping the dyke was a rite of passage for a four year old and you just had to do it.

The leap was from the wash-house roof, which was sloped, across a four-foot gap onto the roof of the enclosure where the bins were kept. It was quite a jump for us youngsters and the big danger were the spiked railings between the wash house and the bins enclosure.

One day when I was making this jump, I slipped off the wash-house roof and landed on the spikes below. I'm howling in terror, sitting on the spikes thinking they had gone right through my backside. I can't get off the spikes and there's blood on my hands.

As my screams got louder, I saw Bella waddling across the backcourt, rushing to see what had happened. She had bowlie legs and I always said that if she'd had them straightened she would've been eight foot six.

'What happened, what happened?' she's shouting.

'I was trying to jump off the wash-house roof,' says I, in between sobs.

Well, what a slap she gives me and says, 'You've no right to be up on that roof. Hell mend you.'

As it turned out, the spikes had only nicked my bum as the spike had gone through my trousers.

It was like that if you got the belt at school. You never told Bella because you would have got another skelp off her for getting the belt. Her view was that you must have been doing something bad to get the belt in the first place.

Bella's house was a happy house and there was always laughter there. Yes, we were poor, but we didn't know we were poor because you didn't know any other life. But we got our meals every day – you could cut Bella's porridge into slices and put it in the drawer for the next day – we were looked after and got plenty of cuddles and if anyone was in a bit of bother everyone mucked in and helped.

I never felt poor. I never felt underprivileged and I was never abused in any way. I was always loved and there was affection in abundance. But if I did something wrong, there would be retribution. I may have got a slap on the legs from time to time, but nothing that could ever be described as a beating. It was a great upbringing and if a fairy came and said I could go back to 1941, there's no way I would change a thing.

Chapter 2

LAUGHS, LIFE BOYS AND FALLING IN LOVE WITH MY TEACHER

THE PACKED CINEMA WAS IN DARKNESS, APART FROM THE FLICKERING shafts of light coming from the screen and bouncing off a sea of eager faces in the audience. The latest cowboy film had just started and I was on my hands and knees crawling up the outside aisle, hugging the wall, hoping no one would notice I had sneaked into the Rio cinema without paying.

The excitement gripped me as I thought I had made it without being caught, when suddenly I was looking at a pair of size ten brogues standing in my path. I stopped and slowly looked up as a torch was shone in my face. Through the beam of light, I could just about make out the cinema usher's uniform and the milk-bottle glasses on his face. I'd seen this guy before and he was trouble.

I jumped up and started to make a run for it, but the usher grabbed me and decided to give my hasty retreat a helping hand by booting my backside all the way down the aisle, out the door through which I'd come and into the street. He wanted to show everybody what would happen to them if they tried to sneak in without paying.

For days, my backside and the tops of my legs were black and blue – I was aching. What an evil bastard that usher was. All I wanted to do was see a cowboy picture even though I was skint.

I had just turned ten and this was the daring, resourceful Andy Cameron at his youthful best – well, almost. I thought I had done it and what a story it was going to be when I told all my pals. I hadn't told any of them I was trying this scam. It was hard enough getting myself in, never mind half a dozen of us.

The auditorium of the Rio in Rutherglen had a side door which opened onto the street, and slightly overlapped the step down to the street when it was closed. I had discovered that if you were able to lift the door slightly you could get it off the latch and open it. Armed with a piece of wood, I did just that. Levering the door up and off the latch, opening it just enough for me to sneak in, I thought, 'Ya beauty.' That was until I crawled right into the legs of the infamous usher. What a hiding he gave me and I couldn't even tell Bella about it because she would have given me another doing for trying to get into the pictures without paying.

Life for me growing up in Rutherglen in my primary school days was one big adventure – I just loved it. School was great, as was joining the Life Boys (which was for primary school kids not old enough to join the Boys Brigade), going to the swimming baths, playing in the street and going on holiday with Bella and my cousin Campbell Gordon. Halcyon days indeed.

I went to Farie Street Primary School in August 1945, just a couple of months before my fifth birthday, which was on 13 October. Then, I was still calling Bella and Old Andra my mammy and daddy and my aunts and uncles were my big brothers and sisters. There wasn't a cloud on my life's horizon.

The school was only 100 yards from my tenement close and every playtime at 11 a.m., Bella and all the other mothers would walk to the school gates with a big enamel mug full of tea and a playpiece for their kids. It was the only thing you stopped playing football for during playtime. During the lunch-break – or as we called it, dinner time – it was the same. A dash along the street, gulp down your soup and back to the playground.

I was so excited about going to school for the first time – no tears from this boy. It was an incredible experience for me and my eyes were like saucers waiting to hear what the teacher was going to tell us next.

The boy beside me started greetin' and I asked, 'What's up with you?'

He said, 'I want to go home.'

'You go home at 12 o'clock,' I replied.

'No,' he sobbed. 'You're here until you are 15!'

Farie Street School was a big, grey sandstone building and when you went in the front door there was a big assembly hall. Miss White played the piano and all the kids marched in for assembly every morning. Then you marched out and into the classroom. It was a wee bit regimented, but it taught you discipline.

My first teacher was Miss Marjoribanks, who was absolutely brilliant and all the kids loved her. She was so warm and caring and never shouted at you. In Primary Two I had Miss Hay, who should have been in the German SS she was so different from Miss Marjoribanks.

You were put at desks in alphabetical order and I was third desk along in the front row. Miss Hay was like a beanpole and her nose was always running. She would blow into a paper hankie and say to me, 'Cameron, put this in the bin for me,' handing me the tissue.

I used to hang around with my two cousins Sandy Cameron and Campbell Gordon. We were very close and our birthdays were within two months of each other. Sandy was a really good singer and was a natural at harmonies. We would sing as a duet in school doing Burns songs and Al Jolson numbers. Campbell was a really good football player and I'll never understand how he never made it professionally. His other claim to fame was that he was the first child in Lanarkshire to get 100 per cent in the Cycling Proficiency Test. His picture was in the local papers and he was a bit of a celebrity in school for a while.

I was quite clever in primary school. I always wanted to be top of the class and a competitive streak would sometimes show itself. I used to sit beside Josephine Gardner, who was a real bright girl. We would be given an exercise and if she finished before me I would be raging with myself. Imagine getting beat by a lassie! My mission that school term was to finish my schoolwork before Josephine Gardner.

When it came to Primary Seven and I saw my new teacher, Miss

Peters, I thought I'd died and woken up in Hollywood. What a looker she was – a real film star. She was absolutely gorgeous, with a personality to match. We were her first class as a primary school teacher. She must have been about 21 years old and all the boys fell in love with her.

Miss Peters must have been well qualified to be given a Primary Seven as her first class, but she was brilliant. She never gave the belt, she never fell out with you and she was your pal. One of the first things she did was to take us all on a trip to watch the launch of a ship – the SS *Windsor* – on the Clyde, at Scotstoun. She took the whole class of 30 excited and chattering kids on a tramcar and after the launch we went to Victoria Park and had a picnic. She was entirely different from any other teacher we ever had.

A great thing she did on a Friday afternoon was to get all the class together for some play-acting. We would choose a different subject every week and then play out the parts. One week, we were all going on an aeroplane and she chose Wull Stewart to be the airline pilot while the other kids would sit in chairs behind him like they were on a plane. Miss Peters asked Wull how long it would take to fly to America.

'I don't know, Miss,' says Wull. 'We'll have to stop for firewood.'

'Firewood?' asks Miss Peters.

'Aye, Miss. We need firewood to make the engines go!' says Wull as he made ready for take-off.

Another Friday, we were acting out being a shopkeeper dealing with customers. We were all getting a chance of being shopkeeper and it came round to Andy Kilpatrick, who was as rough as a badger's whatsit. Andy is standing behind the counter when one of the pupils acting as a customer asks for a pound of sugar. When I was that age, ration books were no longer needed, but Andy says, 'Where's your ration book?'

'Ration books aren't in any more,' says the customer.

'You need one in my shop,' replies Andy.

'No, you don't,' retorts the customer. 'Ration books went out ages ago.'

'I'm telling you,' says Andy, getting very irritated, 'you need a ration book in my shop.'

'You're just trying to be smart,' says the customer.

To which Andy shouted 'Listen, you don't get f****n' messages without a ration book.'

The whole classroom fell into a shocked silence. I think Andy actually believed he was a shopkeeper that afternoon, but we couldn't believe our ears at what Andy had just said. Miss Peters calmly stood up and told Andy to sit at the back of the class on the right-hand side. We all carried on and after a while Andy said, 'Please Miss, can I go back to my own seat? This is the girls' section.' The teacher replied, 'That's right. If you are going to behave like a hooligan I want you to sit beside the girls and you might learn to behave better.'

Andy had to sit among the girls all afternoon and what a big reddy he had at the end of the day. I don't recall him ever swearing in front of the teacher again, though.

Miss Peters was another one who had a great influence on me and it was quite sad when I had to leave Farie Street School and her classroom.

Years later, I was doing a live radio programme in Fife when this lady came up to me and said, 'Hello, Mr Cameron.' I looked at her and said, 'If you're going to tell me you're Miss Peters I'm going to faint at your feet.' It was Miss Peters right enough, and she had hardly changed. I told her I had been in love with her as a wee boy in her class at school and she said, 'I wish I had a penny every time a former pupil had said that to me.' We spoke for about half an hour and she admitted she had been spoiled by our class because we were always willing to have a wee concert and take turns singing. There was nothing like that in the next school she went to.

Since boys will be boys, we all used to think it was a big deal to use swear-words that we heard the older boys using and I only found out about the following story in 1981 when I was in Canada visiting my Great-uncle Duncan. Apparently, Andra had told Duncan this story in the Quarry Bar a few hours after it happened.

Andra had been looking after my cousin Sandy Cameron and me one day when we were about six years old. Andra was in his usual chair by the fire and we were sitting on the floor playing with our cars. I said to Sandy, 'Say f**k.'

Sandy says: 'No, my Uncle Andra will hear me.' To which I replied, 'Don't worry about him, he's f****n' deaf!'

Old Andra, to his eternal credit, just sat there and must have had a right giggle to himself. He never said a word until he got to the pub that night and had a laugh telling his brother what had happened.

Football played a big part in most young boys' lives in those days. I wasn't very good at playing football, but my ambition was to get in the school team. Every school in Rutherglen had a team and they competed for the Burgh Cup. We had a terrible football team at Farie Street when I was there – apart from Jim Finnie who was the young David Beckham of the day with his blond hair and silky skills. The only problem was that Jim came from a family of pigeon flyers.

Jim would be in the middle of a game and if he saw a pigeon flying overhead he would stop, look up at the sky and start making coo-ing noises. He even did that in a Burgh Cup game played at Rutherglen's Glencairn's Park. One minute, he's running and dribbling with the ball, the next, he's started his coo-ing at a passing pigeon. Everybody thought he was off his head.

One of the top teams in the area was St Columbkilles. They were always well kitted out, as the teacher who took the team would organise fund-raising social nights in the chapel hall to buy new strips for the boys.

Our school team had pre-war strips and the jerseys had more holes in them than our defence, which was saying something. All the same, I thought it was a great honour to play for the school team. We were ten and in Primary Six when my cousin Campbell and I first made it into the team. I played right-half and the best you could say was that I was a tough-tackling hamper boy. My Uncle Jim and Uncle Joe used to come and watch our games and encourage me from the sidelines. That year, we were put out of the Burgh Cup in the first round by Calderwood, who beat us 3–0.

A year later, we did a lot better and got to the Cup final against St Columbkilles. They had a boy who was only about eight and he was playing directly against me. By the end of the game they had to unscrew me out of the ground. This wee guy was magnificent and we were defeated 4–1.

That same wee guy went on to become one of Scotland's top footballers, a legend in fact. He was Bobby Murdoch, who played for Celtic and was one of the Lisbon Lions who won the European Cup in 1967. I always called him wee Bobby Murdoch, but he took a right stretch in his teens and grew to over 6 ft tall.

The Murdoch family lived two doors along from my Aunt Cathy and Uncle Duncan and when I went to visit them with Bella I would play football with Bobby and his brothers, Jim, Matt and Billy. We used to play games of Rangers versus Celtic. They all wanted to be Charlie Tully and I wanted to be Willie Waddell. We did have one daft boy who wasn't quite right and wanted to be Dougie Wallace of Clyde. Geordie Simpson and his family were all great Clyde supporters. More to be pitied than scolded, I suppose.

Along with my two cousins Sandy and Campbell, who were my best pals, I had another good friend, Rab Kerr, who was the best fighter in the school. There were other boys we would hang around with. We were a group, but not a gang going round causing mayhem.

There were always playground fights at school. I was never a great fighter, but my Auntie Isa taught me to hit them first and negotiate after. One day, I was having an argument with Wull Stewart, who was a bit of a bruiser and I was a wee skinny thing. I knew it was going to end in fisticuffs so I whacked him on the chin and followed it up with another punch. He never got up for more, so I had won that one.

But on the way home from school after the fight I was walking down the road with Campbell and I started crying. He asked me what was wrong. 'What's your problem? You won the fight fair and square. Wull Stewart's not going to come near you again.'

I replied, 'When Bella finds out I've been fighting I'm going to get a real doing off her.'

Campbell still talks about that day. I won the fight and it's me that ends up greetin'.

Another incident which had Campbell doubled up with laughter was when I jumped off the school roof and got stuck in a bunker and couldn't get out. We used to get onto the roof by climbing onto the bunker, which was against the wall, and then pulling ourselves up onto the roof.

I was up on the roof – goodness knows why – and the bell to go back to class rang. I was about eight at the time and I jumped off the roof onto the bunker. But the bunker lid couldn't take my weight and I went right through and couldn't get out.

Everyone else was in their lines waiting to go back after playtime and Campbell couldn't tell the teacher what had happened for laughing. It was ten minutes before the janitor, Matt Walker, came round to pull me out and what a row he gave me for being up on the school roof. I was taken to the headmaster's office and given a right telling off, although, for some reason, I never got the belt.

Primary school was when you first started to notice girls and every other day you were falling in and out of love with some wee lassie and passing notes to each other in the classroom.

One girl, June Clark, was my girlfriend when she was having her 11th birthday party and we were all invited round to her house. I ended up getting a rather stern look from Mrs Clark after I suggested we should play Dustman's Knock instead of Postman's Knock because it was a wee bit dirtier.

Now here's another memory of my schooldays – the belt. The belt is now banned in schools and a lot of people say it's cruel. But I don't agree. Not many of our teachers actually gave you the belt. It was the threat of getting the belt that really worked.

One of the teachers in Farie Street had a terrible reputation and the kids would say she gave you sixers – six slaps with the belt. She left before I got to her class and it was only after she left that we realised she had never given anyone the belt – the threat was enough to make her pupils behave. She used to hang the belt up in front of class, dip it in vinegar and warn them it was for anyone who misbehaved. But no one ever remembered her giving anyone the belt.

Going to the Calder Street Swimming Baths was another source of great joy for us young lads. Willie McDonald lived in the same close as me. He was four years older and the organiser of all the trips to the baths. There would be about 12 of us and we would walk to Toryglen to catch the number 12 bus to the baths. What an adventure.

The older lads had a sure-fire way of making you learn to swim – they threw you in at the deep end. When you were thrown in your natural survival instinct made you swim to the side of the pool. How did we learn to swim? Shove, splash, there you go wee man – start swimming.

When I got thrown into the deep end I swam to the nearest side of the pool. After I climbed out of the water I was thrown straight back in and told to swim to the far side. That's when you conquered your fear of the water and you could learn to swim properly. Willie McDonald took me to the shallow end, held my chin up out of the water and showed me how to do the strokes.

John McIntyre was the same age as me and stayed in the next close. He was a real tough boy and could run and fight for Scotland. He came along to the baths with us and declared no one was going to push him into the deep end. I couldn't believe it when he climbed the stairs to the top dale – to me that was up in the sky – and jumped off into the water. He swam to the side and like the rest of us never looked back.

When we headed off for the baths we would be given a shilling. The bus there was 3d, then it was a tanner to get in and 3d for the bus fare back home. But by the time you came out the baths you were starving and we would spend our bus fare home on a bag of chips and walk back to Bouverie Street.

We would walk to the Bungalow Café in Victoria Road, get a bag of chips and walk home with our pals. Nowadays, kids have their own ways of entertaining themselves – they sit with their thumbs going on the video games. We used to get out and about using our legs – it was marvellous.

Believe it or not, we had a beauty queen living in a tenement in Bouverie Street – Annie Brown was her name. She was a real looker: dyed-blonde hair, always wore make-up and done up to the nines in the latest fashions. Sometimes, she would ask the kids in the street to run an errand for her and one day she rattled the window at me and asked me to go to Mr Ogg's shop for a pint of milk and two well-fired rolls.

When I came back, I knocked on the door and Annie opened it wearing a housecoat. To my horror, the housecoat accidentally fell open and I saw she had nothing on underneath. My eyes must have popped out of my head because I had never seen pubic hair before and here I was looking at what appeared to be a big hedgehog.

She started laughing and told me to put the milk and rolls on the table. I couldn't get out of her house quickly enough I was so embarrassed and as I rushed out the door she said, 'You'll remember that when you're a man.' And she's right, I still remember it. That was my first inkling that you could get hair other than on your head.

The Bouverie Street tearaway was undoubtedly Billy Donaldson, who was four years older than me. If ever there were any shenanigans he would be the one to start them. We went through a phase where everyone wanted to have a bow and arrows. We made the bow out of bamboo cane with a piece of string stretched from one end to the other, and the arrows were made of bamboo too. Billy thought he would get his arrow to go further than the rest of us if he could put a bit of weight on the end of it. He rummaged about the midden and found the top off a tin can, which he folded over and hit with a hammer until it made a diamond-shaped arrowhead. This was stuck on the top of the arrow and boy, did that thing fly through the air.

We all got a shot at firing it into the air and the next thing we hear is another of our pals, Frankie McLaughlin, screaming and there's an arrow sticking out the top of his head. He was taken to hospital and had stitches put in his head. For years after the incident he was called Frankie Two Skulls, because when he got back from hospital he bragged that the doctors had told him he had two skulls.

Billy Donaldson was also involved in one of the most amazing sights I ever saw as a wee boy. There was an old character in Rutherglen called Nana Anderson and his party piece after coming out the pub at night was to bite the head off a rat. Nana was a fair age and he only had three teeth at the front and they were black. His gums must have been like rocks. The first time I saw Nana doing this was on a summer evening outside the Quarry Bar when all the men were standing around talking about football. Suddenly, someone shouted, 'Nana's going to bite the head off a rat.'

So Billy Donaldson goes round the corner to the corporation cleansing yard, which was full of rats, caught one, knocked it out and brought it round to the front of the pub holding it by its tail. Nana shook the rat, put his mouth over the rat's head, bit it off and spat it out. He threw the rest of the rat's body into the street. I think Nana only intended to do this stunt with the rat for a dare once, but because of his bravado he couldn't get out of repeating it when he was asked – it became a ritual.

A year later, I saw Nana do the same thing again. This time, I thought I was a bit braver and wanted to help Billy Donaldson catch the rat for Nana. The two of us went round to the corpy and started banging things to scare the rats and make them run. Billy had a bin and scooped up one of the rats before stunning it with a stick while it was in the bin. As soon as I saw the rat, though, I was off – my bravery suddenly deserting me.

Sure enough, Billy brings the rat to Nana and he bites the head off, saying it was the last time he was going to do this. But he always said that.

There were some memorable characters in Rutherglen at that time. I can even remember my great-granny Campbell – Bella's mother – sitting at the close mouth during the summer smoking her clay pipe. She had a mass of silver hair tied in a bun. She lived until she was 83 and died shortly after she fell down some stairs and broke her leg. I was only six at the time, but I've been told that she never really got over the accident.

At that time of my life I really looked forward to going on holiday with Bella, Campbell and his mother, my Auntie Sarah, who was my granny's sister. We regularly went to Stevenston, in Ayrshire, for the Glasgow Fair fortnight and we always stayed in digs with the Cassidys – Mary and her husband Barney.

The Cassidys stayed in a council house and I don't think it was legal taking in lodgers for the Glasgow Fair. But when you went there hundreds of families from Glasgow stayed in the council houses in the seaside town.

We would get on the train at Glasgow Central and you could smell the engines. Paisley Gilmour Street was the first stop, then Beith and Dalry. The Cassidys were a lovely family and couldn't do enough for you. There was always a great welcome for you and great warmth in the house. They were an Irish family and had a big picture of Pope Pius XII at the top of the stairs. It was a huge picture – CinemaScope. I didn't know who it was at the time, but it terrified me. Mrs Cassidy used to say to me that if I didn't eat my mince and potatoes, he's going to get you and she'd be pointing at the picture of the Pope at the top of the stairs.

We weren't brought up in any kind of sectarian way because there was a real mix in our family, with people marrying Catholics and taking their religion. So that kind of stuff wasn't an issue with us at all.

These holidays were so carefree. You had the run of the place and nobody bothered you. You would go down to the beach, splash in the water and build sandcastles while my granny and auntie would be sitting on the beach knitting.

A great organisation I have always been glad I was involved in was the Life Boys and then the Boys Brigade (BB). When I was six, I joined the Life Boys of the 1st Rutherglen BB. It was the start of an association with that organisation which continued until I was 20 and I am forever grateful to people in the BB for what they did for me and what they taught me.

I met my best pal George Dunn in the Life Boys and George to this day is still my best friend. We would go to the Life Boys between 6.30 p.m. and 7.30 p.m. every Friday. For the first couple of years, either Bella or one of my aunties would come to collect me, but when I reached the ripe old age of eight I was allowed to extend my Friday evenings beyond the Life Boys.

Four of us – George Dunn, Campbell Gordon, John McIntyre and I would come out the Life Boys and head straight for Clark's Café in Rutherglen Main Street and ask for a Dig Deep, which was a mug full of hot peas drowned in vinegar for tuppence.

The café had marble-topped tables and you rang a bell if you wanted serving. There we were with our short trousers wearing sailor hats and hanging around a café making our Dig Deeps last for ever because there were lots of older people there and we were able to mix with grown-ups.

The Odeon Club on a Saturday morning was another favourite haunt. We would watch our heroes Johnny MacBrown, Hopalong Cassidy and Roy Rogers and his horse, Trigger. There would also be a competition every week and Sandy Cameron and I would often win it with me singing the melody of a song and Sandy doing the harmony on stage. The prize was a tub of ice cream – well, you've got to start somewhere!

I can still remember the Odeon Club song:

> We come along on Saturday morning, greeting everybody
> with a smile,
> We come along on Saturday morning, knowing it's well
> worthwhile,
> As members of the Odeon Club we all intend to be, good
> citizens when we grow up and champions of the free,
> We come along on Saturday morning, greeting everybody
> with a smile, smile, smile,
> Greeting everybody with a smile.

When we weren't getting involved in all these different activities we would be up at the quoiting green playing football, rounders or cricket with an old tennis racquet. There were old railway sleepers at the back of the clay head and we painted wickets on them. Oh yes, and we also played quoits at the quoiting green.

There were other games we played which perhaps we shouldn't have been playing. One was KDRF – Kick Doors Run Fast. Someone would go to the top flat of the tenement, someone on the next landing and so on to the bottom of the close. The boy at the top of the stairs would shout for everyone to knock all the doors on their landing and everybody would have to run down the stairs before anyone came to open their doors. More than once the boy at the bottom would knock his door before the signal and run away. The woman whose door he chapped would already be out in the close before the boys upstairs had even knocked their doors. She would be waiting for them to run out the close and would give them a dull one to help them on their way.

Another prank we would get up to was when you tied a button in the middle of a long piece of thread and used chewing gum to stick one end of the thread as high up someone's window as you could reach. Holding the other end of the thread you would hide under the window, pull the thread and make the button click off the window. It would really annoy people continually coming to their window to see who was knocking it and not seeing the thread hanging down.

One day when I was seven, my world was thrown into confusion when someone at the school said Bella wasn't my real mother. I was really upset and came home and told Bella. 'They said you're not my mammy.'

'No,' she said. 'I'm your father's mammy. Your father stays in London and he's Hughie. You've heard us talking about him.'

'Well, who's Dougie then?' I asked, because I'd heard my aunts and other people using the name Dougie. You can imagine how this was so confusing to a seven year old. I asked Bella where my mother was and she said she had got lost in the bombings – obviously not wanting to go into any details. And to confuse matters even more, Bella took the opportunity to tell me my father was getting married again and was coming up from London to visit us.

It was all getting a bit too much and I began to have some fearful thoughts that maybe my father and his new wife were going to take me back to London with them.

Time went on and a few months later the father I never knew existed came into the house with a lady with glasses and long red hair down to her waist who spoke very politely, and was really nice to me.

I suppose I was excited at the thought of this man who was my father coming to see me, but there was also a lot of apprehension. My Uncle Jim picked him up from the railway station and Bella's house was spotless for the welcome home party.

When my father came through the door he tried to hug me, but I was holding back because I wasn't really sure what was going on. His first words to me were, 'Hello, how are you? You're getting big.'

He was told by my aunts that I was a good singer, so I had to stand there and sing a song for him. I didn't know this at the time, but he had been sending Bella money to help pay for my upkeep and the aunts and uncles probably mentioned my father in a natural way hoping I would pick up on it.

The confusion began to disappear as I got to know my father and his new wife, Doris. They wanted to take me back to London with them, but Bella put her foot down and said no. They were embarking on a new life, they would soon have a family of their own and I had been living in Rutherglen for seven years. There was no point in upsetting everyone's applecart. In any case, wild horses wouldn't have dragged me away from Rutherglen. I was having the time of my life.

Money was tight and neither my father nor Bella could afford to be coming back and forward to and from London so I could see my father. Then Uncle Joe came up with the idea of me going to visit my father on the next Quarry Bar Wembley bus. Everybody was desperate to go on the Wembley weekend to watch Scotland play England and the men saved up to pay for the bus down south. That was my first real geography lesson when the carry-out was finished we'd be at Motherwell.

My father went back to London, but I wouldn't see him for another two years, as Scotland didn't play England at Wembley until 1949. But when the time came I was at the back of the bus with Uncle Joe and Uncle Jim amidst a throng of tartan-clad football fans heading for the big match and me going to see my father. My bi-annual trip to London on the Wembley bus went on for years when I was young.

In between times, I would speak to my dad every Thursday night at 7 p.m. from a phone box in Mill Street, Rutherglen. Bella would take me there and make the transfer charge call to my father's house in London and he would be kept up to date on how I was getting on.

In later years I was told I had two new stepbrothers. Ian was first and then Stuart came along. I keep in contact and we phone each other every week.

Both my father and I accepted that, because of circumstances, we would never live together. He never, ever forgot me and was as proud as punch when I was on *Top of the Pops* with 'Ally's Tartan Army' all those years later.

I got to love my father dearly and was extremely sad when he died in 1979. We were close like any father and son – we just didn't stay in the same house.

Chapter 3

ROMANCE IN THE BACKCOURT WASH HOUSE

I'M STARING AT THE ALGEBRA TEST PAPER LYING ON MY DESK, UNABLE TO
make head nor tail of what looks like a foreign language to me.
Everyone else has their head down, arms hooked round their
papers so nobody can read their answers and scribbling away
furiously.

Me, I'm drumming my pencil on the wooden desk and staring
out the window looking for some divine intervention – or even a
clue as to what I should be doing would have been fine. I'm so
useless at this stuff it took me ten minutes to realise that the test
paper was UPSIDE DOWN!

Even with the test paper now the right way up, it made little
difference and I was still struggling to come to terms with the
equations. For all I knew, The Equations could have been a 50s
American rock 'n' roll band.

There were no surprises when I got the result of the maths-test
paper in my first year at Rutherglen Academy – 13 out of 100.
Bella's not going to be happy when she hears this. I could count in
my head and was good at mental arithmetic when I was at Farie
Street Primary, but 13 out of 100 and probably 10 of those marks
for spelling my name right was a real shocker. It's fair to say my
first year at Rutherglen Academy was what you call coming down
to earth with a bump.

I had passed my qualifying exam with flying colours and the teachers at Farie Street had encouraged me to opt for the more academic curriculum of the Academy instead of going to the local junior secondary Gallowflat, where all my pals were heading. In fact, I was the only pupil from my class in Farie Street to go to the Academy.

All of a sudden, when I moved from primary to secondary school, education was a problem for me. But I had turned up at the Academy on the first day after the summer holidays with the same enthusiasm I had when I started at Farie Street Primary.

During the summer break, the only thing I worried about was if Bella could afford the navy blue blazer, grey trousers and the blue and yellow tie that was the Academy uniform. But true to form, Bella had me turned out spick and span.

I made the mistake of gravitating towards the boys who were cheeky to the teachers, had a bit of patter and were gallus – the ones who were repeating first year. I didn't have the gumption to realise why they should have to repeat first year and I was heading the same way. I should have sat beside guys like James Birrell and Bruce Muir who got stuck in at their lessons and didn't let a good carry-on in class take precedence from the hard work that was necessary. Bruce was a lovely wee guy, but had Glasgow eyes – one is going for the messages and the other is coming back with the change – and the kids would tease him about his lazy eye.

However, I sat next to the wrong type of boys – for me anyway. They were the show-offs and a bit like myself, I suppose.

Our maths teacher in first year was Miss Smith, who was called Chop-Chop because of the way she gave you the belt. She held the belt with both hands like an axe and tried to hit your hands with it. Invariably, she would miss and this caused even more derision among the boys for her.

Chop-Chop appeared to be naive in the early days of her teaching career and she couldn't control some of us in the class. She used to sit on the front of her desk facing the class unaware that she was showing a bit more of her thighs than she should. You never saw so many pencils, rulers and erasers being dropped on the floor by giggling boys.

My first year at Rutherglen Academy was a great disappointment to everybody and I had to repeat it. Maybe it was the fact that I'd loved the togetherness of my primary school class with the same teacher every day and then moved on to a different teacher every hour that made my first year at secondary school so hard for me.

Things did change when I repeated first year and probably a lot to do with it was the style of teachers I had then. My new maths teacher was Dan Livingston and he couldn't have been any more different than Chop-Chop. He had a fearsome reputation for bringing the belt out if you misbehaved in class. I never actually saw him give anyone the belt, which hung down beside the blackboard. It was that old threat thing again that did the trick.

The first time he walked into our class he took a look round and asked who was repeating first year. Three of us put our hands up and he sent us to sit as far away as possible from each other. Right away, I realised he knew what he was doing – making sure there would be no interruptions to lessons. That year, I flew through maths because Dan Livingston taught you well and if you had a problem he sat down with you and explained it.

By the time I had finished my repeat of first year and moved into second year I had settled down a bit and got on with the work, although I was never going to be considered an academic success.

Perhaps Bouverie Street was the wrong side of town for someone to be going to Rutherglen Academy. The school was full of kids who had an inside toilet and real fruit on their dining-room table even when nobody in the house was ill, whereas Gallowflat was full of kids like me – rough and ready and more than just a wee bit gallus. However, despite this, I still enjoyed my time at the Academy.

There were times when I wished I had gone to Gallowflat though. They had a rather famous teacher called Alastair MacLean who wrote books like *Where Eagles Dare* and *HMS Ulysses*. My pals at Gallowflat said he was a great teacher and they spoke about him in awe.

But then again, I had another well-known teacher when I was at the Academy. It was Norman Buchan, who went on to become a long-serving Labour MP. He taught history and the only problem was that you didn't want to sit in the front three rows of his class because he slavered a lot when he was talking.

He was a great teacher and I really enjoyed his lessons. There was a connection between us because Norman was a great folk music enthusiast and I knew all the bothy ballads from hearing my Auntie Isa singing them when she came home from the Land Army.

The great trick in his class was to get Norman talking about folk music and the history lesson was out the window. You got a history lesson all right – the history of folk music and not 1066 and the Battle of Hastings. Norman was a lovely man and very intelligent. You could tell he really enjoyed teaching because we enjoyed being taught by him.

One great thing about being at the Academy was the organised football teams – especially as I was picked to play for the school. We played against some really talented kids and a few of them went on to football glory when they grew up. Probably one of the best school teams of that era was Our Lady's High, in Motherwell. When I played against them their half-back line was McNeill, Cushley and Rooney. Billy McNeill went on to play for Celtic and became a Lisbon Lion – captain of the first British team to win the European Cup. John Cushley played with West Ham and Benny Rooney was a hero with Morton.

My years at Rutherglen Academy were important to me because it determined I was never going to be academic. I had left Farie Street as someone who had a chance to be academic, but as they say what's meant for you, won't go by you. It wasn't a blow that I left the Academy at 15 after third year with only a Leaver's Certificate. Who knows, if I had become a bit of a swot and gained O levels and Highers, then gone on to university, I might not have ended up the entertainer I am today.

Reading American comics was a favourite pastime with us lads. And one boy in particular, John Rainey, always had a big supply of titles like *Nyoka the Jungle Girl*, *Captain Marvel*, *Superman* and the *Archie* comics. The shop we used to buy the comics from was at 89 Springfield Road, Dalmarnock. We always used to say 'are you going to 89?' and everybody knew what you were talking about. We would walk from Rutherglen down through the Soda Waste behind White's Chemical Works, along the banks of the Clyde to Dalmarnock power station and down to Springfield Road.

This was a big thing for youngsters in the early '50s and the man who owned the shop would do you a favour by taking the comics back off you after you had read them and give you money off the next batch you bought.

John Rainey was certainly the boy who was the most avid reader and he would pass the comics round his pals to give them a read after he had finished. But you had to make sure you were careful and not tear any pages as he might want to take the comic back to 89.

We would sit under the gaslight in the close and read these comics and you could feel the excitement among us when it was time to head for 89 to get a new batch of adventures to read.

In the days when I was growing up there was plenty of room in the street for playing football – not like today where car after car is parked on either side of the road and it's too dangerous for youngsters to play in the street. Even older boys in their late teens would play football there. Every Sunday, there would be a crowd of them standing at the corner of Bouverie Street before their weekly game of football.

One time, they didn't have a ball and, as it happened, I had just been given a brand new red football. My Uncle Jim came round the backcourt and asked me for a loan of the ball so he and his pals could have a game. The deal was that all 16 of the boys would give me a penny each if I let them have my ball. That was too good an offer to refuse. One and fourpence for the loan of a ball? That'd do me.

That was, however, until Willie Kilpatrick blootered the ball right through Bella's window. The sound of breaking glass was the signal for the older boys to head for the hills knowing full well what Bella's reaction was going to be. So I was left standing in the street when Bella came out of the close like a whirlwind looking for me. She picked the ball up off the bedroom floor and recognised it as mine and, thinking I was the guilty party, came out on the warpath.

I was rescued by my Uncle Jim, who came out of nowhere and

assured Bella it hadn't been me who kicked the ball through the window. However, to pay for the new pane of glass Bella took the one and fourpence off me and said she needed the money for the glazier's bill. I didn't know whether to laugh or cry as I hadn't got a doing for breaking the window, but I'd just lost all my riches to pay for the new one.

Growing up meant doing the things young boys maybe shouldn't be doing and learning a hard lesson along with it. I had just started at Rutherglen Academy and was out playing with my cousin Campbell Gordon. He whispered in my ear had I ever tried smoking and I said no. Then he produced five Woodbines he had stolen from his dad's stash in the house. We both decided it would be a good idea to practise being an adult and smoke the cigarettes. Off we went to the Grand Central Cinema and smoked the five Woodbines between us. Talk about technicolor. When we came out the cinema we were as green as the grass on Ibrox Park and as we walked home along Rutherglen Main Street we were being sick all over the pavement. It was like something out of *The Exorcist* and people were stopping us to ask if we were all right.

We managed to get home and into our beds without anyone else realising what had happened – or so I thought. A few days later, I came home from school and was about to go the messages for Bella when my Auntie Isa grabbed my ear and dragged me into the bedroom.

'You've been smoking,' she said.

'No, I haven't,' says I.

'Oh, you certainly have,' says Isa. 'I was talking to someone who saw you being sick all over Main Street and you were stinking of smoke.'

I exited the bedroom courtesy of a kick in the backside from Auntie Isa and I've never touched a cigarette since.

One day, when I was about 12, I volunteered to help out in Kerry's Chip Shop at the bottom of Bouverie Street. They were short-staffed and I agreed to wrap the chips and fish suppers for the owners Peter Kerry and his sister Rena. But little did I know I was about to start World War III between Peter and a drunken customer.

The drunk saw me behind the counter and took umbrage to a wee boy working there. He had a go at Peter for having the audacity to hire child labour to wrap the chips. One word led to another and before long there was a real ding-dong between them. I joined in and told the drunk, 'Mister, shut up – I like working here.' He then threatened to tell Bella and I replied, 'Listen, just f***k off – I told you, I like working here.'

At that, the two of them started laughing and that was the argument over. But it wasn't the end of the matter for me. A few weeks later, I told Bella I was going to the chip shop and she said, 'That's fine, but remember, don't be telling anybody to f**k off.'

That was another lesson I should have learned a long time before – Bella would always find out through the jungle drums what I'd been up to.

Making extra pocket money was always a great pastime and pleasure for me. When I was in primary school I would join a group of lads combing the terraces of either Hampden, Shawfield or Cathkin Park looking for empty beer bottles to collect and take back to the Quarry Bar to get tuppence a bottle.

Our transport was an old pram, which we would use to cart the bottles from the football grounds all the way back to Rutherglen. It was a great day out. We'd get lifted over the turnstile by an adult, get to watch the game and when it was over collect the empty beer bottles or screwtops as they were called then – and exchange them for money.

The Martin Brothers – Davie and John – ran the Quarry Bar. Davie would only take back the bottles of the beer they sold, so we would wait for John to appear at the counter since he would take any empty beer bottle and give us the cash for it. The Quarry Bar is quite unique in our family because Old Andra drank there, his father as well, it was my local pub for many years and occasionally my two daughters go there too.

But back to my childhood. Since I was about to become a teenager, collecting empty beer bottles wasn't for the more mature entrepreneur that I'd now become at the ages of 12 and 13. So I graduated to being a paper boy.

Angus Mackay had the busiest wee paper shop in Rutherglen.

He had five or six paper boys delivering morning and night and they were all built like me – for speed. So when East Kilbride changed from being a quiet little Scottish village to a vibrant, bustling New Town in the early '50s, I had five years of running all over the Royal Burgh under my belt. From a skinny little 8 year old I had grown up into a skinny little 13 year old.

Delivering newspapers in the '50s was magic. It kept you fit, you met interesting people and you got paid for it. And if you were a smooth-tongued wee patter merchant like me, you could get a tip for a bit of flattery. I would tell a 70-year-old granny she looked like Betty Grable if it would get me another tanner!

I remember Angus's big car with leather seats drawing up and me jumping in before I was whisked off through tenement streets and into the countryside heading up the hill to where a brand-new community had started to be built in East Kilbride.

It's the early '50s, and if a motor drove up in our street there would be people at their windows to see who it was. Not many folk went to their work by car in those days – far less a 13-year-old lad from Rutherglen heading for East Kilbride. But that was me every day after school – being chauffeured to my work by the boss, no less.

My job was to deliver the *Evening Times* and the *Evening Citizen* to West Nerston – one of the first areas to be built in the New Town development. Delivering papers wasn't a job – it was an adventure. From Rutherglen to East Kilbride is nothing nowadays, but in those days it seemed like a long way off.

I got a shilling for my wages and that was a lot of money for me in those days. My favourite time was a Friday night going to collect the money. If you got one penny or two pennies for a tip you thought you were well off. And if women gave you a threepenny bit as a tip, you thought you were a millionaire.

There's a petrol station across the road from the houses in West Nerston now and when I've been in there filling up my car I've looked across at those houses. I get a great feeling of nostalgia remembering these great days. They may not have actually been that great, but that's how I remember them.

Having a paper round gave me a work ethic. And the work ethic to me is the most important thing we have in Scotland. If you learn the work ethic you learn you don't get anything for nothing. The paper round also taught me to be nice to people and to always go that wee bit extra for them and that way you always got a bigger tip and your rewards were greater.

After I was a paper boy, I got a job as a milk boy, which meant early rises for yours truly. I worked for Perratt's – owned by the father of the now well-known racehorse trainer Linda Perratt. Working for George Perratt meant getting up at 4.30 a.m. for a 5 a.m. start, doing your round, which would finish at about 7.45 a.m. and returning home for a quick breakfast before going to school.

The other lads on the milk float were Shuggy Donnan, Benny McEwan and Benny York with George driving. He was a gruff old bugger was George. Once I suggested he paint a sign on the side of the milk float which would read, 'We Perratt On Your Doorstep' and his reply was, 'You're off your f*****g head – get on with your work!'

My career as a milk boy caused me to end up in hospital and miss my Uncle Jim's wedding. It was very foggy one morning and George was driving the milk float down the road. He turned a corner and crashed into the back of a lorry, which was parked and didn't have any lights on. With the motion of the crash I was thrown forward and a metal milk crate came sliding backwards, hitting me on the side of my face close to my eye. The blood was streaming from the wound, but acting the hero I got a plaster over the cut and carried on with the milk round.

The following morning, the side of my face began to swell, although I still did the milk round. But when I got back to the house Bella took one look at me and said I didn't look well and ordered me to my bed for the day. When she came back later that afternoon, my face was in a real bad way and Bella sent for the doctor who said I had a skin infection called erysipelas and I would have to go to hospital.

I thought erysipelas was a Greek football player – I'd never heard the word before – but it certainly had me floored and I was in Ruchhill Hospital for several days with an eye so swollen I couldn't see out of it. And while I was lying in my hospital bed feeling sorry for myself, the rest of the Cameron clan were celebrating Uncle Jim's wedding.

Moving from primary to secondary school also meant leaving the Life Boys and joining the Boys Brigade. This was how I met the man with the biggest influence on my life outside my family: Alex Montgomery, Captain of the 189th Glasgow Boys Brigade. Alex was a real Christian and not just on a Sunday. He practised his Christian values seven days a week, twenty-four hours a day and he did his best to prepare us young lads for the life that was ahead of us.

I remember saying 'Jesus Johnny' one night and Mr Montgomery – as he was to me then – quietly took me aside and told me not to take the Lord's name in vain. He was strict, but fair and had an even-minded approach to everything in life, making sure he heard both sides of the story before coming to a decision. Sadly, Alex is dead now and I haven't met a boy in the 189th BB who doesn't say they miss Alex Montgomery.

Even as an adult and 30 years after I had left the BB, Alex Montgomery still had an effect on me. He wrote to me at the BBC and asked if I would speak at a dinner he was organising. Straight away, I dialled his number and said, 'Hello, sir, this is Andy Cameron.' It was like we were back in the church hall all those years ago.

I told him I would be delighted to speak at the dinner and no way would I be charging a fee after all he did for me. That afternoon I went over to his house for a cup of tea and a long chat about the old days in the 189.

So, it comes round to the dinner and I'm sitting there with Norma listening to other speakers and it suddenly dawns on me that I can't do my usual routine in front of my old BB captain. At that time, part of my routine was about Bella's method of swearing without using any actual swear-words. I would get a laugh saying she never used the 'f' word, instead replacing the 'f' with a 'p'. 'That's puckin' terrible,' she would say. I would tell the story that when visitors were in the house she would show off by saying the 'p' word in between bigger words. Lots of old Glasgow women do this and say things like dia-puckin-bolical and anti-puckin-quated.

I also did a few gags which had swear-words in the punch line and I became more and more embarrassed as I realised I would be saying these words in front of Alex Montgomery. I was starting to panic and in my mind I was putting together a routine that wasn't risqué or didn't have swear-words in it. Norma's advice to me was that I should just go ahead and do my usual stuff. It wasn't until I was on my feet, though, that I decided just to stick to my normal routine.

Even before I started, I told the guests I was terrified about doing my usual material in front of my old BB captain and half expected to get three days' jankers washing dishes at the next BB camp. But the one who laughed the loudest was Alex Montgomery. He told me later that I was no longer one of his boys, I was a friend and an adult now.

I got my sense of fair play from Alex. If you did something wrong he would never berate you in front of other people. He would ask for a wee word, take you aside and explain why what you had done was wrong. It was so logical when he explained things that you accepted he was right. There was something special about him – he saw the best in people and the good in everybody.

At the Saturday BB dances, he would address the company the night before and say that if he came into the hall and saw all the boys lined up against one wall and the girls against the other wall the dances would stop. He said he wanted to see a bit of social intercourse and naturally we all started giggling and he got a wee bit embarrassed, but he was making sure the boys and girls mixed and that would be a valuable lesson for later years. These BB dances not only got us adolescents over our awkward shyness with girls, it taught us how to dance properly, which stood us in good stead a few years later when we would be going to places like The Barrowland and other dance halls in Glasgow.

Another lesson he taught us was during one BB summer camp, in Macduff, in the north-east of Scotland. I played drums in the pipe band and we were wearing T-shirts and shorts as we stood in a circle practising in the street. Alex gathered us together and suggested that next time we were playing where the public could see us, we should be dressed in trousers and shirts so we all looked the same, explaining it would reflect better on us all. We all just looked at each other and said, 'Aye, you're right, Mr Montgomery.' He was such a common-sense guy and I still think about him a lot.

At his funeral last year I stood in the crematorium and watched his coffin disappear and there was a lump in my throat the size of a tennis ball because of the effect that man had on my life. As we filed out I turned to my cousin Campbell Gordon and said, 'I don't know what stopped me from saluting as that coffin disappeared. I really had the urge to do that.' Campbell said he felt exactly the same way and so did the rest of the former 189th BB boys who were in the crematorium that day.

Yes, the BB played a huge part in my formative years and I met Tom Broadley, one my lifelong pals, there – although the first time we set eyes on each other we had a square go after an argument. I punched him, but Tom said he'd better not get into a fight because his brother had just spent a small fortune buying him an American jacket. From that moment, though, we have been great friends and Tom was the best man at my first wedding.

The discipline I got from the BB was important because I was turning into someone with a devil-may-care attitude who was only out for a laugh. Goodness knows where I would have ended up if that hadn't been tempered by the BB. Initially, I was in the 204th Glasgow BB, but soon joined the 189th as most of my pals were in that company. The BB summer camps were great and we went to places like Girvan, Carnoustie and St Anne's, in Lancashire. We did luxury camping, staying in church halls instead of in tents in the middle of a field. We all agreed that fields were for sheep, cows and farmers. But we still slept on top of a palliasse filled with straw and wrapped ourselves in a blanket.

Undoubtedly, my favourite camps were at Macduff. We went there three years in a row when I was 13, 14 and 15 and it was magic. We all had a great time and we really got to know the eccentrics among us. One of these guys was Tom Smith, who would keep you awake with his rendition of a Soviet Union radio broadcast. 'This is Radio Moscow calling,' he would shout in a

Russian accent. He was off his head, with just that lovely wee bit of eccentricity about him.

When we were in the hall at night, you could also hear the rustling of boys doing what teenagers do beneath the covers. There was one boy who seemed to be doing it all the time and I'm surprised he didn't have one arm longer than the other. I used to shout to him, 'Betty Grable!', 'Marilyn Monroe!' and when he asked me why, I told him it was so he could think of a different girl every night. He denied he did anything, but I told him you could hear him halfway down the high street.

We had a great time at Macduff going to Tarlair outdoor swimming pool, which was cut out of rock and had a café with a jukebox. We'd be there every day, although the water was so cold you could almost skate on it. On a Saturday night, we would go to the dancing at Macduff Town Hall and try to get off with the local talent. The girls were lined up along one wall and the boys along the opposite. You would position yourself opposite a girl you fancied hoping you'd be first to ask her for a dance. When the MC said take your partners it was something out of a John Wayne picture with a mad charge across the dance floor. If you weren't careful you'd end up dancing with one of your pals.

During one camp at Macduff, I ended up all at sea in a lifeboat with one of the BB officers. I had asked one of the younger boys to sweep the church hall floor, but he did a runner and I was the only one left. One of the officers, Roy McGregor, then told me I was to do the chore and I said no way and headed out the door as well. He chased me all the way down the hill to the harbour and I was running full pelt when I saw a lifeboat, which I thought was tied to the quay. I jumped on board and Roy leapt on just after me. He was just about to grab hold of me when we felt the boat moving and before we could do anything we were heading out to sea. We had unwittingly joined a trip the Lifeboat people had put on and it was 40 minutes before the boat came back to the harbour.

Another incident at the harbour ended with one of the BB lads being hailed a hero and getting himself in the local paper. There was some kind of gala event at Macduff and a wee boy fell into the sea at the harbour. The story goes that one of our boys, Lee Porte, dived in and saved him and when he got him to safety everyone was patting him on the back telling him how wonderful and brave he was. But the reality was that when the wee boy fell in, we were all looking at him splashing about in the water and Tom Smith – our Radio Moscow correspondent – pushed Lee into the sea saying, 'Lee, Lee, you can swim – go in and save him!'

When you left the Life Boys and joined the older lads in the Boys Brigade, you also graduated from Clark's Café and the Dig Deep hot peas to Marie's Café in Stonelaw Road, Rutherglen. You really began to feel grown-up because there were lots of older teenagers hanging around the café, and all the latest songs were on the jukebox. My favourites were Jerry Lee Lewis and the Everly Brothers. But when I first heard Bobby Darin singing that was me hooked and to this day he is certainly my all-time favourite singer.

I have a very catholic – oops, better watch what I'm saying! – taste in music and I often listened to my Uncle Jim's Will Starr and Jimmy Shand Scottish country dance music.

But back to Marie's Café. A tanner would get you a glass of paraffin, as we would call it. Never really knew what it was, but it was a soft drink coloured pink. Although Marie, an old Italian woman who owned the café, was a bit grumpy, you could always get round her with a bit of patter and the atmosphere was great. I used to put my arm around her and ask for a cuddle and tell her she must have been stunning when she was younger. Once, when I was showing a girl in the café how to do the Moonie dance, Marie decided she was having none of that kind of stuff in her café and ordered us to stop dancing. So I moved some chairs out the way, got hold of her and started dancing with her. She softened, and said we could dance in the corner. Even at that early age, I was using patter as a negotiating tool and to make things happen. Mainly, it would be to try to get off with a girl and, usually, failing miserably.

Another favourite pastime I had in my early teens was going skating at Crossmyloof Ice Rink, where you would find me whizzing round the ice several times a week. I had learned to skate pretty well – crossovers, skating backwards, the hockey stop, when you would spray ice up at the girls when you suddenly stopped in front of them. One of the great advantages of being able to skate well was being able to show off to the girls and skate backwards in front of them as they made their way anti-clockwise round the rink.

Although we were now in our teens, we still played stupid pranks like we were still daft wee boys in the close. One night at Crossmyloof, we set off all the fire extinguishers at the same time. It was a Saturday night in the middle of winter and it had been snowing quite heavily, so there weren't many girls there to keep our attention. We were becoming bored and decided on the prank. The rink had a balcony round it and we placed about ten fire extinguishers on the balcony all round the rink. On a signal, we ran round them all pressing the plunger and setting them off before we disappeared out the door. A bit of devilment, but immature all the same.

At the age of 14, I was to be found sporting my first pair of long trousers and at the same age I lost something – my virginity.

Oh, romance was nowhere to be seen the first time. It was up against the sink in a darkened wash house in the backcourt of a tenement where the girl lived in Govanhill. And it was over in seconds – quicker than running a wet shirt through the mangle, which was only a few inches away from us.

I had lumbered the girl at the skating after I had been checked by the stewards for skating round the ice with a bottle of Coke in my hand. After I'd been told off, she came up to me and said, 'You think you're great, don't you?'

'As a matter of fact, I am,' says I, nonchalantly.

To which she replied, 'What makes you think you're so great?'

And my riposte was, 'Are you daft? You've just got to look at me.'

After that, we skated round the ice together and I asked her if she'd ever been kissed while she was skating. She dared me and that's just what I did – planted a smacker on her lips as we skated round. That's when I knew I'd be taking her home.

We were walking through Queen's Park and I was trying my luck with her, but she said no, I'd have to wait. When we got to her tenement she led me by the hand into the wash house. She had obviously been in this film before because she was older than me and had a way of locking the door from the inside.

So much for the earth moving for us. The only thing that moved was a washboard as it fell off the sink onto the floor. However, I felt 10 ft tall and a real man as I walked home and I don't know how many times I told my pals about it the next day. I was almost going to put an advert in the *Rutherglen Reformer* that week to tell everybody.

The one thing I remember about her – well, I remember her name, but I'll spare her the embarrassment of having had it off in a wash house with a skinny wee Andy Cameron – was her beautiful teeth. She had terrific teeth and me the Buck Teeth, the Boy Wonder.

I never went out with her again and if we were at the skating we would avoid each other. It was a strange situation and introduction to the wonders of love and romance.

Chapter 4

WHEN BOYS BECOME MEN

THE BIG BROWN COFFIN SEEMED TO FILL THE ROOM OF THE SINGLE-END house where Willie McEwan had stayed. Willie was laid out in the coffin and surrounded by his workmates drinking whisky and beer chasers regaling each other with tales of his life in Sir William Arrol's Dalmarnock Iron Works and laughing with each memory. A typical Glasgow wake.

I had never seen a dead body before and I was looking everywhere but at Willie in his coffin with its lid leaning against the wall. Fidgeting in my seat and looking very ill at ease, the rest of the men noticed and one of them dug me in the ribs and said, 'Away and have a look at old Willie and pay your last respects.'

Half an hour earlier, I had walked into the single-end and had been confronted with a sight I had never encountered before in my 17 years of life. As soon as I got through the door there it was, a dead man lying in a wooden box. Although I was eight when Old Andra died and he was laid out in the back room, I had never been allowed to see his body, as Bella thought I was too young.

A few days before, Willie and I had been having our usual banter at Arrol's, where I was an apprentice plater. But now Willie was dead and the other men had insisted I come along to his house in Bridgeton for the wake the night before he was to be buried. A wake? I didn't even know what that was until that day, but I went along just the same. I thought a wake was what happened when the alarm clock goes in the morning.

I was scared to look at Willie and the rest of the men knew it. But they weren't letting me away with it. All eyes were on me as I got out of my seat and stepped over to the coffin. I was surprised how normal he looked and one of the guys said, 'He's got a wee smile on his face.'

'Aye,' says another. 'He's obviously no' realised he's no' getting any overtime this Saturday and Sunday.'

I'm trying desperately not to laugh and then I notice someone has stuck a bottle of whisky inside the coffin with Willie. 'What's that for?' I asked.

A knowing smile between the men and one told me, 'That's for Willie to take with him when he gets to heaven. It's just like Ne'erday – you don't get in unless you take a bottle for a wee hauf with you.'

'Right enough, I think I'd heard about that before,' I said, taking it all dead serious – if you'll pardon the pun.

About 10.30 p.m., the drink was finished and we were about to leave when one of Willie's brothers took the bottle of whisky out of the coffin and started pouring everyone a drink. I suggested we should leave the whisky in the coffin for Willie, but was told, 'Don't worry, he'll get a carry-out in the morning!'

What a squad they were in Arrol's. They even got a laugh out of a funeral and Willie would have been just as bad if it was someone else being laid to rest.

This was just one of the new experiences that life as a fully fledged working man had in store for me. I'd left school at 15 and it soon became obvious that I should have gone to Gallowflat Junior Secondary and not Rutherglen Academy. What I needed was knowledge of technical subjects as I was trying to win an apprenticeship as a pattern maker at the famous engineering company Weirs of Cathcart.

I had joined Weirs working as a store boy, but had ambitions of being an apprentice. The problem I had was that while I had been getting taught things like French, Latin and algebra, the test to become an apprentice was all about mechanics, and because I hadn't been taught anything about mechanics I failed miserably and it was back to taking drawings back and forward to the store. If I'd gone to Gallowflat, I would have been taught the technical subjects I needed. The boys who had come to Weirs from Gallowflat passed the entrance exam with flying colours and I didn't.

I stayed in Weirs for six months, with Bella constantly telling me I should get a trade and have something to fall back on. My Uncle Joe suggested I should get a hump on my back – a right joker he was.

I got a break and was accepted as an apprentice plater at Sir William Arrol's. You started as a plater's helper and, like all new starts, you got to run all the errands for the journeymen. That continued until someone younger came in and you moved up the ladder and they had to do the fetching and carrying.

Willie Clifford was the young boy who took over from me and he was three weeks into his role as the unofficial message boy. Big Sanny Cowie was a steel erector and he sent Willie out to the shop for cigarettes. 'Get me 20 Capstan full strength,' he says. 'And if they've no Capstan, get me anything.'

Well, they didn't have any Capstan, so Willie brought him back a pie instead. What a sight – big Sanny chasing Willie round the factory trying to hit him with the pie.

As in all workplaces in those days, there were the initiation ceremonies, like having your wedding tackle covered in axle grease by the older guys and being told it will make it grow. And there's being sent to the stores to ask for a long stand and you're left standing for half an hour or being told to fetch a left-handed screwdriver and a bucket of blue steam. I was caught out with all that kind of stuff when I started at Weirs, so I was a bit wise when the men tried it on at Arrol's.

Sammy Lynn was my journeyman and he was Celtic daft. So you can imagine the banter between the two of us because I supported Rangers. There was an old guy worked in Arrol's called Jock Lyons, and he was in the Orange Lodge. He saw me wearing a Rangers scarf one day and pulled me aside and said it was good that I was wearing the colours. Then he went on to warn me to 'watch out for those Papes in here' and I asked him how would I know who was a Catholic and who wasn't. He claimed that Catholics had their eyes closer together. I told him to give himself peace and not to be so stupid. Sure I was a Rangers fan, but that didn't mean I shouldn't like Catholics.

In fact, one of my best pals in Arrol's was a slinger called Mick Cassidy and, as you will have gathered from his name, he was a Catholic. His patter was great and he used to wind me up rotten. I was just a naive teenager and he would come up to me and say, 'Your team's f****d now. Celtic have just signed a centre-forward from Ireland, 8 ft 6 in. tall and scores goals with his head from 200 yards.'

I was going, 'Aw no – what are we going to do about him?' swallowing the story hook, line and sinker.

Mick had cauliflower ears and a bashed nose, having been a boxer, and he claimed he had fought the great Benny Lynch three times in the boxing booths. 'The first time,' says Mick, 'Benny gave me a hell of a doing for three rounds. The second time, he knocked me out in the second round and in the third fight, the only time I laid a glove on him was when we shook hands at the start.'

I never believed him and for years I would wind him up about fighting Benny Lynch. Years later, I was reading a book about Benny Lynch, which listed everyone he had ever fought and sure enough, Mick Cassidy's name was there. Mick had died by this time, but I knew his son stayed in Castlemilk, so I got in touch with him and gave his boy a copy of the book with his dad's name in it.

There were some real funny guys working at Arrol's, but the funniest was undoubtedly Dan Irvine. Dan was a welder and worked part time in the Bridgeton pub owned by former Third Lanark and Scotland international footballer, Jimmy Mason. Every Friday and Saturday night, Dan would be behind the bar pulling pints, pouring halves and holding court with his fantastic stories. People would go into the pub just to hear Dan's patter and I'm sure that's one of the reasons Jimmy Mason was so keen to have Dan working in the pub.

The lads in Arrol's told me that if you ever went to see Clyde you would find Dan standing on the same spot on the terraces at home games. So, one mid-week when Rangers weren't playing, I decided to go to Shawfield and watch the game with Dan. I got into the Shawfield and made for the spot where Dan would be standing, but I couldn't get near as there was a crowd surrounding him listening to his patter.

He would shout things like, 'Cross a ball? He couldn't cross a f****n' postal order.' And, 'Look at that goalkeeper; he's fumbled more balls than Rita Hayworth.' I was just a young lad and I was fascinated. I had never heard anything like it before. I'm sure lots of fans turned up at Shawfield to hear Dan and never mind the football on the park.

He would come into his work in the morning and would always greet you with a joke or some bit of patter. He met me at the start of a shift and said a woman had just asked him if the factory horn had blew. 'So I just told her,' says Dan, 'I've no idea what colour the horn is.' Absolutely daft, but I still laugh to myself when I think about it.

When we were working nightshift at Arrol's we would crowd into the bothy at 1 a.m. for our tea and pieces. We would be desperate to hear some of Dan's patter to keep us going through the long night. Someone would lob a verbal insult at Dan and that would set him off – it was like flicking a switch and the place lit up with his humour.

As a comedian, I now recognise that Dan's timing was terrific – he was a natural. He could do what all great comedians do and that is being able to tell a story you have heard before, but still getting you to laugh. With a crowd round him, Dan was fantastic, but suggest he should go on stage and tell some jokes and he would run a mile. He was quite happy making the tears of laughter run down the legs of his pals at work, at the football or in the pub. Dan died about ten years ago and I'm sure the angels in heaven are laughing till their wings shake at Dan's patter.

There were plenty of characters in Arrol's and plenty of guys who were dead ringers for Walter Mitty. As Dan used to say, you could throw a stone anywhere in Arrol's and it would hit a champion. But there was one guy, Sammy Scott, who claimed he was a shipmate of the famous actor Kenneth More during the war. He would come into work and talk about the latest war film starring Kenneth More and again tell us the story of how he sailed the seven seas with this film star. 'Aye, right,' we would say. 'And John Wayne was up in our house last night for mince and potatoes!' And just as the ribbing he was taking off his workmates reached a crescendo, Sammy turned up one day with a huge photo of him in his Navy uniform on the deck of a warship and who would be beside him – none other than Kenneth More.

When I was working at Arrol's, we were making the steel sections for the Forth Road Bridge. We had a guy, Tommy O'Hare, whose party piece was to crawl up behind people and paint their heels white. You would be standing talking to someone and the next thing you know your workmates are sniggering and there's Tommy sneaking off with a paintbrush in his hand.

And he didn't stop at playing that trick on his workmates. Oh no, Tommy had to make sure the management got the treatment as well. He managed to paint the heels of Frank McCrae, the general manager of Arrol's, and Bob Kerr, the civil engineer who built the Forth Road Bridge. No one was safe from Tommy and his paintbrush.

Then there was Herman the German who worked the saw that cut the giant steel beams. He had found God and walked about Arrol's holding a Bible and quoting from it. We would have to throw rivets at him during our tea-break to make him shut up and give us peace. He was called Herman the German because he talked with a German accent when he was reading out the Bible. I never found out his real name because no one ever called him anything else but Herman the German.

Working at Arrol's was a huge awakening, making me realise there was a huge world outside my tenement close at Bouverie Street. I was meeting people from all different walks of life, with a different outlook and a different view of life from the relatively sheltered one I had been experiencing.

The excitement of it all was the journey from adolescence to manhood and as I was about to find out it could be a real rough ride. But in my early years as an apprentice, the joy of earning money and being able to choose clothes and pay for them myself will always stay with me.

My first wage was £1 17/6d and it was a great feeling as I ripped open the pay packet every Friday to find a pound note, a ten-shilling note and three half-crowns inside. In time-honoured tradition, Bella said I could keep the first wage packet for myself, but from then on I would give Bella my wages and she would give me money for myself from it. The reality was while I handed over £1 17/6d, I probably got about £3 back off Bella when everything was added up.

But having that first wage packet to myself was something to savour. I used the money to buy a new pair of shoes out of Saxone's. They were casual slip-ons, oxblood in colour, had wedged heels and cost me all of 25 shillings. Boy, did I feel a real dandy walking around with those on. I couldn't believe the thrill of handing over the money to the girl at the counter and walking away with them in a box under my arm. Up until then, Bella had bought everything for me and buying these shoes was a big turning point in growing up.

By the time I was 16, I was grafting hard at Arrol's since we were on piecework. But it also meant more money in the wage packet and more visits to the trendy clothes shops in Glasgow city centre. A favourite of mine was The Esquire Shop, in Cambridge Street. It was run by a Glasgow man who spoke with an American accent when he was serving you. When you walked in he would greet you with, 'Hi, how y'all doin'?' The place was full of the latest fashions of American shirts, which was what we now call polo shirts. They're ten-a-penny now, but in those days they were a new style and something special. They were £2 each then and I would get a new one almost every week.

Once I got this real cracker and couldn't wait to wear it to the skating that night. I've got it on sitting in the house waiting for Bella to put down the mince 'n' tatties for my tea.

'Where's the brown sauce?' I asked Bella.

'I forgot to get a bottle,' she said. 'You'll have to use tomato sauce instead.'

'You can't have tomato sauce with mince 'n' tatties,' I said. 'Away down to the shop and get me some brown sauce.'

Well, one word led to another and I ended up shouting, 'You can keep your mince 'n' tatties – if there's no brown sauce I'm not eating it!'

To which Bella picked up the plate of mince and poured it over my head. The mince ran all down my face and over my fancy new shirt. Maybe tomato sauce might not have been too bad after all.

Although I was becoming more independent, I was still relying on Bella for the important things in life – like getting me up on time in the morning. I would normally get up about 6.30 a.m. for work and one morning Bella came into my room and shook me. 'Quick, get up,' she says. 'Hurry, you've slept in.'

I rushed around getting ready and Bella made me extra pieces since I didn't have time for breakfast and she pushed me out the door with me still half-sleeping. It was a cold and foggy morning and there's me standing at the bus stop in Mill Street noticing there are not many people about. Two policemen came on the scene and eyed me suspiciously. 'What are you doing?' one of them asked.

'Going to my work,' I said.

'What time do you start?' he enquired.

'Quarter to eight. Why? What's the problem?' I replied.

'Well, you've a while to wait,' the policeman said. 'It's only a quarter to two in the morning!'

Bella's clock must have been upside down and she had put me out to work in the middle of the night. It was good to get back into bed and have another few hours' kip, though.

The first time I ever had a drink was as a 16 year old. One of the guys in Arrol's was getting married and his stag night was at the Viking Bar in Rutherglen and I was invited. The barman there knew I was under age and he told me to sit in the corner and behave myself. All I had that night was a half of whisky and a half pint of beer, but that had me birlin'. Some of the boys brought me home and as I staggered through the door I shouted to Bella, 'That's me in. I'll see you in the morning.'

She knew right away something was wrong because I would

normally have sat and had a chat with her. And something certainly was wrong as the ceiling was going one way and the bed the other. I knew I was going to be sick, but the one thing uppermost in my mind was not to be sick in the house. I threw open the bedroom window and was sick into Bouverie Street. The next thing I remember was waking up in the middle of the night, freezing and lying on the floor. I climbed into my bed and the next thing I hear is Bella shaking me and saying in a stern voice, 'Get up, get up.'

'What for?' I ask. 'It's Saturday and I'm not going to work.'

'Get through to that kitchen,' orders Bella.

And there on the table was a great big plate of steaming hot porridge with the cream off the top of the milk poured over it. 'Get that down you,' says Bella. 'And in future, you watch yourself with that drink.'

I confessed I had been sick out the window and Bella said, 'I know – I've been out and cleaned it up.' That was the way of Bella. She wasn't going to let any of her family be seen making a fool of themselves.

As a teenager, I wanted to be a patter merchant and make people laugh and emulate guys like Dan Irvine, but I would have died if someone had suggested I go on a stage and tell funny stories. Perhaps being exposed to this wonderful humour and story-telling was subconsciously preparing me for the day when I would make a living out of being funny. This was, of course, allied to the fact that I was a natural show-off and you have to be to make it in show business.

Among friends, it was different. I was a performer all the time, especially in Marie's Café as I retold all the stories I had heard at Arrol's, to everyone's amazement. And during the summer, I would come off the bus in Rutherglen and meet up with my pal George Dunn, who was working in his Uncle Jimmy's shop. We would stand outside the shop watching the girls walk by and I would tell George about all the characters and goings-on at work. He never tired of hearing these stories, as it was a completely different world from his as he stood behind the counter of the shop. He had never experienced what went on in the world of factories and industry.

In my mid-to-late teens, I was leading two lives. One was in the rough and tumble of Arrol's with the swearing, bragging about girlfriends and everything that goes with being in a big workplace. My other life was in the Boys Brigade with its discipline, being on your best behaviour on Friday nights, gleaming belt buckles and shiny shoes.

Slowly but surely, however, the two lives were beginning to mix. Some of the BB stuff was being taken into Arrol's and some of the Arrol's stuff was coming to the surface in my BB life. It was just like a great big melting pot, although some of the lads at work would wind you up by asking how the hymn singing was at BB camp during the Fair. These lads would come back after the summer holidays with tales of derring-do with the ladies in Blackpool, when in fact they probably hadn't been any further out of Glasgow than Calderpark Zoo!

At that time, as far as I was concerned, you could keep Blackpool and all your other fancy resorts because the two-week long BB camps were terrific. Of course, the ambition of the BB lads from the big city was to impress the local talent and get as far as we could with them in the romance stakes, which frankly was never very far. At Macduff, you'd take a girl for a walk and be sitting on top of the hill with the big monument overlooking the sea and you only had one thing on your mind. But the girl had something else on her mind – 'No, you've no chance.'

Two years in a row I went out with a girl from Macduff called Nan Munro and in between the holidays we would write to each other. All we did was go to the pictures or meet up at the swimming pool and we thought we were in love. There was no chance of sex because her family was in the Brethren and she wasn't even allowed out on a Sunday.

About 30 years later, I was doing a show in a bingo hall in Dunfermline and I went through the usual routine of putting my hand out and saying to the women, 'Do you want to touch me? Go on, touch me if you want.'

I did this to one woman and she said she had already touched me in Macduff. I looked at her until it dawned on me I was looking at the very same Nan Munro. This time she had her lorry-driver husband – six feet across the chest – sitting beside her, so I made up a few jokes about him being there. After the show, Nan and her husband came backstage and we had a cup of tea and talked about old times. Sadly, a year later, I received a letter telling me Nan had died of cancer.

I was still spending a lot of the time at Crossmyloof Ice Rink, even after I started work. Although I was bringing in a wage, there were times when I would be skint and would have to adopt some unorthodox methods of getting home.

One night, Johnny Duncan and I were at the skating and when we got out, we discovered we only had 3d each to get home. We were 18 at the time and decided we would have to pretend we were under 15 and ask for half fares on the bus. We asked for two three-penny halves and the conductor duly obliged. He walks up to the front of the bus and on his way back he turns to us and says in a stage whisper, 'See tomorrow when you're shaving, gonnae stand a bit f*****g closer to the razor!'

It was brilliant: a typical Glasgow response. He knew fine well we were too old for a half fare, but didn't want to put us off the bus. However, at the same time, he wanted to let us know that we hadn't fooled him for a minute.

Although I loved going to the skating, as I got older the dancing began to take preference. Well, it was warmer for a start and there was physical contact with the opposite sex when you were dancing. The big recreation of the day for us young lads was trying to get a lumber.

I was just 15 when I started going to The Barrowland in Glasgow for dancing. I would be wearing my BB blazer and the rest of the guys had the fancy suits. So I was not really properly attired in the hunt for girls. Thanks to the BB dances I had been to, I knew how to step out around the floor, but I was still a bit nervous about asking strangers to dance and I would get a bit tongue-tied. Despite this, I still looked forward to queuing up outside Barrowland, in the Gallowgate, climbing up the stairs as the music of the big bands playing got louder and louder. You could feel the excitement as you caught your first glimpse of the couples dancing round the floor and the ever-optimistic idea that this might be your lucky night with the fairer sex.

I would go to The Barrowland with a couple of workmates from Arrol's – Jimmy Hunter and Bobby Brown. Jimmy was another really funny guy and always had a joke to tell you. He would come away with stories like the woman who shouted at a conductress asking if her bus went to Castlemilk, and the clippie said no.

'But it says Castlemilk on the front,' says the woman.

'It may well do,' says the conductress. 'But we've got Omo on the side and we don't take in washing!'

There were some great characters who regularly went to The Barrowland and you would recognise them every week. There was a guy called Chick-Chick who was so ugly he was like a Bud Neill drawing, but boy, could he dance. He might not have been handsome, but he was such a great dancer he never got a knock-back from any of the girls.

As well as the girls, another big attraction for me was the music. My favourite was Billy McGregor and the Gaybirds. They were fantastic musicians and played Woody Herman and Benny Goodman swing music, which was great to dance to. There was also a girl singer, Helen Thompson, who would bring the house down. She's probably better known to most people as Lena Martell who made her career singing what I would call pseudo-country songs. She was so good that people would stop dancing sometimes to listen to her.

I don't know how many times I've said to Lena that she should bring out an album of big band songs. Then people would realise just how good a singer she really is. But she never thought there was a big enough market for that kind of material. I have got to beg to differ on that one, as I'd be first in a very long queue to buy an album of Lena Martell singing the big band classics.

Monday night at Dennistoun Palais was a must, since it was Glasgow's first disco – before they called them discos. Instead of having a band, Jack Anderson from Rutherglen played records of singers like Ella Fitzgerald and Billy Eckstein. So we'd have a few pints and head for The Palais on a Monday for the record night. There was a corner in The Palais where all the pretty people stood and they all looked liked they'd just stepped out of a Burton's window. It was a real posers' corner with the lads in their Italian suits and the girls dolled up to the nines and looking magnificent. Nice looking they might have been, but they couldn't dance properly to save themselves. The only dancing they did was the Moonie.

One of the girls in Posers' Corner caught my eye one week. She was an absolute stunner and, in terms of looks, she was right out of my league. But I was desperate to ask her to dance. Well, it took me three weeks to pluck up the courage to ask her for a dance, instead of watching her from the other side of the dance floor. When I did and she said 'yes' my heart was pounding and I couldn't believe my luck that such a beautiful girl was going to dance with me.

When we got on the floor, I started to chat her up as best I could, hoping to make a good impression. 'You'll never guess how long it's taken me to ask you to dance,' I said. 'I've been looking at you from across the floor for three weeks.'

But my illusions were shattered when she replied, 'Is that so? Well I hope you've f*****g seen enough!'

I tried to explain that I meant it had taken me a long time to get the courage to ask her to dance and she said, 'Well, start dancing and stop f*****g blethering.'

Still determined to make a good impression, I continued and asked her where she worked. Her reply was, 'You're a right nosy bastard, aren't you?'

Well, that was it. I'd tried my best to chat her up and all I got was a mouthful of swear-words, so it was once round the dance floor and nothing more. I had thought she was an angel, an absolute stunner – that was until she'd opened her mouth. I imagined it would have been like dancing with a film star, but it ended up like I was dancing with a riveter from the shipyards.

When you were dancing with a girl and chatting her up, the trick was to make yourself sound more interesting than an apprentice plater. So we used to make up exotic jobs for ourselves and tell the girls we had been to lands far across the sea. One night, I was chatting up a girl and I told her I was in the Merchant Navy and had just come home from visiting places like San Francisco, Rio de Janeiro and New York. Oh yes, I explained, we had to lay up for a week in New York and I had visited all the tourist hot-spots.

I was just getting into my stride when she whispered in my ear, 'You're a lying wee s***e. You work beside my brother, Tam, in Arrol's.' Right enough, the course of true love never did run smooth.

When I was a teenager, sometimes you didn't have to cross your own front door to have a good time. I remember some great parties at our house. Everybody would do a turn – either sing a song or play an instrument. When my father's cousin, Jim Robertson, came to the house for a party, he would always bring his accordion and that would kick off a big debate about who was the best accordionist in Scotland – Jimmy Shand or Will Starr.

Jim had a pal, Johnny McTear, who would come to the parties with him and he would always volunteer to compère the proceedings. Now Johnny was from Rutherglen and spoke just like the rest of us. That was until he started to compère, when he would suddenly find an American accent.

'Howzitgaun, Bella?' he would ask on arrival. 'Aye, the wee man's fair growin' up'. But when he rose to his feet to introduce the turns it would be, 'How ya doin' y'all? OK, we're gonna have a real swell party,' in an American accent.

I never understood why he did this and there was never any reaction from anyone else in the room. He must have been doing this for years and everybody just accepted it.

Another great 'act' at parties in Bella's was Jim Bowles. While the rest of us would give everyone a song, his party piece was to put on a Glenn Miller record and conduct it! He would stand up and wave his hands about as if he was in front of the Big Band. Then, when it came to a drum solo, he would pretend he was playing the drums and when the saxophone came on, he'd play that as well. The daftest thing though, was that we would sit and watch him and give him a round of applause when the record was finished. I don't know if he had seen this done in a film, but he did this for years until his wife, Margaret, eventually managed to stop him because she was so embarrassed.

I was 18 when I started going out with May Brodie, who would become my first wife. May was a year older than me and I knew her from going to Marie's Café. She would be sitting with her group of pals and I would be with mine. But since it was Rutherglen, everyone knew each other anyway.

My pal Tom Broadley lived round the corner from May and we were walking round to his house one night when May and her sister were going in the same direction. We got talking and I asked May if she wanted to go to the pictures on Saturday night and she said yes. May was a good-looking girl, was easy to talk to and us getting together was something that seemed to happen quite naturally. Although she was from a Catholic family and her father and brother were Celtic fans, that didn't bother me.

In those days, both sides of the divide were telling their kids not to go out with someone of the opposite religion. It was a terrible situation, but thankfully a lot of the younger generation never paid any heed and defied their parents. There were a lot of mixed marriages, as they were called then. This rebelliousness of the teenagers from that era has gone a good way to diluting the sectarian problem since the '50s and '60s. And when these couples had kids, it meant they had grandparents who were both Catholic and Protestant and they were even more adamant they wouldn't have anything to do with sectarianism. I accept we have a long way to go to completely eradicate the cancer of sectarianism in our society, but it's certainly not as bad as when I was growing up.

So May and I would meet up in Marie's Café on a Sunday after she had been to mass and I had come from Bible class. We went out regularly as girlfriend and boyfriend for about a year until, to everyone's surprise, May and I brought more than a stick of rock back from a holiday in the Isle of Man. We came back with the news that we had got engaged and the only rock to be seen was a diamond, on the third finger of May's left hand.

Chapter 5

BELLA . . . I'VE SOMETHING TO TELL YOU

TALK ABOUT SPRINGING A SURPRISE. MAY AND I HAD LEFT RUTHERGLEN TWO weeks earlier, just another boyfriend and girlfriend heading off for a two-week holiday with our friends. And now here we were pulling into Glasgow's Central Station, excited and preparing ourselves to tell our respective families that we were engaged to be married.

It started off as just another two-week holiday at the Glasgow Fair of 1959, heading for the Isle of Man like thousands of others. It wasn't just the two of us – we went in a crowd, May and her pals staying in one boarding house and us guys staying in another.

We were having a great time and maybe the holiday mood took its grip when we decided we would get engaged. It would certainly come as a shock to everybody back home as we hadn't told anyone this was going to happen. Never mind telling our family and friends – we didn't know we were going to do it ourselves!

The ring cost me £7 – which was a lot of money in those days, and I had bought it out of my holiday money on the Isle of Man. Everybody who was on holiday with us had a big party when we announced our engagement and everything was just hunky-dory – as it is when you are in love and get engaged.

However, when we got back to Rutherglen and told everyone we were engaged, the brown stuff hit the fan because I was a

Protestant and May was a Catholic. Everybody was asking us what we were going to do. Which church were we going to get married in? Was I going to turn and become a Catholic? What was May going to do and what would happen when we had kids? In those days, it was really tough going through with a mixed marriage.

After we got off the train, we first made our way to May's parents' house and told them we were engaged. Ellen and Patrick Brodie were very nice about it and congratulated us. Maybe they thought nothing would come of our relationship because they never made an issue of our religion all the time we were going out together.

Then it was over to Bella's, who said she was happy for us, but warned us not to rush into anything and do anything stupid. If only I'd listened. May's parents were obviously having words with her when I wasn't in their company and telling her not to give up her faith. This was a bit late in the day for May, because she always said if her mother hadn't insisted on her going to mass on a Sunday she never would have bothered going.

Eventually, May's parents said they wanted their daughter to get married in the chapel and I replied that it wasn't a problem as far as I was concerned – but I wasn't going to become a Catholic myself. They insisted I had to, because they wanted the children to be brought up as Catholics, but my view was that when they were old enough, the children could make up their own minds what church they went to.

Obviously, there was a bit of tension between the Brodies and myself, but that didn't deter May and me from doing what all young lovers do and by September – only a couple of months after we'd got engaged – we discovered May was pregnant. So much for heeding Bella's 'don't do anything stupid' warning.

May told her mother and father and I told Bella that a baby was on the way. It was a case of, 'Er . . . we're getting married soon.'

'Why, what's the rush?'

'Well, it's like this – May's er, eh, she's expecting.'

Bella took it quite well, as did Mr and Mrs Brodie. But Bella said to me, 'What have I been telling you for years? A man can put his bunnet on and walk away – a girl carries her shame in front of her.'

That's a great line, but of course, when you're that age you never listen.

I was more worried about my Uncle Jim's reaction. But his attitude was that I'd been a stupid bugger, but it was my life, what was done was done and I'd better just get on with it and make myself a good husband and father.

I felt I had let Bella down after all she'd done over the years looking after me. I was earning good money and was able to give money to Bella and now all the money I had was going to go into my own house. But after the initial shock Bella was great, helping out with bits of furniture and always willing to give us some money until next payday. And to be fair, the Brodies were also good at helping us out.

Society wasn't as sophisticated as it is now about such matters and doing the right thing meant getting married. May was quite happy to get married in Munro parish church, in Rutherglen, in November 1959, but her mother and father refused to come to the wedding because it wasn't in the chapel.

I wasn't ostracised by the Brodies and I was in and out of their house. It's just that they weren't happy about May not getting married in the chapel and not going to the wedding was their protest.

I had just turned 19, but was still quite happy to be getting married and embarking on a new adventure. My pal, Tom Broadley, was the best man and his girlfriend, Sheila – who went on to marry Tom – was maid of honour.

Money was going to be really tight for us newly-weds, so the reception was a meal for the four of us in The 101 Restaurant in Glasgow. After our wedding meal, May and I went back to our new home together, which was a room and kitchen that Bella had got us upstairs from her house.

I was happy to be married with a baby on the way. I thought this was for life and was amazed how quickly I settled and couldn't believe I was going to be a daddy. My first daughter, Ellen – named after May's mum – was born in May 1960. The Brodies really took to their new granddaughter and the religious problem was never mentioned again. It was just like a light had been switched on and

Mrs Brodie was really good to us, looking after Ellen so both of us could go out to work. She turned out to be a great mother-in-law.

Ellen was their first grandchild and as far as they were concerned she was number one. Ellen was never referred to as Ellen – it was always Ellen Cameron, which was a good sign that, at last, I had been accepted.

For the first couple of years, the marriage was great. I was still an apprentice at Arrol's, but the money when you were on nightshift was good. I loved coming home on a Friday with my wage packet. I never went to the pub like many men did – it was straight up the road to see May and Ellen.

There would be a big fire on and Ellen would be in her cot. I would play records and sit on the couch cuddling May. I've always been a romantic and I thought being able to do this in my own home was great.

I might have been the romantic, but May was more practical and worked extremely hard to earn money for the family. And that perhaps is where the seeds of separation and eventual divorce were sown.

I was the kind of guy who would say, 'Right, we've got £3 left until the end of the week – let's go to the pictures.' But May would want to keep the money for messages, despite me saying we could borrow money from Bella until payday. The feeling that I didn't want to be tied to the house was beginning to creep up on me and that feeling was accelerated when, after my time was out at Arrol's, I went to work on the buses.

I started as a conductor when I was 20, and later trained to be a driver. I enjoyed meeting different people every day and the chat on the buses was great. I made friends with some really good people. The two women who had the most influence on me in those days were an older woman called Betty Tait, who was a real family person and warned me not to try anything on with the clippies, and Margaret Baird, who was like the wee sister I never had. Both were great pals and that was as far as it went with the pair of them.

But it wasn't quite so platonic with other women. Only two years after getting married, I began chatting up the ladies with the sole purpose of getting them into bed. Apart from Betty and Margaret, I wanted to have an affair with any woman I came across. And it's something to this day that haunts me and I'm certainly not proud of how I was behaving then.

The first time I was unfaithful to May was in October 1961, when I went over to Belfast with some pals to see Scotland play Northern Ireland. Scotland won 6–1, with three Rangers players scoring all the goals. Ralph Brand got two, Davy Wilson got one and Alex Scott scored a hat-trick.

We stayed at Robinson's Hotel, in Belfast, which didn't have a bar because it was a temperance hotel. The lads were waiting downstairs for me to go out for a few beers, but unknown to them I was upstairs having my way with a chambermaid. She was in my room cleaning up when I gave her a bit of patter and she suddenly came on to me. She locked the door from the inside and said she wasn't going to let me out until she had me. The temptation was just too much and I obliged her request.

When I eventually got downstairs, I was afraid to tell the rest of the boys what had happened – they would have been shocked. None of the other guys were chasing women, they were there for the football and a few bevvies.

But I had got away with it. And if you can get away with it once, you think you can get away with it again and again. The shame of what I did that night didn't hit me until three or four years later, when I was being unfaithful on a regular basis – even when May was pregnant the second time. All of a sudden, I realised the mistake I'd been making and I said to myself, 'This isn't right. It's so unfair on May.'

But in the years between the sinning and the shame there were many times I would sneak off with other women. I've got to be honest, at the time, the feeling of having affairs and the fact you are attractive to women was magic. I think it's just a male thing. But when I think about it now, I realise what a terrible thing I was doing.

By 1963, May was expecting again and we had moved to a new house – a prefab in Liddoch Road, Rutherglen. My second daughter, Marion – named after my Auntie Marion – was born in

December of that year. I had been playing the loving husband at home, while playing an entirely different game away from home.

One morning, I reported for work at the bus garage at 3.55 a.m. I was due to leave the garage with a conductress at 4.20 a.m. to be at Castlemilk at 5 a.m., taking a busload of cleaners into the city. As I was bringing the bus to the front of the garage, the conductress – who shall remain nameless – was making a cup of tea. When I jumped out of my cab to get her, she said we wouldn't have to leave for another 20 minutes because there would be nobody to pick up on the way to Castlemilk and we would get a clear run.

Jokingly, I said, 'We've got time for a wee cuddle then.' And by the way she said 'don't you start' I knew it was more than a wee cuddle she was interested in. So there we were at quarter past four in the morning having it off on the table in the bothy at the Glasgow Corporation bus garage in Battlefield Road, Langside.

My shift finished at 11.30 a.m. and I was on what was called a spread-over – a rather apt choice of words, considering what had happened earlier that day – which meant you didn't start the next part of your shift until 4.45 p.m. so you had the afternoon to yourself.

I was having a cup of tea in the garage before I headed home and this other conductress began chatting to me. She was saying she wasn't going to bother going home before she started again at 4.45 p.m., as there would be no one in her house. Since I was going her way in any case, I said I would give her a lift to her house if she changed her mind about going home.

When we got there, she asked me in for a cup of tea and before the kettle had boiled we were in bed together. I bid her farewell and headed to pick up Ellen who was being looked after that day by Bella. I got back to my house and made her tea waiting for May to come in from her work.

Off I go to work again and pick up a bus with another conductress and after the shift is finished about 9 p.m., I offer to drop her off at her house on my way home. On our way, she asks me if I want to go for a drink so we stop off at the Albert Bar. I had a Bacardi and Coke and she had a Snowball. We're sitting there chatting and I jokingly suggested she was planning to take me to her house and interfere with me.

She laughed and said, 'You'd like to think so, wouldn't you?'

I said that I wouldn't be buying her any more drink unless she said she would take me home with her. It was just a bit of patter and when I asked if she wanted another drink she said, 'I thought we were going back to my place.' And that was it.

Three women in the one day. At the time I was thinking, 'Yes, ya beauty – you've knocked it off again.' I can't explain it, but that was how I felt at the time.

I'm certainly not proud of it and since then I have thought about how I behaved and I am thoroughly ashamed. In fact, when I do think about it, I cringe. I did a terrible thing to my wife, who was pregnant with our second child, working hard to earn money for our family and I was trying to get anything female that had a pulse into bed.

For a time after Marion was born, I stopped the womanising, but eventually I was on the philandering trail again. I may have been a bad husband because I was being unfaithful, but I always made sure the family were looked after. I always had a job and there was money coming into the house.

By the end of 1963, I had found myself a much better-paid job on the production line at the Rootes car factory in Linwood, Renfrewshire. And, of course, the one-night stands continued. There were plenty of women working at Rootes and I soldiered on trying to bed as many of them as possible.

I would work a twilight shift and tell May I was going to a workmate's stag night when, in fact, I was heading to the dancing in Glasgow looking for a lumber. One night, I came out of The Locarno with a girl on my arm and who should be standing there but May's sister, Ellen. She saw me, but never uttered a word about it to May. Maybe she should have.

I hid the fact I was having affairs very badly. May would smell perfume from me and she wasn't daft. Maybe she was like a lot of women in that situation who turned a blind eye, as long as it didn't affect their family. It got to the stage that, no matter where I was working, I would be having an affair with some woman or other.

I even went on holidays myself. The car factory would take the Paisley Fair – the first two weeks in August – as an annual holiday and my wife would get the Glasgow Fair, which is a fortnight earlier. May, Ellen, Marion and Mrs Brodie would go to Rothesay for the Glasgow Fair and I would head off somewhere else with one of my pals for the Paisley Fair.

Once I went on holiday to Margate with a pal of mine, Dougie Murphy. Then I discovered May's sister, Ellen, was there as well. It was like something out of a James Bond film, me looking over my shoulder to make sure she didn't catch me sneaking away with another woman.

The realisation that I shouldn't be behaving like this and carrying on behind May's back hit me in 1968. I had been seeing someone and I decided I should come clean and move out of the house and stay with this other woman. That didn't last. After a fortnight, I was back home with May, but now that it was all out in the open, we confronted the problems we faced in our marriage.

It was the first time she admitted that she knew I had been going out with other women, and I promised it would stop. By this time, we had moved to our third home. It was a two-bedroom council house in Alloway Crescent, in The Spittal area just outside Rutherglen near Croftfoot. But a new house sadly didn't mean a new start for May and me. By then, the damage was done and the marriage was over.

After 14 years of marriage, we separated and two years later we divorced. It was my fault, I was the one who had been unfaithful and it wouldn't be fair to blame May for anything.

It was all over, but in reality the marriage was over long before that. May and I had grown apart over the years – she wanted different things from life. I was facing a brick wall and I had to climb over it and get on with the rest of my life. On the one hand, when eventually we admitted to each other the marriage was over, there was a sense of relief within me. On the other, though, it broke my heart to break up our family, because I dearly loved our two girls, Ellen and Marion. I knew they loved me and we had great times together when they were young.

By the time we had separated, I had left Rootes and had various jobs as a delivery driver. During the school holidays, the girls would come with me in the cab of the van and we would drive all over the west of Scotland singing songs as we made our way to the next shop to make a delivery. Sadly, Marion took the break up of our marriage much worse than Ellen. Even after all those years since my marriage broke up, to the girls and to May I would still say 'sorry' – I never intended to cause them any pain or heartache and I never would. I will never forgive myself for what I did to them. I broke up the marriage and I blame myself for that.

My feelings for May now are of admiration. She has always been a hard worker and has now settled down, having remarried. It's the kind of marriage she always wanted. She wants a structure to her life and she's happy for a man who will go for a couple of pints and always come home to her. And if they go to The Glens social club on a Saturday or Sunday, then she's happy.

Although I didn't realise it at the time we got married, I have a different nature from that. I wanted more from life. May's nature was that she is not a very demonstrative or touchy-feely person and I am. I would never leave the house without giving May a kiss and a cuddle and I would do the same when I came back in. But May wasn't like that. When she was growing up she became a sort of mother figure to her brothers and sisters since both their parents would be at work. I don't know if May didn't get a lot of cuddles when she was growing up, but she was never one for showing affection like that.

We would still be married if it had been up to May, because she was one for believing marriage is for life – just like her mother and father, who didn't believe in divorce. I admire that in May. But after all the nonsense I got up to, the marriage just couldn't last.

However, I stuck with it for 14 years and whatever might have happened in that time there are two good things to come out of it. I have two fantastic daughters from that marriage and I still see them regularly.

When we broke up, I certainly couldn't afford to run two houses, so May and the girls moved back to her parents' house and I stayed on at The Spittal.

As well as the '60s being a time of womanising for me, I also joined the Freemasons and, unknown to me, the harmonies, which take place after meetings – when everyone has a drink and relaxes – would be the start of what would end up being a total life-changing experience for me.

While other guys would get up and sing songs, I would do what could be loosely called a routine and tell jokes. This went down a storm with the guys and when we visited other lodges I was always asked to tell a few gags at their harmonies. This was happening on a more regular basis and it was quite well known among the Masonic fraternity that there was a funny wee guy from Rutherglen who would give you a laugh after the meetings. I didn't know it, but that was me on the way and taking the first step into showbiz.

I know that Freemasonry sometimes gets a bad name and is the butt of many jibes, but I joined the Masons for one reason and that was curiosity – I wanted to find out what it was all about. My Uncle Jim and Uncle Joe were in the Masons and they invited me to join. I think Freemasonry is a good thing – although some people give it a bad name by abusing their position and the privileges of being a Freemason. But if you live your life by the tenets of Freemasonry, you won't go wrong because it's all about doing good charitable works and respecting your fellow man.

I enjoyed it and became an office-bearer, putting other new members through their degrees. It also got me out on a Friday night and I could have a wee drink with the boys.

But there's something else I'm not proud of. I would tell May I was going to a Masonic meeting when, in reality I was going to meet another woman. No, I'm definitely not proud of having used the Masons as an excuse for even more inexcusable behaviour.

Another sign of things to come was the day a nosy neighbour caught a glimpse of Andy Cameron the would-be performer, thinking he's Bobby Darin at the Copacabana. We were living in the prefab in Liddoch Road at the time and I was working nightshift. I had got up just after 3 p.m. and, since it was the middle of winter and snowing heavily, had the fire blazing and the tea ready for May coming home from her work.

I had put on a Bobby Darin record – my all-time favourite

singer – and was cleaning the hearth with a brush. One minute I'm holding a brush and the next it's suddenly become a microphone and I've been transported onto the stage of the famous New York nightclub, the Copacabana. Oh, yes, the Yanks would have loved me. I was singing along to the record adamant that the brush was a microphone, eyes closed and doing all the moves around the front room which, of course, was really a stage.

Suddenly, I became conscious of someone looking at me and when I turned round there was this wee woman staring through my window. The snow was dripping off her nose and her face had a look of incredulity on it. She could see me dancing about the room singing into a brush, but couldn't hear the record playing.

She must have thought I had just come out of the madhouse and the last I saw of her was as she was trudging through the snow shaking her head. I wonder if she thought I was any good.

Chapter 6

FUN AND LAUGHTER ON THE BUSES

THE BUS ROLLS THROUGH THE TEATIME RUSH-HOUR TRAFFIC AND PEOPLE IN the queue at the bus stop in Argyle Street in Glasgow city centre are eager to get on board and head home after a long day's work.

The bus is almost full to the gunwales. I can see there are about 30 people hoping to get on, but there's only room for another two standing passengers. There's going to be a few disappointed faces. I'm driving one of the new one-man operated (OMO) buses, although for the initial settling-in period there's still a conductress on board. It's a big change from being a driver stuck in a cab at the front of the bus, not being able to talk to anyone and it certainly makes your shift go quicker. In these OMOs, the driver sits opposite the door and you can chat to the passengers as they come in.

I pull up at the bus stop and Rene Watson, the conductress, shouts that there's only room for the first two passengers in the queue. There's more than a few grumbles and the woman who is third in the queue asks, 'How long is the next bus going to be?'

Well, I couldn't resist it and I probably should have kept my mouth shut, but I told the woman, 'The same length as this one!' I was about to drive off, having a right good chuckle to myself thinking that was a right clever reply, when the woman shouted, 'And will it be a f*****g monkey that's driving that one as well?'

You just can't beat Glasgow folk for their patter and their off-the-cuff put-downs. I've used plenty of stories and funny lines that have come from my own life experiences and that was just one of them. I use that story in my act and it's absolutely true. That's what makes life worth living – wee compliments like that.

They say truth is stranger than fiction and I can tell you that truth is also a lot funnier as well. The things that happened and the things people said when I was either on the buses, working in the Rootes car plant, or driving delivery vans would keep a comedian in material for almost a lifetime.

As I have said, as soon as my apprenticeship was finished by late 1960, I joined Glasgow Corporation Transport, first as a conductor and then as a bus driver. The camaraderie was great and the fun even better. There were people with the same sense of humour as me who loved to laugh at daft things.

I was driving a bus before I ever drove a car and having a Public Service Vehicle licence meant I could drive a car as well. I spent four weeks at the bus-driving school and there were several of us taking our test on the same bus. We would swap over in the driver's cab once we had finished our part of the test. Everybody had to do a reverse, but really, my bus-driving test consisted of me taking the bus from a bus stop outside the Carlton cinema in Townhead up to Royston Road, turning right and pulling up at the first bus stop, making sure the platform was in line with the bus stop. That was it – I went upstairs and the next guy took over from me.

When I eventually got my first car, which was a Mini, I found it difficult because it wasn't as long or as broad as a bus. One day, when I was driving to my work, there was a bus behind me and as I was passing a bus stop this guy put his hand out to signal to the bus. Did I not just go and pull in to pick him up, forgetting I was driving a car not a bus. I was so embarrassed that I pulled back out into the traffic driving the car from beneath the dashboard so no one would see me.

And anyone who has watched the TV sitcom *On the Buses* will know the relationship between bus drivers, conductresses and their inspector can be a fraught one, to say the least. The first buses I drove were the old-fashioned double-deckers with the open entrance at the back and I would be sitting in a separate cab up the front with passengers sitting through the window behind me. There was always an understanding between a driver and his conductress that they would look out for each other. If an inspector was standing at a bus stop waiting for his next victim to come along, the first person to see him would be the driver. Apart from checking passengers' tickets, there were certain rules and codes that had to be adhered to or you could be in trouble. If a conductress was caught sitting down that could mean you would get a line and had to report to the chief inspector and possibly face a suspension if you didn't have a good reason for it.

We operated a code that if a driver spotted an inspector he would knock on the window behind him twice with his elbow, warning the conductress that an inspector was about to come on board. One day, as I was approaching a bus stop, I spied the tell-tale hat of an inspector standing there, so I duly banged on the window behind me. But instead of just making the required amount of noise to signal a warning, the window flew open and hit a woman passenger on the nose.

Unknown to me, I was driving a bus which was sometimes used to train drivers and the window opened so an instructor could talk to the learner bus driver. The window hadn't been locked and when I gave it a dunt with my elbow, it swung open back inside the bus and gave this poor lady a right sore one.

There was blood and snotters everywhere and all hell broke loose before the poor woman was taken to the hospital casualty department. I got a line for that incident and ten days later I was standing in front of the grim-looking chief inspector. He told me that the woman's nose had been broken and she also had to have stitches.

'What happened?' he asked.

'Well, the window just suddenly flew open,' I said. 'I might have accidentally hit it and it couldn't have been closed properly when the bus was last out on a training run.'

Fortunately for me, the chief inspector had come from the days of the tramcar and had no idea about the early warning procedure when an inspector appeared on the horizon. I got away with a few stern words but no suspension, and was immediately back behind the wheel keeping my eyes peeled for inspectors.

One of the inspectors at our garage was folk singer Alastair McDonald's father. He was called The Professor because he wore his glasses at the end of his nose and looked over them to see the number on the front of the buses. I was based at Langside garage and when I was there they called me Sanny.

There were plenty of tricks bus drivers and conductresses played to avoid having a packed bus which meant having to march up and down both top and bottom deck taking fares and pulling up at every bus stop. One scam was that when you knew the bingo was about to come out in the city centre, you would do your best not to be the first bus on the run. The trick was to press the starter motor when the engine was running and this would invariably jam the starter and cut the engine. Of course, it would take a while for the mechanic to come out of the garage to fix it and by this time the bingo punters were already home and the coast was clear for an easy run.

I was a victim of this ploy and the fly man was a driver who lived with his conductress. That was really unusual in those days but the two of them didn't give a hoot what anyone said and they just got on with it. The driver pulled the starter trick when he was at the terminus at Castlemilk and I was the mug behind him who was slaughtered with a double-load of passengers going from the city centre to Castlemilk.

I was raging when I found out and when I got to Castlemilk, I saw his bus and I got out the cab and went over to give him a piece of my mind. But he was nowhere to be seen and neither was the conductress. I was standing on the downstairs deck of the bus when I felt the bus moving from side to side. I looked upstairs and I couldn't believe my eyes. There are the two of them going hammer and tongs on a bench seat on the upper deck. The bus is shaking and there're people standing at the bus stop waiting to get on.

There was a scam that some of the conductors and conductresses worked with old tickets. Passengers would stick their ticket on the back of the seat in front of them and when they got off, the clippie would collect them and put them in his or her bag. The next time a passenger came on and asked for, say a fourpenny one, they would be given the old ticket and the fourpence would go into the clippie's pocket. They would maybe do this three times in the one run, but it was a dangerous game to play. You could easily be caught if the inspector came on and checked the passengers' tickets. You would get the sack for just a few shillings. When I was a conductor, I certainly wasn't into anything like that, having been the good BB boy and all that.

Playing cards was a favourite pastime for bus drivers at the Langside garage and sometimes the stakes would get really out of order. In my early days as a conductor, my driver took me up to a card school in King's Park. It was our spread-over day and we had a few hours between our morning runs and 4 p.m. when we were due to start again. I was never a great one for poker and certainly not gambling my money away – I needed it for things like paying the rent and, at the time of course, feeding my family. I was sitting in this house watching the guys play and I still had my bag with all the money in it from the morning runs. The game was starting to get a bit tense, with some guys losing a lot of money. My driver was one of them.

'Sanny, give us ten pounds out your bag,' he said to me, and I told him to go and take a f**k to himself. There was no way I was going to put my job on the line so he could lose another hand of poker. I was raging with him and I walked out of the house leaving him behind.

Later, when we met up at the garage for the second part of our shift he said to me, 'You did the right thing with that tenner.'

I was still angry and I said, 'Don't ever ask me to do that again – not with their money. Don't ever ask me to dip the bag.'

Now, there's a fine line between genius and insanity and one conductor in particular walked that line. He was one of the brainiest guys I have ever met and had been at university. But he had decided the academic life wasn't for him and he signed up to be a conductor. He was certainly a real brainbox, but he left his common sense on the mantelpiece when he came to his work every day. How he ever became a conductor I'll never know – he was scared of a crowd of passengers and they would poke fun at him.

Once when I was driving and he was my conductor, we pulled into St Enoch's Square at teatime and the bus filled up in no time with people heading home after work. You're only supposed to allow five people standing and I was waiting on the bell for us to go and I looked in the wing mirror. The bus was packed like sardines and there were folk hanging off the bus platform.

I got out my cab, came round to the door and shouted on this conductor, as I couldn't see him anywhere. Then I heard his voice: 'I'm under the stairs – I can't get out!' He had gone under the stairs and was sitting on the box that held all the tickets while it seemed half of Glasgow decided to squeeze their way on to the bus. The passengers pushing their way onto the bus must have been too much for him and he obviously thought the best place for him was under the stairs. When passengers had a go at him he would never growl back. That kind of thing happens all the time, but when someone can't give as good as they get it can be really cruel.

I would never wish any harm on him, but he had some really strange ways. He would never open the canteen door because he didn't want to touch the handle. He would wait until someone else opened the door and he would walk in behind them. When he got into the canteen, he would get a cup of tea and two cakes, only this guy would eat the cakes with a knife and fork – he didn't want to touch the cakes either.

At the front door of the garage, there was a big barrel of water for drivers to fill their radiators. With no explanation, he would clean his metal case that contained his spare rolls of tickets and other bits and pieces by dipping the whole case into the barrel of water. The rolls of tickets inside would be soaking. But that was the way he was and he got away with all his little foibles. For all that he was a real brainbox. But the last I heard was that he was caught swimming naked in the Queen's Park boating pond one Christmas Eve.

The Glasgow bus drivers and conductors had a very competitive football league and I loved playing for our garage's team. We won the treble – league and two cups – one year and when we were playing games everybody would pile into a double-decker bus and drive to the match. One game we were playing was against the Parkhead garage at Helenvale and we were winning 7–4. That's the kind of scores you'd get. They got a soft penalty and mayhem broke out, with fists flying, but nobody got booked or ordered off.

Their guy is about to take the penalty and one of our players, big Gus Hoban, walks up to their penalty-taker and says, 'By the way, I'm sh*****g your back end. I'm giving your back end one.' The back end was the name given by drivers to conductresses.

The guy swallows it hook, line and sinker and is so angry at what Gus is saying he puts the ball ten feet over the bar. Then Gus says, 'It's all right, mate. I'm only kidding.' I don't know if that kind of thing goes on in professional football, but as a tactic it worked great for us.

Whenever we would win something we would all adjourn to the Albert Bar and have a right good session.

I left the buses at the end of 1963 and went to work in the Rootes car plant in Linwood as a machine operator on the line that made the Hillman Imp. What a place that was. Butchers, bakers and candlestick makers – anybody, in fact – were hired to work machinery they had never seen in their lives before as they made cars. And they wondered why they couldn't get good workmanship.

Working in the factory was a whole new life for me, a massive learning curve and another part of growing up. There were some real strange goings-on in Rootes. The place even had its own unofficial, official bookie. The management knew what was going on but they turned a blind eye to it. All this guy did all day was stand in the toilets and take the lines from the guys, then nip out to the bookies to place the bets.

There was one gaffer that nobody liked and everyone talked about him behind his back. One day, he called us all together and said, 'I know there's people talking about me behind my back and they're making certain allegations and if I ever catch the alligators . . .'

Well, we all burst out laughing when he said this. He was really angry and started throwing things at people and shouting, 'You bastards!'

I know the alligator line has become a bit of a cliché, but that's exactly what he said. That's probably where the story started, but nowadays every second workplace has had someone say that.

Working in Rootes is where I found out that Johnstone people don't like Paisley Buddies. Hughie Campbell was from Johnstone and you should have heard him slagging off Paisley folk for being tight-fisted. That was the first time I heard the saying that when Paisley folk go on holiday the seagulls take their own pieces.

I got lots of material for my act in later years from remembering the patter that went on in Rootes about Paisley people. They would come out with stuff like a Paisley man dropped a two bob bit and he got down to pick it up that quick, it hit him on the head.

And there's the one about the Paisley man on a night out in the pub with his pals who always asked for a Horlicks when his mates were having a pint. By the time it got to his round he was asleep.

I never really believed all that stuff about them being tight-fisted, but it was a great source of laughter. I've met some smashing Paisley guys in my time and there was one Buddie in particular who soon put a stop to a heckler who had been plaguing me all night in a social club years later when I was trying to do my act. More of that later.

However, one Paisley man did nothing to contradict the myth of Buddies being tight-fisted. I used to buy the broadsheet *Scottish Daily Express* every day and it had a pull-out racing section. I wasn't that interested in racing, but I began to notice when I got home that this racing section was missing.

I was standing at my machine one day and I watched this Paisley man take the paper out my jacket pocket, take the racing section out and put the paper back in the pocket. I followed him into the toilet and he's in one of the cubicles. I told him to get out and bring the racing section he had nicked from my paper with him.

I told him that if he'd asked I would have given him the racing section and, in any case, why didn't he buy the paper himself. 'I'm not paying threepence for a racing section,' he replied.

There was one unit machine-block manager called Davie Ferguson – or Grey Fox as we would call him. And a sly fox he was. He would get you to do anything for him he was that fly. One day, he came up to me and said, 'I can't get anyone to work Thursday on an all-nighter. Will you do it for me?'

I asked him what the rate was and when he said it was time and a half, I told him I wasn't interested. He came back ten minutes later and said, 'I'll give you time and a half and a guarantee of the next six Sundays overtime.' Now, Sunday working was a great earner and I agreed to the all-nighter on the Thursday. However, as was typical with the Grey Fox, come Friday he came up to me and said, 'You'll never believe what these bastards have done – they've just gone and cancelled all the overtime on a Sunday!'

I was always cracking jokes and coming away with patter like the rest of the guys, and Margaret Murnie – who worked on the machine opposite me – was the first person to tell me I should go on the stage because I made her laugh so much.

I spent three years in Rootes, but got totally sickened by the wildcat strikes and the guys walking out for really daft things.

'We're out on strike, Andy.'

'What for?'

'I've got cheese on my piece!'

There was one guy on nightshift who actually made himself a bed with curtains round it and he would spend the night sleeping. He was caught in a sleeping bag with his overalls off having himself a nice wee rest. Naturally, he was sacked and that caused another strike. It turned out he had another job during the day and just came to Rootes for his kip.

I got fed up with the constant walkouts, so in 1966 I decided to get back on the buses. This time, I got a job at the Corporation Buses' Bridgeton garage, but for some reason it wasn't as much fun the second time around. Because I was at a different garage I wasn't seeing all the old faces and the football team had disintegrated.

I lasted two years there and in 1968 I got a job driving and making deliveries with Coca-Cola, who were based at Thornliebank. It was better money than working on the buses and there was a certain freedom being a delivery driver – almost like being your own gaffer – which I liked.

I stayed with Coca-Cola for 18 months, but I was chasing better money. I knew Bobby Gilchrist, from Rutherglen, who worked with the refrigeration company Craig Nicol, from Polmadie in Glasgow, and he told me they were looking for a driver-labourer and the money was good. They were a company that supplied and fitted large refrigeration units, cold rooms and patisserie cases to shops, schools and restaurants. One of the advantages of working with Craig Nicol was that you were given a certain time to finish the job, but if you worked hard and completed the work earlier, the rest of the time was yours.

Officially, the management didn't know about this, but I'm sure they did and turned a blind eye since the work was being done. Once we went to Blackpool to fit some gear into a shopping centre. We had ten days to do the job, but we worked our backsides off from 6 a.m. to 6 p.m., had a couple of pints at night and were in our beds by 11 p.m. ready for an early rise the next day. We completed the job after seven days and it was back up to Scotland for three days off.

We travelled all the way to the Western Isles to do a job in Stornoway and for the first few days we worked our socks off to get the job completed early. We still had some work left to do by the time we finished on the Saturday night and we told the guy in charge we would see him in the morning. 'You can't do that,' he says. 'You're not allowed to work on a Sunday – it's the Sabbath.'

'What do we do all day then?' I asked, since I knew all the pubs were shut because they didn't allow Sunday drinking.

'Don't worry about that,' he says. 'You can come with me to a place where we can get a few drams and we'll enjoy ourselves.'

I couldn't believe it. We were stopped from finishing the job because you weren't allowed to work on a Sunday, yet the guy was going to take us for a fly bevvy session.

After the Craig Nicol job, I went back to straight driving and delivering to shops, cafés and restaurants. The first of these jobs was McVitie's Cakes, which only lasted about six months, and then Rowntree Mackintosh, where I stayed until 1972 when I made a great decision and joined bakers Sunblest as a delivery driver.

Although I wouldn't dream of doing these things myself, there were loads of scams going on with the drivers making a skin. Well, they had to because the basic money wasn't that good, but you could make up for that in other ways. The drivers had their own outlets for bread, cakes or sweets that weren't sold at the end of the run. Some places you delivered to would have ordered too much and they didn't need the full order. So it was thank you very much, there's a wee café or corner shop that will take these off your hands.

As I said, being of a sound, Christian upbringing I would never have got involved in such matters and anyway, Bella would have battered me if I had got caught.

Now, anyone fancy a couple of dozen boxes of McVitie's Jaffa Cakes . . .?

Chapter 7

NO JOKING, I WANT TO BE A COMEDIAN

I COULD ALMOST HEAR MY HEART THUMPING ABOVE THE DIN OF A PACKED social club. There were dozens of tables set out round the carpeted perimeter of the rectangular dance floor. And at each one of those tables, laden with pint beer tumblers, glasses of whisky, vodka and Bacardi sat the men who could either make or break a budding entertainer's career, before it even got off the ground.

Among the would-be showbiz stars about to perform in front of this audience, there was definitely an air of excitement tinged with apprehension and in some cases abject terror. Eleven of us were sitting at three or four tables together waiting on our turn to be called to the stage where we would give it everything in the hope of breaking into the burgeoning clubland entertainment scene which was so popular in the late '60s and '70s.

The audience was a mix of locals and a small army of social club conveners from all over Scotland looking for acts to book into their clubs. Make a good impression here and you're on your way.

I toyed with a long-john glass of soda water and lime, swirling the sparkling liquid round and round, making the ice cubes click-clack together. I might not have appeared nervous, but my insides were bubbling up just like the glass of soda and lime. There was a bit of chat between the singers, musicians and stand-up comics as we waited for the showcase at Cambusnethan Miners Welfare

97

Club to begin. Other acts were obviously far more experienced than me and they chatted to each other about clubs they had played in and agents who had promised them work.

It was early in 1972 and this was the real thing as far as I was concerned. I fixed my eyes on the stage bathed in coloured lights at the far end of the long, narrow social-club hall. In my mind, I rehearsed the jokes that made up my 20-minute routine. I even imagined the audience roaring with laughter, then the doubts crept in and I thought to myself, 'What will I do if I bomb and they think I'm rubbish?'

Cambusnethan Miners Welfare was a great club: well run, with a great atmosphere and none of the acts had to pay for a drink all night. Being asked to perform in this showcase was my big opportunity to break into the club scene as a proper stand-up comedian. We were allowed to bring a friend with us and my pal John Walker was sitting beside me offering words of encouragement in between gulps of his pint of heavy.

John asked why I wasn't having my usual Bacardi and Coke and I told him I didn't want to get up on stage with a drink in me; I had to have all my wits about me. Anyway, I didn't need alcohol when there was so much adrenalin pumping around my body.

I was told I'd be on fourth after three singers and soon I was up there on stage, bathed in spotlight, wearing my best suit and giving it all the patter I've got. I was doing all the jokes I'd heard in Rootes about Paisley folk being mean and then routines about going on holiday to Blackpool and the dancing in Glasgow. Then I moved on to some football jokes. I told them I was a Rangers fan and asked if there were any Motherwell fans in the club. Of course, there's a roar since Cambusnethan is near Motherwell. I told them a story about how the last time I was going to Fir Park I got lost and when I asked a policeman for directions he told me just to follow the crowd and I ended up in Woolworth's.

I was getting a good reception and plenty of laughs and that encouraged me. I would have tried anything that night to get a laugh. I even walked up to the bar and asked for a pint of heavy. 'Just take it out my wages – I'll give you the rest later.' That went down well.

The performance was a mixture of anticipation, excitement and a bit of relief at the end of it that it had worked. I hadn't failed, and that voice inside me telling me I wasn't going to fail had been proved right. I was giving it my all and must have spoken at a hundred miles an hour – just as well they could understand my accent.

It was a defining moment in my life when I stepped off the stage with the sound of laughter and applause ringing in my ears. That was it, I said to myself, I'm having a go at this.

On the way home in the car, John Walker was enthusiastically telling me how well I'd gone down and I could see the new horizon in my life I was heading towards. But how quickly I would start on that journey would depend on how good all these social conveners sitting in the audience of the showcase thought I was. Impressing your pals with some fancy patter was one thing; impressing these guys was another. But I didn't have long to wait to find out.

It was an entertainment agent called Ian Wilson who had arranged for me to perform at the showcase after he had seen me tell a few jokes at a stag do the week before. He hadn't even been there to see me – he was there to listen to a girl singer, Lee Anthony, who was the main spot of the night.

The morning after the showcase, I was back at my work at Sunblest when there was a message for me to phone him. I got the message when I came back from my morning delivery run to phone a Mr Wilson. I was a bit wary at first because they were always playing jokes on you at Sunblest – telling you to phone a Mr Lyon at this number, which would turn out to be Calderpark Zoo.

Anyway, I checked the number with the one Ian Wilson had given me and I phoned. The number was for MK Entertainments in Wishaw and the guy who answered the phone was Ian Wilson's partner in the agency, Sam Young. He was a farmer from Mauchline in Ayrshire. 'Great spot last night,' he said. 'I think Ian's got a wheen o' work for you. Wait till I pass you over to him.'

Ian Wilson came on the phone and his words to me were, 'You were definitely the hit of the night. I've got 21 bookings for you.' Well, you could have knocked me down with a pan loaf. I was on my way.

It couldn't have come at a better time as my life was in turmoil with my marriage breaking up. I had been in a whirlwind not knowing what to do for the best with the situation between May, the kids and myself. But now I knew exactly what I wanted to do – I had a real purpose.

I'll always be grateful to the guys who ran Cumbusnethan Miners Welfare Club. I still see them because every so often I'll do a show for them. They were good to me that night of the showcase and I'll never forget that. They also gave me a gig, which was very nice of them.

The invite to the showcase at Cambusnethan came right out the blue after I'd done that turn at the stag do. That came about by chance. I was in the Rutherglen Glencairn Club when a guy who had seen me perform at the Masonic harmonies asked me if I would do a turn at his stag do there the following week.

I didn't even know who he was, but when he said he would pay me a fiver I agreed. He had already booked Lee Anthony and I think a comedian was an afterthought and he was looking for the cheapest option. Lee Anthony was a great singer and a cracking-looking girl: vivacious, blonde, falling out her dress, she had the lot for a cabaret singer. She was quite well known in the pubs and clubs and was a regular at the Crazy Daisy in Sauchiehall Street, Glasgow.

I did about 20–25 minutes and the more they laughed, the more jokes I told. I had finished my spot and the crowd were shouting for more. So I told them a few more jokes and ended with a routine about drink driving and getting stopped by the police. It was stories like sitting in the car in a lay-by with a bird and the police pulling up and knocking on the window. The cop says, 'Will you blow into this bag, sir?' And me replying, 'Are you kidding? I've just thrown it out the window.' When I came off stage it suddenly dawned on me that I had just given my first encore, but hadn't realised it.

Although Ian Wilson was there to see Lee Anthony, he was soon chatting to me and offering me the showcase at Cambusnethan the following Wednesday. When he came up to me he asked if I fancied doing a showcase and I replied, 'What's a showcase?'

That's how naive I was about the world of entertainment. It was like a football scout going to see a midfield player and during the game the centre-half catches his eye.

After I agreed to do the Cambusnethan gig, it meant five days to think about what I'd let myself in for. During the day was fine because I was at my work and when you were busy it kept your mind occupied. But as soon as I was driving home from work, my mind started to race about the showcase. I was going from being excited about the chance to be a performer to thinking I'll go up there and they won't like me and start shouting, 'Hey you, get off that stage.' I feared I would make a fool of myself and nobody would ever ask me to tell a joke again. All those things go through your head.

I must have pre-run the showcase in my head a hundred times. But in reality you can't really rehearse a stand-up comic routine. As I later discovered, when you've got some new material the only way to find out if it's any good is to try it in front of a live audience as part of your routine. They'll soon tell you if it's any good.

I had come a long way from holding court in Marie's Café telling funny stories to all my friends or being the centre of attention in someone's kitchen giving an impromptu performance at a party. Looking back, I suppose there was a progression, because after performing for my pals, I became more confident telling jokes and doing a routine at the Masonic Lodge harmonies. It started with just a few jokes and developed into a five- and ten-minute spot and even longer.

The harmonies really were a big step in my development, although I didn't know it at the time. They got me telling jokes and stories in front of strangers as we visited other lodges throughout the west and central Scotland. I even heard that before a visit to a lodge in Alloa, the guys there were phoning up asking if the funny wee guy from Rutherglen was part of the visitation group. When they were told I was, apparently there was a great turnout, with the attendance rocketing because they wanted to hear me at the harmony after the lodge meeting. They knew that I did a turn telling jokes because about three months earlier they had visited our lodge and heard me do my stuff.

That was another progression for me and probably when I stood on that stage at Cambusnethan, subconsciously I was just bursting to be a comedian. I had always felt that I wanted to do something with my life and earn a living doing something that wasn't a normal job. From a young age, I always wanted to be different and when it came to work I hated clocking on and clocking off. I wanted a job where I had some measure of control over what I did.

I was given some sound advice from the lodge secretary, Willie McChesney, about a year into me doing the clubs. By then, I was very active in the Masons and was a junior warden with responsibilities. He said I had to make up my mind whether I should continue being so involved in the lodge or concentrate on the comedy work: 'You've got a decision to make. But really there's only one decision you can come to. We need you here on a Friday and these clubs you are doing are Fridays, Saturdays and Sundays. Freemasonry is a hobby and what you're doing now is business and that has to come first. You've got a family to look after so make sure you attend to your business.'

It was a good shout from Willie, so I scaled down my involvement with the lodge to concentrate on the comedy.

Although the stag do and the showcase at Cambusnethan was the first time I had appeared on stage as a bona fide stand-up comedian, it wasn't the first time I'd had a mike in my hand talking to an audience.

Two years previously, in 1970, I had been asked by my pal from the lodge, Sam Steel, to go for a pint one Sunday lunchtime at the Rolls-Royce Club in Paisley Road West, Glasgow. Now, the Rolls-Royce Club was a big venue at the time and there were some really good acts appearing there in cabaret. The club also had floor singers – people getting up from the audience and doing their bit.

I'm sitting there having a pint, enjoying the chat when Sam turns to me and says: 'I've put your name up so you can tell a few jokes.'

'I can't get up there and do that,' I replied.

'Well, you'll have to. I've told them you'll do it.'

Sam had seen me performing at the harmonies and had got me along to the club on the false pretence of an afternoon pint. So I got up on stage, took the mike in my hand and the adrenalin kicked in. I must have done all right because they asked me if I'd compère the Sunday-afternoon and night-time shows after that.

I didn't look upon the Rolls-Royce Club as a gig, nor did I see myself as a stand-up comic. I was just there to introduce people on stage and I wasn't doing gags, although I did take the opportunity to wind up the guys I knew who happened to be in the club at the time. It did pay, though – I got a fiver for compèring at lunchtime and another for doing the night-time spot.

Two years later, I was still compèring at the club on a Sunday and by this time all the regulars knew who I was and that I was a real Bluenose. The day after Celtic won their eighth league title in a row I was on stage congratulating the Celtic fans, but telling them it was difficult to say it when your teeth are stuck together. Then I told the audience that the lunchtime show was over and I would see them tonight when so-and-so would be entertaining them.

I was just about to walk off stage when one of the club committee men, Peter Burnette, came on and took the mike out of my hand and told me to wait a minute, he had an announcement.

'Ladies and gentlemen,' he said. 'Many of you won't have realised that Andy has been doing this for exactly two years to the day. You know how good he has been and he's attracted a big crowd on a Sunday. So we've decided to give Andy a present to mark the two-year anniversary.'

I got a lump in my throat and started thanking everybody profusely, saying how touched I was and what a wonderful gesture it was from the club. I was about to walk off the stage when Peter said, 'Are you not going to open your present in front of everybody?'

So I took the fancy wrapping paper off the box, opened the box and there was another box inside that. I took the wrapping paper off that box and inside there was another smaller box. The wrapping paper came off that and inside there was a box of After Eight mints. Celtic had won eight in a row and I'd been done up good and proper.

The material I used when I started doing the social clubs as a comedian came largely from my experiences in life – the characters I'd met and the funny things they would say and do. The places I had worked in were always a great source of jokes people told or strange and amusing things that had happened. I would string a series of jokes and stories together from those experiences and that made up a routine. I would then have routines about other things and that's what made up my two half-hour spots for the clubs.

There was always the Paisley folk being mean stuff, plus my experiences at primary school. I would say I went to Farie Street School – F-A-R-I-E Street. And don't let the name fool you, it was a right tough school. We had one holiday a year and that was Al Capone's birthday. I wasn't really the Thief of Bad Gags, but if you heard a good line somewhere you would adapt and use it in your own act. However, I would never steal a routine from anyone.

I did take one idea from one of Scotland's best comics of the day – Hector Nicol. He would dress up as a policewoman or a boxer and do a routine around that character. I thought it was a great concept, so I decided that I would be a football hooligan. I would tell loads of football gags wearing Bay City Rollers trousers and a hard hat, and have all the scarves of Scottish football clubs tied to my arms. I always tried never to say 'there's a wee boy going into the school' or 'two guys walked into this pub'. I put myself in the story, and said that I was in the school or the pub when the funny story happened to me or to someone else.

Before I became a comedian, I was a regular at theatre shows and social clubs so I had seen and heard many of the top acts in those days. Clem Dane was a big influence on me. He had a great delivery and was a really good comic. I would go to clubs to watch him because I thought he was very funny. Another hero of mine from the old days was Lex McLean – his sketches were great. Other Scots comics I would see at the theatre would be Rikki Fulton and Jack Milroy as Francie and Josie and I liked Johnny Beattie as well.

When it comes to ad-libbing, no one beats Bob Hope and Bing Crosby in the series of *Road to* . . . films. They were brilliant and when I saw them I would think to myself, these guys are great at making the script seem as if they are just ad-libbing. Years later, reading their biographies, I discovered that often they actually were ad-libbing, and a lot of their funniest stuff wasn't in the script – they were just batting off each other.

George Burns is another comic with superb timing. He would stand there with his cigar, say a few lines, pause and then hit you with the punch line – superb. When I first started doing the clubs, I was firing out jokes like a machine gun – bang, bang, bang – and never giving the audience the chance to laugh or even think about the joke before I was on to the next one. I thought it was a case of hit 'em loud and hit 'em quick and they'll think you're good.

But it's not like that at all. Proper timing is an all-important asset to a comedian. But it can be quite daunting and courageous when you're out there in front of an audience to hold back and wait for the right moment to hit them with the punch line.

The best example of using timing to get a laugh was Jack Benny during a radio show. The sketch was that he would go over to his neighbour, Gilbert Rowland, who had just won an Oscar, and ask to see the Oscar. Jack then said Rochester, his servant, had never seen an Oscar before and could he take it over to his house to show him.

Jack Benny takes the Oscar, shows it to Rochester and returns the award to Gilbert Rowland. On his way back to his own house, you hear footsteps and a rustle and this robber jumps out in front of Jack Benny. 'Your money or your life,' says the robber.

Silence for ten seconds. And that's a long time to hear nothing on radio.

'Give me your money or your life,' says the robber again.

Another ten seconds of silence.

'Your money or your life,' for the third time.

And then Jack Benny says, 'I'm thinking about it.'

All that silence, nothing, just to tee-up the punch line. It must have taken a lot of courage to try that and I admired him for it.

Another great British comic who had a lot of influence on me was Jimmy Tarbuck. He was abrasive, cheeky, but at the same time brilliant and the audiences loved him.

In the early years, I began to develop my own style, but I modelled myself on these great comics. I would love to have the courage to try the Jack Benny and George Burns style of relaxed and laid-back comedy, but it's not really me as I'm still doing the rat-tat-tat when it comes to performing.

However, if you ask me whom I admire most in comedy, I would have to say anybody who has got the balls to stand up on a stage, face an audience and tell them jokes. Because I know what it feels like to go up there and die on your arse!

And talking about dying on stage. Although I was getting several gigs a week all over Scotland and gaining a reputation as a good comic, you didn't always leave 'em rocking with laughter. Oh yes, I have died a death many times. And any comic who tells you they haven't died in front of an audience is a liar.

Normally, you can feel that something is not quite right before you go on. You'll walk into a club or a hotel where you're speaking at a dinner and there will be something about the atmosphere that's different from how you normally feel. You can't put your finger on it, but there will definitely be something there. When you get on stage and the first few gags have hardly raised a laugh, your mouth dries up and you start talking quicker. Your brain is working overtime to try to come up with more gags that will hit the target, so your mouth tries to catch up and it doesn't do you any favours.

Comics like Hector Nicol wouldn't let dying on stage bother them – they would carry on regardless. I've seen people walk out in the middle of Hector's act because of his double-entendre routine, but he just soldiered on – just kept doing what he knew was a good routine and never let it bother him. He was the master at staying alive on stage.

Experience is a great teacher, but you have to go through the horrors of dying in front of an audience to learn how to deal with it. In the early days, there were times I would turn up at a club and the social convener would say, 'What is it you do, son?'

'I'm a comedian.'

'Aw, this is not a comics' club. They like singers in here.'

And then you say to yourself, 'Oh, oh, we've got a problem tonight.'

When that happened, I learned how to deal with it, because

there were certain clubs whose audience preferred a singer instead of a comic and vice-versa. When I was in a club that preferred singers I would tell the band what I was doing and tee them up for the start routine. I would come on the stage and start singing really badly and after a few lines of the song the band would stop playing and walk off stage. I would turn round and shout to them, 'What's up? Do you not know this song right through?' Straight away, the audience knew you were a comic and hopefully you'd get a laugh and that would set you up for the rest of the spot.

The first time I died in a club it came as such a shock to the system I almost chucked the business altogether. I had gone more than a year doing the circuit and was going great guns. And by this time I was going out with Norma, who would become my second wife. I had two gigs one Sunday. The afternoon gig was at Danderhall Miners Club in Midlothian and the night-time gig was in the Ochiltree Club in Ayrshire. I get on the stage at Danderhall Miners thinking everything's going to be fine, because there's a busload in from Kirkcaldy and I always went down well in Fife. But after a minute I knew the game was up – I was dying a death. I don't know why it happened – it just didn't happen for me that day and I could hardly raise a snigger never mind a laugh.

I know now that if you're struggling you stay calm, change the routine and try to get on a theme they like. But that day I just got faster and faster in my delivery and I did 20 minutes' worth of gags in 15 minutes. I could see them sitting there nursing their pints and turning to each other saying, 'Where did they get this guy from? He's f*****g hopeless.'

I'm sitting in the dressing-room at the interval and one of the club committee men comes in and says, 'Here's your money, son. They don't fancy you out there.' I get into the car and say to myself, driving home, 'That's it. I'm chucking it. I'll just concentrate on my real job at Sunblest. I'll go in tomorrow morning and say I'll take the supervisor's job they offered me. I'm not doing these clubs any more.'

I hadn't taken the supervisor's job because I was doing so many clubs at night, coming home at 3 a.m. to get a wash and shave before heading out to the bakery, I couldn't give the Sunblest job my undivided attention.

I was due to have my tea at Norma's house before heading off to Ochiltree and when I got there she knew right away that something was wrong. I told her I had died on stage and that was the last gig I'd ever do. I was even about to phone the Ayrshire club and cancel my gig that night. But Norma got a hold of me and said, 'There's no way you're finished. You have a bad gig at one club after all this time and you want to pack it in. You're going to Ochiltree tonight and I'm coming with you. It's like falling off a bike – you just get back on it and pedal away.'

So we went to Ochiltree. I went on stage, did the first half-hour spot and I slayed them. There was a lot of anger in my set that night because I was so annoyed at the audience not liking me earlier in the day. I gave it everything I had and at the end of the first set, for the first time, I got a standing ovation. At that time, the clubs in Ayrshire were great and they provided you with a high tea at the interval in the committee room. So I had my break and couldn't wait to get out there for the second half.

My second half-hour turned into 45 minutes. There were things coming into my head while I was on stage that got me great laughs. I was digging wee women up about their frocks and poking fun at people in the audience, which they loved. I had gone down a storm – the best reaction in my career so far. Norma and I were leaving the club and as we were getting into the car she shook her head and said, 'And you were going to chuck it!' That taught me a great lesson and, as Norma had said, if you fall off your bike you get right back on it.

That episode didn't stop me dying on stage again, but it meant I could handle it better and not let it affect me so badly. The worst ever was doing a show for the squaddies at Redford Barracks. They were heading for a tour of duty in Northern Ireland and this was a going away do for them. It was 6 p.m. and they had been drinking since nine in the morning. Most of them had their heads down because they're heading for Northern Ireland and I'm getting no reaction to the gags. But by this time I had learned how to cope so I just kept at it. The next thing this soldier gets up and starts dancing in the middle of the floor while I'm telling jokes. There's no music or anything, but I must have had an excellent delivery because he kept a right good rhythm.

I've seen really good comics dying on stage and it was nothing to do with the jokes they were telling. I always liked to see other comedians and I'd heard of a duo from down south called The Harper Brothers who later went on to find success as Cannon and Ball. I went along to see them one night and they died a death – even though I was almost rolling about the floor laughing at the antics of Bobby Ball because I thought he was fantastic. I'm not a slapstick type of person, I prefer smart lines, but there was just something about him. I thought he was hilarious and he really made me laugh.

But what had happened that night was that the audience couldn't quite understand their Yorkshire accents and after ten minutes they gave up watching them and started talking to each other. What a horrible feeling you get when you die in front of an audience. Although it's not pleasant, however, it's certainly a worthwhile experience because you can learn a lot from it.

Later in my career, I always insisted on doing one, one-hour spot instead of two half-hour sets. It's not that I was getting to be a Billy Big Time, but that worked better for everyone – the comedian and the audience. It's always more difficult doing a second spot because the audience have had more drink, they've not won anything at the half-time bingo, they've already heard you and although it's entirely different material there's a feeling of, 'Oh aye, it's him again.'

When I first started going to clubs, my pal John Walker would come with me and act as my spy. I would do the first set and in the interval John would hang about the bar with the locals or go to the toilet to hear what they were saying about me. He would come and see me before I went back on and tell me what went down well, what didn't and what kind of material he thought they wanted to hear.

Some of the guys who ran the clubs would give you as good a laugh as the acts themselves. In the mid-'70s, there was a singer doing the circuit and he called himself The Voice from Nowhere.

He was one of the first acts to have a radio mike, which meant he could sing into the mike from anywhere in the club, and wasn't restricted by a mike cable.

His big entrance was that he would be introduced and he would start singing behind the door to an ante-room of the club and after a verse he would come on stage. The punters didn't know about the radio mike and when they heard the singing start they were wondering where the hell it was coming from.

I was doing the stand-up and he was the singer one night at Tannochside Miners Club. He had asked me to do the introduction for him straight after my spot. He said, 'As soon as you're finished, take a bow and introduce me as The Voice from Nowhere. I'd rather you do it because you know what these committee guys are like. They'll labour it and go on about getting peas with the pies and all that.'

So he's positioned himself behind the door as I'm about to finish my spot and I say, 'Ladies and gentlemen – the star of tonight's show and he's absolutely brilliant. You'll love him, so please welcome . . . The Voice from Nowhere!'

The next thing they hear is him bursting into song: 'Tonight's the night . . . open the door. Tonight's the night . . . open the f*****g door!'

He was locked out after one committee man had unlocked the door for the big entrance and while I was doing my routine another one came along, noticed it was open and decided he would lock it.

One of the biggest acts to tour in the '70s was Neville Taylor and his band, The Cutters. Neville was a fantastic singer with a big, deep, booming voice. He was 6 ft 2 in. with a physique to match, after all. He came to Glasgow just after the Second World War from the West Indies and studied law at Glasgow University. Despite getting his degree, he never practised law. Instead, he went on the road with his band and did all the big venues around the country.

I can't believe I'm on the Neville Taylor tour because he's one of the biggest acts in clubland and it's going to be a delight to watch him perform every night. We're in Crosshill Miners Club and big

Neville is into his third song and he's giving it laldy. But all you can hear above his singing is, 'Wullie, it's four pints of lager, a packet of plain and three packets of cheese and onion.'

I'm raging and I grab hold of the MC and tell him it's a bloody disgrace all that noise going on while one of the best acts out is performing. He agrees and says he's going to sort it out right away. The MC jumps onto the stage while Neville is still singing, grabs the mike out of his hand and bellows into it, 'Order, order! You know the rules of this club – give the big man a f*****g chance!' Then he hands the mike back to Neville and says, 'Right, carry on, son.' You couldn't make that up.

The Paisley man who saved my bacon when I was getting a hard time from a group of hecklers was boxer John Cowboy McCormack. He was working at Mosmorrran petrochemical plant at the time and he came to see me at Lumphinnans Social Club. He knew my pal Andy Bain, from Bridgeton in Glasgow, who was also there that night.

During the first set, I was getting some grief from a heckler who wouldn't shut up. 'You're f*****g rotten,' he would shout, full of bravado because he was sitting at a table with all his pals. 'Get yoursel' away back to Glesga'.' The guy wasn't even funny with his heckling, it was just one insult after another. I'd tried all the one-liner put-downs, but they hadn't worked and I'd eventually run out of them. One of the club committee asked if I wanted the heckler put out of the club because he was spoiling it for everyone, but I said no because he was there mob-handed and it could have caused a right rammy.

I came out for the second half and I saw Cowboy and Andy sitting at a table at the back of the hall. I'm just about to launch into a routine when the heckler starts again. 'I telt you in the first half you were s***e,' he says. 'You'll probably be no' much better this half either.' At that, I could see Cowboy McCormack get up off his seat and drag it across to the table where the heckler was. I don't know what Cowboy said to him, but it certainly shut him up because he never uttered another word all night.

I bought Cowboy and Andy a drink at the end of the night to thank them. Cowboy said, 'He didn't want to listen to anybody, never mind you, but the rest of the audience did. Mind you, if you had been rotten and dying on your arse, I wouldn't have bothered to rescue you, but you were doing well and he was spoiling it for everyone.'

John was a great boxer and a really good guy. He stays in Glenburn in Paisley and is a regular at the St Peter's Club up there. He's had me do a few gigs in the club and it's always a good night.

Dealing with hecklers is part and parcel of the business and if you can come with a few one-liners as put-downs the audience love it and they're on your side. What I can't abide is fellow professionals who turn up and heckle you from the audience. There was one Scots comedian – who shall remain nameless because I don't go around bad-mouthing people – who almost got a good hiding from me backstage at the Gaiety Theatre in Ayr.

I was doing a spot in the first half and he came in and sat in the stalls. Every time I told a joke he shouted, 'Heard it.' and then it would be, 'Heard that one as well.' I cut the spot short, introduced the next act and came backstage seething that he would be so unprofessional as to do that to a fellow entertainer. I got a hold of the theatre manager, Bernard Cotton, and said I wanted the guy thrown out of the theatre or I would go out and do it myself. At the interval, the so-called fellow comedian came backstage and he obviously had a good drink in him. 'Can you not take a bit of fun?' he asked me. I grabbed him and put him up against the wall and said, 'F**k you. If you ever do that to me again I'll break your jaw.'

The more successful I became, the more money I was earning and eventually I had to register for value added tax (VAT). The clubs had to pay me the extra tax on top of my fee, although they could claim it back on their VAT returns. It wasn't quite as simple as that, however. I was doing a show at a smashing big club in Fife. I had finished my act and was in the committee room waiting to be paid. One of the committee handed me my money and I said, 'I'm registered for VAT now – I've got a receipt book and I'll give you a receipt.'

'No, no,' he says. 'Just stick it in your pocket, son. It's cash, ye ken.'

'You don't understand,' I said. 'I've got to charge you VAT. I'll give you a receipt and you can claim it back from the government.'

'No, son. You don't understand,' he replied. 'We had a committee meeting about the VAT and we decided not to join it!'

Working in the clubs all over Scotland was also a great lesson in life for me and it taught me to be grateful for what I have. This was never more highlighted than when I was appearing at Lumphinnans Social Club on another occasion. Things went really well that night and I did an hour and fifteen minutes instead of just an hour. One of their guys came in to pay me and he's saying, 'You were brilliant. You did an hour and a quarter, that was great. Oh, you were just brilliant.'

'Thanks very much,' I said. 'What do you do for a living?'

'I'm a miner, son,' he told me. 'Work at the coalface. I'll be there tomorrow morning, six until two o'clock in the afternoon.'

I said, 'You're the guy that should be getting the pat on the back. You're down there digging coal and not seeing daylight for eight hours and you're telling me I'm brilliant.' I was probably getting more for that one night than he would be getting in a week. That's what I call being lucky.

Chapter 8

I'VE MET THE GIRL OF MY DREAMS

HE'S A GIANT OF A POLICEMAN, 6 FT 4 IN. AND BUILT LIKE THE GABLE END OF a house. Norrie McDonald had a stern and, to put it mildly, disapproving look on his face as we sat face-to-face in his back room. I'm now getting to know what it's like to be interrogated by the polis!

A few minutes earlier, I had turned up at his door out of the blue and told him that although I was still a married man with two children, I wanted to get engaged to his daughter, Norma. Now that was bad enough, but I was 32 and she was only 18. Needless to say, Norrie was doing most of the talking and I was doing the listening, nodding my head, agreeing with everything he said and trying to make sure I ended up on his good side.

I might have been a bit of a patter merchant, but that night was no time for funnies. I had fallen in love with Norma, who was working as secretary to the sales manager at Sunblest, 14 years my junior, and I was damned sure I was going to marry this girl. Of course, there was still one problem stopping me – I was still married to May, although we had been separated for some time. But that hurdle was nothing compared to the task of persuading Norma's dad I was the right guy for his daughter and to have him give our relationship his blessing. Oh, aye, and then I had to get her mother, Agnes, on my side as well.

That evening was a defining moment in the relationship between Norma and me that had begun a few months earlier. I had seen Norma around the Sunblest bakery when I started work there in 1972. There was a bus strike in Glasgow the following year and staff were finding it difficult to get in to work. I was living in The Spittal, which is not far from Castlemilk where Norma lived. The sales manager asked me if I would give Norma a lift into work during the bus strike, take her to Sunblest in the east end of Glasgow near Parkhead and take her home at night again. I was happy to oblige.

No one realised the bus strike was going to last for ten weeks and certainly no one would have thought these lifts to and from work would have been the start of a relationship which has given me 28 years of blissfully happy married life. Every day, I would pick her up and on the journey to Sunblest we would talk about the normal goings-on at work and, of course, I would be giving her a wee bit of the Andy Cameron patter as well. I fancied her, of course, but I told myself there was no chance she would want to go out with me.

One morning on our way in to Sunblest, Norma said she had heard that I was a comedian and performed in the clubs. I told her that I had just started, only did it for pin money and I wasn't really all that good. But she said she would like to come and see me perform in one of the social clubs. 'What do you want to do that for?' I asked. 'People will think you're my daughter.'

But she insisted and said she still wanted to come to a club along with a pal and the pal's boyfriend. Who was I to argue? An 18-year-old girl wanting to come and see a 32-year-old man telling daft jokes – either she's lost her guide dog or I'm better looking than I thought I was.

So a date was set and Norma – with pal and boyfriend – came to see me at the General Motors Club in Holytown, Lanarkshire, a few days later. In the early '70s, the drink-drive thing wasn't as strict and I would often have three or four Bacardis before I went on stage. And that's exactly what I did that night, with Norma sitting at the same table as me listening to the other acts that were on before me.

I got on stage and started my routines. It was one of those nights when I could have said anything and the crowd would have laughed. It couldn't have gone better – especially with Norma sitting in the audience and me trying my hardest to impress her.

At the interval, I had another two or three Bacardis and I went on to do my second spot which went down just as well. After the gig, I was feeling well pleased with myself and when I asked Norma's friends what they thought they said I was great. After I dropped Norma's pal and the boyfriend off, I asked Norma if she would come out and have dinner with me. But she said no and to add insult to injury she said, 'See what you did tonight, you could earn a living at that, but not if you take four or five Bacardis before you go on. You did two gags in the second spot that you had already told in the first half and that was because of the drink. You don't need drink to be good at what you do.'

The next morning, I picked Norma up to take her to work and I asked her if she meant what she said about me being able to make it as a comic and she said yes, but repeated her warning about not drinking before a show.

'Right then,' I said. 'If you come out to dinner with me, I won't take a drink the next time I go on stage.'

'No,' she says. 'The next time you go on stage, I'll come to see you and if you don't have a drink, then I'll come out to dinner with you.'

Sure enough, Norma came with me to my next gig at the Greenfield Social Club in Burnbank, Lanarkshire. I drank soda water and lime all night and the performance went down very well. I was determined to get Norma out on that date and I had made my mind up not to touch alcohol that night. It made no difference. As soon as I stepped onto the stage, the adrenalin kicked in and off I went.

The social convener, Charlie Dunn, said he had heard I was good, but I had been magnificent. Charlie was surprised when I told him I hadn't had a drink all night and it was the first time I'd done a spot without a wee charge. He said, 'Well, now you know the secret.'

Norma had given me the best advice I have ever had. And since that day I have never taken alcohol before going on stage to perform – it's a rule I have never broken. Although, if someone wants to buy me a wee refreshment afterwards, I won't object as long as I'm not driving.

Needless to say, Norma kept her side of the bargain and we went to the Berni Inn in Hope Street, Glasgow, the following Saturday. I was on my best behaviour – so much the perfect gentleman it wasn't true. I respected Norma and the old randy Andy Cameron was nowhere to be seen.

One date followed another and after a few months it was obvious to both of us we were made for each other. By that time, I had told Norma I loved her, wanted to marry her and that we should tell her parents about us. The age difference was a big deal to me, but it didn't bother Norma. Big Norrie and Agnes knew their daughter was going out with someone, but didn't know who it was. Norma kept saying she would tell them, but she never got round to it.

I was getting impatient that Norma hadn't told her parents about me and one night I suddenly decided I would take the bull by the horns and I made an unannounced visit to their door that fateful night. I was having a couple of pints in Rutherglen and was heading home in the car. As I got near The Spittal, for some unknown reason instead of turning right, I carried straight on heading for Norma's house. I had got it into my head I was going to bring everything into the open with Norma's parents and I was going to do it now – at a quarter to ten at night.

I parked the car and as I walked up the path took several deep breaths and knocked on the door. Big Norrie answered it asking, 'Who are you?'

'I'm Andy. I'm going out with Norma and I need to talk to you,' I answered.

'You'd better come in,' says Norma's dad with a suspicious look on his face.

I walked into the living-room and Norma was sitting on the couch watching television and her mother was in a chair having dozed off. Norrie woke her up and she wanted to know who this stranger was in her house.

I could see Norma was appalled at me turning up like this. But I sat beside her, held her hand and told her I loved her. I told her mum and dad I was married, but the marriage was long over and I planned to start divorce proceedings because I wanted to marry their daughter.

Big Norrie said, 'You had better come with me.' And he led me into another room and gave me a real talking to. 'You'd better be what you say you are,' he warned. 'This is my daughter we're talking about.'

Big Norrie must have smelled the beer from my breath and asked me how much I had had to drink. I told him a couple of pints of Guinness and that I needed that to give me the courage to come and speak to him. He wasn't too happy about that and said he would have had more respect for me if I hadn't come to the house with a drink in me. I apologised for that and he said, 'I think it's about time you left.'

I was feeling like a wee boy who had been caught doing something naughty and I was trembling with fear and trepidation. I stood up and said, 'I came to say my piece and I've said it.'

On my way out, I popped into the living-room and said sorry to Norma. By this time, the bus strike was over and Norma was making her own way to work. When she saw me the next morning, she said, 'You're taking me to lunch, but there won't be much eating going on. I want to talk to you.'

I don't think Norma was too impressed by my sudden impulse to tell the world we were in love, but I explained something had to be done or we would have been in the same position in three years' time, still going out together and not having told her parents. But the next day, Norma was sitting in her room when her dad came in and asked her one question: 'Is he the guy for you, is he the one?' She said yes and Big Norrie replied, 'Right, that's OK then. You better bring him up for his tea on Sunday and we can speak to him.'

I turned up on the Sunday with a box of chocolates for Norma's mother and she eyed me up suspiciously. The look on her face said you won't get round me with a box of chocolates. It took them a while to get used to the idea of their daughter going out with me, but when they did come round they were lovely people and always good to me.

In fact, before we got married, Agnes told me not to let Norma make me give up going to the football. 'What do you mean?' I asked. And Agnes replied, 'I know you love going to see Rangers and Norma will try to stop you.'

Norma has admitted she never liked the idea of me going to the football because she had seen the state of her dad's police uniform covered in spit after he'd been on duty at a football match. While I was going out with Norma, but before the night I knocked on their door, I had seen her father. I was walking to Hampden for an Old Firm cup final and I walked past a policeman with his police dog. I looked at him and I knew that was Norma's father because they were so alike. He didn't know me, but I knew it was her father. I walked a wee detour round three streets in case the dog took a disliking to me.

Meeting Norma's parents was a daunting task and there was just one more to complete, which was for Norma to meet Bella – who wasn't too enamoured that I was going out with another woman when, officially, I was still married to May. I had been going out with Norma for two years and she still hadn't met Bella, so I hatched a plan for the pair to meet without telling either of them.

I had a Volkswagen Beetle at the time and Bella had asked me to take her to the shops, in Rutherglen. As I was driving her home, I carried on down Main Street instead of turning. 'Where are we going?' asks Bella.

'I've got something to do,' I replied and continued heading towards Shawfield. Bella's getting impatient and she says: 'Where the hell are you taking me? We need to get home.' I just carried on and said I was going to pick someone up.

That someone was Norma, who had moved to a new job at Thorn Lighting, in Shawfield. I parked the car and waited for Norma to come out of her work and when she did, Bella got out the car to let her in the back. I introduced Norma and there was a cursory 'hello' from Bella.

There was polite chat on the car journey back to Bella's and all three of us headed upstairs to the house. I told them they both had to meet some time and now was as good a time as any. Norma, being the clever person she is, decided to break the ice and offered to make a cup of tea for everyone, so I showed her the kitchen and where everything was.

Now, Norma is 5 ft 9 in. and with the high platform shoes she was wearing was taller than me. Not a word was being spoken between Bella and me. I looked at Bella and all she said was, 'She's too big for you!' I'm 34, Norma's 20 and Bella's saying she's too big for me.

I started laughing and Norma came through to ask what all the hilarity was about. I said I would tell her later, but Bella butted in and said, 'Never mind telling her later – I'll tell her what I said. You're too big for him!'

Norma burst out laughing and so did Bella. Thank goodness that was the ice broken and another mountain conquered.

We had our cup of tea and Bella asked what was happening between us. I told her that Norma was still staying with her parents and we weren't going to live together before we got married. The only other question Bella asked was how did Norma get on with the two girls – Ellen and Marion. I told Bella Norma had only met them once, but she got on well with them. At that, Bella seemed to be quite happy and from then on she got on great with Norma.

At the beginning, there was a bit of frostiness between all the old aunties and uncles and Norma. I think it was because they came from an older era where men didn't go out with girls a lot younger than them and because I hadn't been divorced I shouldn't have been going out with someone else.

Norma is the love of my life and when I look at her I think I'm the luckiest guy in the world. I'd already messed up my first marriage and I didn't deserve a second chance. But Norma gave me that second chance and I grabbed it with both hands. I married her as soon as my divorce came through in 1975. She's the best thing that's ever happened to me, keeping me on the straight and narrow. In fact, I would go so far as to say that she rescued me. If I hadn't met her I might have just disappeared into oblivion with the bevvy. I never had a problem with drink, but I was a typical

Glasgow drinker. I worked all week and Fridays and Saturdays were for drinking. Sundays were for getting your head together for work on a Monday morning.

There's a rule that everyone should adhere to and that is to try harder in your second marriage. If you don't, you'll end up with two failed marriages. I certainly tried a lot harder the second time around and I did something with Norma that I never really did in my first marriage and that is to listen. I listened to my wife. You always worry there are going to be problems when you marry for a second time and there are children from the first marriage. But Norma, Ellen and Marion have all made concessions and they have been absolutely brilliant with each other.

From the start, Norma knew that all I wanted to do for a living was to be a comedian, but she knew I would be successful and she gave me 100 per cent support. But she wasn't like some other comedians' wives who would be seeing their husbands perform for the umpteenth time and they would be clapping and cheering louder than anyone else. Norma would applaud normally. For most of these wives, their husbands couldn't do anything wrong, but Norma wasn't like that and afterwards she could be very businesslike, telling me which jokes didn't work with the audience.

In the early days, like all the other comedians, I did Irish and Pakistani gags, although I would argue that the jokes I did were never meant to hurt anyone's feelings and they weren't really racist. Times have, of course, changed and your act changes, so I don't do any of that stuff any more.

Although Norma could be critical of my act she was never slow to spring to my defence if she thought I was being wrongly attacked for my material. There was one dinner in The Albany Hotel in Glasgow and I told a joke about why there weren't any Asian footballers playing in Scotland. The punch line was that it was because every time they get a corner they open a shop. There was definitely no malice in the joke, but I suppose in today's climate some people may argue it was mildly racist. After the dinner, I was standing in the bar with Norma and some other people when I noticed a girl of about 20 holding a pint of heavy and staring at me. She wasn't drinking the beer and I thought that there was something not quite right about the whole scenario.

She started walking towards me and I told Norma to walk away from me when I told her to. She wondered what was going on, but I insisted that she did what I was telling her. The girl was getting closer and closer and I said 'go' to Norma and she walked away. At that point, the girl tried to throw the pint of heavy over me and shouted, 'You're a racist.'

Fortunately, she missed and the beer splattered all over the wall. Norma was raging and she asked the girl what she was talking about. But the girl was drunk and a couple of women ushered her away and into the ladies' toilet.

I didn't know what had happened next until a year later, but Norma followed the girl into the toilet and ripped right into her – nothing physical, because Norma's not like that, but she gave her a real tongue-lashing and told her I was the least racist person she would come across. Aye, when Norma's got her dander up she'll look you right in the eye and tell you what she thinks and I don't care who you are, you won't be interrupting her.

I've had a wonderful marriage with Norma and we have three great children – Jennifer, who was born on 22 October 1976, Elliott, who was born on 27 September 1980 and Spencer, born on 16 October 1982.

Who would have believed this could have happened to me? And it all stemmed from driving Norma to and from her work during that bus strike. I've got a lot to thank those bus drivers for who hit the cobbles all those years ago.

Chapter 9

YOU SILLY BUGGER, THEY'RE LAUGHING AT YOU

THE STAGE OF THE PAVILION THEATRE IN GLASGOW IS BATHED IN LIGHT. There's not a spare seat in the house and the singer Fiona Campbell is on the last number of her spot. I'm standing in the wings waiting to go on for the biggest gig of my career so far. The excitement and nerves are rolled into one amazing feeling and I feel like a boxer ready to take the ring for a world championship fight or a footballer standing in the tunnel waiting to go out for the World Cup final.

The gags are racing through my head and my heart's beating faster and faster as Fiona gets further into her final song. It won't be long now, I think to myself. I'll step into that spotlight and hit them with everything I've got. Just then, the star of the show, country singer Sydney Devine, comes up to me and says, 'A tip.'

'Yeah, sure. What is it?' I ask.

'I've seen you in the clubs and you come out and you just batter the audience into submission. Well, there's no need for that tonight.

'When you're performing in the clubs you're fighting lager, waitresses, guys talking to each other, but in a theatre it's not like that. Sure, they've had a drink before they come into theatre and they'll have a drink at the interval, but they're not drinking now, they're not sitting talking. They're here to see a show. They might have come to see the Sydney Devine Show, but you're a bonus and they're watching you. Just take your time, do a gag, let it wash over them and let the laughter wash over you. You'll learn tonight it's all about timing.'

I barely had time to take in these pearls of wisdom from Sydney when he's got a mike in his hand and he's introducing me: 'Ladies and gentlemen, a young man trying to make his name in comedy – Andy Cameron!'

The band strikes up the *Scotsport* theme tune and I bounce on stage dressed as the football hooligan. What a roar I got from the crowd and yes, I could feel the laughter wash over me. What Sydney had told me a few minutes before I stepped onto that stage suddenly became clear and I heeded every word of his advice: calm down, take your time and give the audience the chance to enjoy the gags.

I used to walk up and down at a fast pace when I was doing my act, but that night at the Pavilion I strolled around the stage. I had planned enough routines and gags to last my 20-minute spot. But because I took my time and did it properly, I only used up half the jokes I had planned to tell. It couldn't have gone better and the audience's reaction to me was fantastic. When I came off stage I was as high as a kite and Sydney said to me in the wings, 'Brilliant, wee man. You gave them just what they want. Now you've set them up, I'll go out and pick the apples off the tree.'

That was when I learned another lesson. A lot of performers would have said, 'I don't want to have to follow him, he was brilliant.' But Sydney showed me that night it's really the other way around. You want to follow someone who has just brought the audience way up there and all you have to do is keep them there. If someone dies a death on stage, you've got to go on and pull them up, which is a lot harder.

That night in the Pavilion in 1975 was a real turning point for me. I had moved on to a different level, literally a bigger stage and I proved to myself I could handle it. Amazingly, nine hours before I went on that stage I was delivering bread in a Sunblest van. Half four in the morning I started and you never saw a bread man deliver his loaves so fast as that day. I don't remember a minute of that morning, as all I could think about was the show later that night. I was finished by 10 a.m. and had squared up my money at the depot and headed for the Pavilion and the band call.

After I parked my car, I almost forgot to take off my Sunblest coat and when I remembered, I threw it in the back of the motor. You could certainly say there was plenty of variety in my life in those days.

I had been doing well in the clubs around Scotland and had been getting plenty of bookings and making a name for myself. But the chance to do the Sydney Devine Show came right out of the blue. Phone calls from entertainment agents to the Sunblest depot were reasonably common and quite often there would be a phone number for me to call when I got back from the bread deliveries late morning or at lunchtime. One day, there was a message for me to phone a Peter de Rance who was booking acts for Sydney's show at the Pavilion. I had a dog at the time and would go home at lunchtime to let him out, so I phoned Peter de Rance from home. He asked me if I wanted to do the Sydney Devine Show and I didn't hesitate in saying yes. An added bonus was that Sydney had personally asked for me to be on the bill.

I knew this was going to be a big one and the theatre would be jam-packed with Sydney fans as he was a huge, huge draw in clubs and theatres at the time because he was such a fabulous entertainer. It was initially for a week's run, but the ticket sales were so good they added another three days on the Thursday, Friday and Saturday of the following week. It was a full house every night and Sydney just packed 'em in. What a boost this was going to be for me. I would have a ready-made audience in the theatre to see me and what a chance this was to further my career. From the moment I put the phone down from speaking to Peter de Rance, the excitement was building.

At first, I thought I would have to get a new image for the show and I said to Norma that I would have to get a dinner suit. At the time, I was doing the football hooligan routine and dressing up in the daft clothes and football scarves. But Norma told me to hang on a minute and remember it was the football hooligan act that had got me this far and that's what got people laughing. So the fancy gear would have to wait for a while longer.

There was another reason why Sydney's Pavilion show was important to me – for the first time, Bella was coming to see me perform. Her first concern when I told her I was playing the Pavilion was that I shouldn't give up my job at Sunblest, but she was satisfied when I told her that I wouldn't do that.

On the night, my Uncle Jim and Aunt Pearl brought Bella to the theatre and after the show they brought her to the dressing-room to see me. 'Well,' I said, 'what do you think?'

'You're a silly bugger behaving like that,' she said. 'No wonder all these folk were laughing at you.' My Uncle Jim just shook his head and the look on her face said it all – 'He's been more trouble than all my other children put together, but I still love him.' Bella's parting shot was, 'And remember, don't you be doing anything stupid like giving up your job at the bakery.'

After the show, people were patting me on the back and I also got good reviews in the newspapers the next day. I really appreciated that, because the people the praise was coming from had been writing about show business for years. The *Daily Express* showbiz writer Neville Garden took me to lunch and did an interview. The photographer with him that day was a guy called Ron Burgess and after he had taken his pictures, Neville turned to Ron and said, 'What do you make of him?'

Ron answered, 'Well, he's not show business, is he?'

I asked him what he meant, wondering if he meant I wasn't good enough, but he explained that I wasn't like show-business people who only talk about themselves all the time. 'All you've spoken about is your granny, Bella, your aunts and uncles and how you're looking forward to getting married for a second time,' said Neville.

'You opened your heart to us and certainly it's about you, but you spoke about your life, not what you want to do in show business.'

This took me by surprise because that was me being me. I'm not show business in that respect and that was the first time I realised I wasn't like most other people in the entertainment world because I'm just not that type of person. I'm glad I came into showbiz at a

Me at nine months old with the man
who won the war — my dad.

Bella and Old Andra round the back — I was probably hanging
off the wash-house dyke when this picture was taken.

This is me showing Scotland's first satellite dishes — look at those ears!

Heading for the Arbroath swimming pool — the last time I saw a pair of legs like that, there was a message tied to them.

The 189th BB boys at Macduff are all smiles — we hadn't yet discovered how cold the Tarlair swimming pool was.

The would-be skiffle group at Sir William Arrol's Iron Works in 1956.
From left: Wee Peem, Sammy McFadyen, Willie Park and myself
— I never could get that shovel in tune.

We will follow on — I'm on the left in Barcelona for the Cup-Winners' Cup final in 1972.
By the way, that's not a tea cosy on my head.

Here's me with Bella just before she started chasing after my hairdresser.
(James Morrison. © *Evening Times*)

Not the best-dressed comic in Scotland as I go
through my paces as the football hooligan.
(© *Daily Record*)

Me handing over the first copy of 'Ally's Tartan Army' to the man himself.
(© *Scottish Daily Express*)

Me as the *Guid Sodjer Schweik* — if I
had been a real soldier, the Germans
might have won the war.
(© *Daily Record*)

Every time I look at this picture, I'm the only one I don't know. I'm on the left in the back row, then it's Jackie Stewart, Gordon Brown and Alan McManus. Front row, from left: Stephen Hendry, Sean Connery and Kenny Dalglish. (© Ian Gavin, Malcolm Sargent House, Prestwick)

One of my best pals: the irrepressible Chic Cherry in *High Road*.
(© Scottish Television)

Me and all my weans — from left: Spencer, Ellen, Elliott, Marion and Jennifer. (© *Rangers News*)

The love of my life — Norma.

late age because by that time I had a strong background and years of living an ordinary life and having to graft for a wage just like everybody else.

Over the years, I discovered that most show-business people make bad audiences. They sit there going, 'Nah – I could do better than that.' I am totally the opposite and when I go to watch comics I laugh my head off. And I can't stand how entertainers love to hear that other comics have had a bad gig and they died on stage. They seem to take a perverse joy hearing about their fellow professionals having an off night. That really upsets me because I've died on stage. I've hated it happening to me and I hate it happening to other people.

The Sydney Devine Show was also good for me because that's how I met Peter de Rance, who went on to be my agent for 24 years. As I was learning all about show business, Peter de Rance was a big influence on me in that respect. I've never had an angry word with him over all the years and he never did me out of a halfpenny, and I wouldn't have done him out of a halfpenny either. We were friends and I liked him as a person as well as for being a good agent. All the best agents are trustworthy, and Peter certainly was trustworthy. I hadn't heard about him before I started with him, but he seemed a good guy, had plenty of contacts in the entertainment world in the right places so I decided to see how it went. Later on, I discovered he was the only agent who brought Frank Sinatra to Glasgow and lost £1,800 on the deal. The reason that Sinatra didn't pull a big audience in 1951 was that he was going through a bad time in his private life. He had left his wife Nancy and was chasing Ava Gardner all over the place and everybody turned against him. In those days, if the public didn't fancy what you were doing in your private life they shunned you. It wasn't only Glasgow where Sinatra bombed. He played to small audiences in Dundee and Ayr as well.

The week after the Sydney Devine Show, I'm sitting in Peter's office and he tells me that Billy Dunlop – who was Lex McLean's producer and also the manager of the Pavilion – was planning a tribute show to Lex, who had died a few months earlier. Peter asked me if I fancied doing the show the following year and I couldn't wait to say yes because Lex McLean was a great comedy hero of mine when I was younger. I had never done sketches before, but it went quite well, was another new show-business experience for me and by and large got good reviews.

Talking about Sydney, it reminds me of a gag I used to do at the time when everyone was having a go at him for being a rotten singer. It didn't do him much harm, though, because everybody would talk about Sydney and his profile would get even bigger. Probably his biggest detractor was his biggest benefactor in those terms – Frank Skerritt, who presented a show on Radio Clyde. He would give Sydney pelters – and then go on to play his records every time.

The gag I used to tell was about one of Sydney's concerts and he's out there with the white Elvis suit on giving it his all, as usual. The place is packed and suddenly someone throws a bottle from the balcony into the stalls and it hits a guy on the back of the head. There's blood spurting everywhere, but Sydney carries on despite the mayhem and the wee guy who's had the bottle on the back of the head staggers up the aisle and shouts, 'Hit me again, I can still hear him!' Don't get me wrong, though, Sydney might not be the best singer in the world, but he can certainly entertain a crowd.

What was happening in my life in 1975 could only be described as a whirlwind in both private and professional terms. Holding down a job in Sunblest getting up at the crack of dawn and fulfilling the many bookings to appear in clubs all over Scotland could not go on for ever and slowly the realisation that I would have to become a full-time entertainer dawned on me.

On the personal side, Norma and I had decided that we would get married as soon as my divorce came through and that meant a new house and a new wife to go along with a brand new career as a comedian. Norma and I had never lived together. I stayed in my own house in The Spittal and she stayed at her parents, although when she wanted a dog, Fred the Dalmatian stayed with me!

I had to travel through to the Court of Session in Edinburgh with two witnesses so I could get my divorce early in 1975. It might come as a surprise to some people, but one of the witnesses was my mother-in-law, Ellen Brodie, and the other was my Uncle Andy. I drove both of them through to Edinburgh in my car that day. May didn't come to the court because she didn't have to be there.

I needed the witnesses to say that May and I hadn't lived together for some time and the marriage was over. I was asked why the marriage had failed and I said there were irreconcilable differences between us, that we'd gone our separate ways and had different ideas in life – all that kind of stuff. The divorce was granted. It was just like shelling peas.

I was looking forward enormously to a new life with Norma, but on that day I came out the court and felt like a phoney because I had failed. I had done something, it didn't work and it was entirely my fault. Millions of other couples have differences and they stick it out and get over it, but I couldn't do that. I had to be true to myself and to my feelings, though, which were that I had another life beckoning and I had to go on from where I was.

There was never any rancour or bitterness from Mrs Brodie – she wasn't that type of person. Even after May and I split up and the whole story came out she was never anything less than pleasant to me when we met. She certainly never felt anything different towards my two girls, Ellen and Marion – she was brilliant with the two of them, as were all the Brodie family.

Mrs Brodie died in 2003 and I went to her funeral. My daughter Ellen was very close to her – after all, she was her gran – and she took her passing very badly.

Ellen was a bit special to Mr and Mrs Brodie because she was their first grandchild – a bit like me with Bella because I was her first grandchild and, of course, when Ellen was born, that made Bella a great-granny for the first time.

Over the years since May and I have been divorced we have always been civil to each other. I might phone Marion's and May has been babysitting my daughter's two kids Taylor and Blair and we will talk like friends. I'll ask her how her husband, Eddie, is and what they're doing for holidays and stuff like that – a normal conversation. It was never like the Wild West with May and me. What happened between us has also happened to millions of other people and I believe in being civilised about it. It's done and dusted and you can never turn back the clock.

Norma and May have met at various family functions and there have never been any issues between them. After all, May remarried and seems to be happy with her lot second time around, just as I am.

When Norma and I became serious about our relationship, I sat her down one night and confessed all about my previous marriage and the reasons for it failing. I told her everything – the affairs, the one-night stands, the lot. I wanted to clear the air, get it off my chest and I certainly came clean that night. I told her I didn't want another marriage where I was going to be Jack the Lad – and since I've met Norma I haven't been. It was important she knew I wasn't going to behave like that again. Thankfully, she accepted what I said.

Although Norma and I were engaged I never got round to getting her an engagement ring. We had decided we would get married, so to all intents and purposes that was us engaged and we told the people who were important to us. At that point, I had just started doing the clubs and couldn't afford an engagement ring.

We bought a house in Hillview Drive, Clarkston for the princely sum of £10,300. That might seem like chicken-feed now with today's house prices, but then it was a king's ransom. We were married at Giffnock Registry Office on 4 November 1975. I always remember the name of the registrar, Zena Livingstone, because of the unusual forename.

There were just six of us at the registry office for a quiet ceremony – Norma and myself, Norma's mum and dad, Norrie and Agnes MacDonald, Norma's sister, Anne, who was best maid and her husband, Dave Biglin, who was best man. I had wondered what to do about the best man. Tom Broadley, who had been best man at my first wedding, was still a close friend but I had to consider other people's feelings because it was my second marriage. But Dave did a fine job and after the ceremony the wedding party went to The Bruce Hotel, in East Kilbride, for a meal. Then it was back to Norma's parents for a celebration with the aunts, uncles, cousins and our friends. But before that we called in to see Bella, who wasn't well enough to come to the wedding.

I couldn't believe my luck. I'd just got married to a woman much younger than me and we were planning to start a family. It was a really happy, happy time for me.

Our wedding night was the first time we lived together and we went back to our new home in Clarkston. But at half past three in the morning the phone rang and woke me up and I sleepily said, 'Who is it?'

'It's Sunblest. Wake up, you've slept in!' the voice said. It was my pal Bobby Maitland up to his usual tricks. 'F**k off, you bastard,' I said and put the phone down.

The week before the wedding, I gave up working at Sunblest to go full time as a comedian. It was like a complete fresh start in both my professional and private life and it was great not having to get up at the crack of dawn after coming home late from a gig.

I had a couple of days off as a honeymoon, but I was soon back on the road performing in clubs all over Scotland. I had been earning a reasonable amount of money adding together the £28 a week I got at Sunblest and the £35 a night I was getting doing shows. At that time, I was doing about three nights a week and one gig was paying more than a week's work at Sunblest. But with the success of the Sydney Devine Show and now having an agent getting better-paying gigs, I was beginning to earn more money than I had been working at Sunblest and doing gigs at night. I was more in demand so that meant Peter could charge more and my earning power was increasing.

Soon, I was getting £100 a show and within a year it was up to £250 a show. After the honeymoon, I worked every night for four weeks, but that was just as well. I had a mortgage to pay and we had spent a lot of money on new carpets, furniture and doing up the house. But once all these bills were paid the number of nights I was working calmed down a bit.

Married life was different second time around. Norma stopped working and we would have the day together at home because most of my shows were at night. I didn't want us to start our married life with Norma going to work and coming home to see me heading out the door to do a gig. After about a month or so we had our first fall-out – I can't remember what it was about, probably something really stupid. But as fall-outs go it was spectacular – bawling and shouting, the whole bit. I stormed out of the house, jumped in the car and headed for the Pop Inn, in Rutherglen.

I knew Alan Elliot who ran the pub and he obviously saw there was something bothering me. 'You all right?' he asks.

'Not really,' I said. 'I've just fell out with her. Just give me a Coke – I only came out to calm down.'

Somebody came in and asked if I wanted a pint of Guinness and I thought I may as well just have the one pint. Next thing, it's half past one in the morning, there's been a lock-in at the pub and I'm birlin'. I'd moved on to the Bacardis. I knew I had to sober up, so Alan gave me a bowl of soup and some crusty bread.

After the soup I must have conked out and I woke up at five to four in the morning and there were still folk in the pub. I knew I had better get home so I left and headed for my car, which now had a big police van parked beside it. I knew one of the policemen in the van and he came out to talk to me, asking what I'm doing in Rutherglen at this time of the morning.

I told him I'd had a row with Norma, had come down to the pub for a blether with some pals and I was just on my way home. I must have been acting sober because he had no idea I had been sozzled a few hours before, otherwise he would never have allowed me to get into my car. After I had driven off, the policeman – who shall remain nameless – went into the pub to check everything was OK and Alan Elliot asked him if he'd seen me and had I got a taxi.

'Taxi?' said the policeman. 'No, he's just away in his motor.'

'You're joking,' says Alan. 'He was birlin' three hours ago and he's just woken up after falling asleep.'

The next time I saw this policeman he told me how he had jumped into his van and driven the route I would have taken. He caught up with me at Prospecthill Road and watched me driving perfectly. He was thinking I couldn't possibly have had all that drink, but stayed on my tail until he saw me park the car in my driveway. Then he warned me, 'You were very lucky. If you'd had as much drink as they said you'd had and you were stopped, you would have been done and lost your licence.'

I'm still grateful to that policeman for double-checking that I got home safely that night.

Anyway, back to my row with Norma. When I try the front door I discover it's locked and as I step back a few paces down the drive to look up at the bedroom window I notice Norma's shadow behind the glass front door.

'Open the door,' I said.

'No,' she says.

'Open the door or I'll kick it in,' I replied.

I take a run at the door, but before I reach it she opens it and I go into the house. As soon as I see her I say, 'I'm sorry. I don't know and I don't care who was in the wrong, we shouldn't have fallen out like that.'

She asks me where I've been and when I tell her I've had a right bucketful of drink she says I'd better get up to bed for a sleep. I say I need a cup of tea and walk into the kitchen.

Now you'll remember how Bella made me a plate of porridge the morning after the first time I had been drunk – well, Norma made me a plate of porridge that morning and we sat at the kitchen table and had a wee heart-to-heart talk.

That chat laid the ground rules about giving each other space, biting your tongue and being willing to give and take. All of these things are about trying harder to make your marriage work. It wasn't so much a bust-up we had, it was more of a collision of two personalities and at the end of it we both learned something. We both had to eat humble pie and go on from there and we made progress. Every married couple has rows, but ours became less spectacular as time went on. Now Norma and I understand each other and I know what makes her tick and she knows what makes me tick.

About three months after we were married, I had come in from a show one night and Norma asked me to sit down as she had something to tell me. I thought something had happened and I said, 'What's up?'

'I'm pregnant,' she said and then burst into tears. I was almost crying myself as we hugged each other. We were both delighted at the prospect of our first child being born.

Jennifer was born on 22 October 1976 and up until then it was one of the biggest things that had happened to me. Not the Sydney Devine Show, nor the Lex McLean Tribute Show. No, it was the birth of our first child and best of all I was going to be at the birth. I'd wanted to be at the birth of my first two children, but I wasn't allowed by the hospital and I don't think May would have been too keen either. This time, however, Norma was quite happy to have me at the birth.

I'm in the labour suite at the maternity hospital in Paisley and Norma's been in labour for 23 hours. I'm holding Norma's hand and saying all the wrong things. I think I'm being a stalwart giving Norma someone to lean on, but I'm not even looking at the business end.

When Jennifer was born weighing 9 lb 1 oz at ten to five in the morning, the tears were rolling down my cheeks I was so happy. When I left Norma to recover, the dawn was hardly breaking and I made my way home to start the phone calls. I was getting people out of their beds to tell them that Norma had just given birth to a wee girl.

The year 1976 just got better and better as far as my career was concerned, and I was earning great money. Not long after this, however, the video age was upon us, and audiences in social clubs began to decline. People who had gone to clubs for their entertainment suddenly realised that staying in at night with a rented video and a carry-out was much cheaper. As the crowds dropped, so did the money clubs could afford to pay the acts. It was boom and bust as far as clubland was concerned.

But I was now getting gigs at bigger clubs and theatre shows as well. I was known well enough to get on the bill as the comedian alongside established entertainers like Andy Stewart, Kenneth McKellar and Moira Anderson. It was great experience for me as it was different from performing in the clubs where you could tell jokes which were a wee bit naughty. I might only have had a 20-minute spot on these shows but it taught me the discipline of choosing my material to suit the audience. I was still doing the football hooligan act, which went down well because nearly everybody in Scotland is football daft. And appearing in the Lex McLean Tribute Show in the summer of 1976 was another big boost to my career.

By this time, I was probably in the top three club acts in Scotland along with comedian Hector Nicol and the singer, Christian. I also started appearing on television with spots on the *Battle of the Comics* and *Joker's Wild* shows. Then I got my own show at the Pavilion, which was another milestone. I was back working with Sydney the year after he gave me a big break in his Glasgow Pavilion show. This time it was on his television series with STV. One of the shows was almost surreal because a special guest was the great jazz pianist, singer and songwriter Buddy Greco. Now, in singing terms, putting Buddy Greco on with Sydney is like Neilston Juniors playing Real Madrid.

Sydney had his own audience and they loved him, but they weren't really into someone like Buddy Greco. However, Buddy Greco did a fantastic jazz version of 'The Lady is a Tramp' and you could hear all Sydney's punters going, 'Aye, he's not bad – who is he? Anyway, when's Sydney coming on?'

An abiding memory for me is the bemused look on Buddy Greco's face – remember, he's played in Las Vegas and all over the world – when he saw me jumping about dressed as a football hooligan and telling daft football gags, followed by Sydney in a white Elvis suit singing stuff like 'Tiny Bubbles'.

I had also had a tilt at getting on national television through the two hugely popular talent shows of the day, *Opportunity Knocks* and *New Faces*. As well as dressing up as a football hooligan I also donned the more mainstream dinner suit and I was wearing a wee mustard number when I did my audition for *Opportunity Knocks*, in 1974.

It was in the Locarno Ballroom in Glasgow and you walked on stage and all you saw was a table with Hughie Green, the show's producer Royston Mayo, and a couple of other people sitting at it. When it came to my turn, I bounded on stage and said, 'Hi, I'm Andy Cameron.'

'Thanks, that's it,' says Hughie Green.

I looked at them bemused. 'Thanks, that will be fine,' he says again.

'Hi, I'm Andy Cameron,' was all I got the chance to say in my audition for *Opportunity Knocks*. I hadn't told a single gag and when I asked what the problem was they said I wasn't what they were looking for. Maybe if I had played the saw or was a singing shepherd I'd have got on the show, but they just weren't interested in hearing my act.

I fared a lot better on *New Faces* a year later. Apart from actually getting on television, I came second to a band called Easy Street, but caused a bit of a row among the judges. The *New Faces* show producer came to see me doing a cabaret in West Linton. It was the ideal place for him to see me because there was an audience there and that was the environment I had been used to. I was on top of my game that night and he fell off his stool laughing. I did the routine about going down to Wembley on the train and saying to the driver when we arrived at Euston that it was the smoothest train journey I ever had, although it was a bit bumpy round about Carlisle. The driver said that was because we hit an Englishman and I asked if he had strayed onto the railway line. 'No,' he replies. 'He was in a field, but we still got him!' It's an old gag now, but it went down a storm with the audience.

I carried on with the football theme – well, I was dressed as a football hooligan with scarves hanging off my arm. I told them the one about going to games with my wee pal Clunt – his name's Willie, really, but we've called him Clunt ever since he ran out of a Chinese restaurant without paying.

Then I went on to the gag about going to bed with a German hooker who's absolutely gorgeous and when I look down I say to her, 'I've never seen one that big before.' And she says that she hopes I'm taking precautions and I reply, 'Aye, I've tied my feet to the bottom of the bed.' These were the kind of naughty gags you could get away with then. The gag ends with the German hooker, after we've done the business, saying she wanted some German marks and I say, 'Ten out of ten.' That daft wee throwaway line had the *New Faces* guy falling off his stool laughing.

Another gag had me at the football with Clunt and I'm

desperate for a pee. Clunt says just do it in the pocket of the guy next to you and I say, 'Don't be stupid. He'll notice.'

'Well, you didn't,' replies Clunt.

After the show, the producer came into the dressing-room and said he thought I was great and he wanted me on *New Faces*. 'But I'll give you one piece of advice – you need to speak slower because the show is recorded in Birmingham and it will be a Midlands audience in the studio.'

I headed down to Birmingham for the show and the panel on the night was George Elrick, Lonnie Donegan, the King of Skiffle in the '60s, John Smith, who was in charge of all the Bailey's clubs in the north of England and the hatchet man everybody loved to hate – Tony Hatch.

I did three minutes of my football hooligan routine and stood waiting to hear what the judging panel had to say. Tony Hatch was first and he says, 'I've heard people say that comedians don't get much of a chance on this show because they only get three minutes to impress you.

'This guy impressed me three seconds after he opened his mouth. He had me in the palm of his hand. He was different and he's a character. Terrific – nine out ten.'

Next up is John Smith. 'I'm sorry to hear Tony saying that,' he says. 'I couldn't put him into any Bailey's clubs because they won't understand him. I had to really listen and I couldn't understand him.' Tony Hatch butts in and argues that the studio audience obviously understood what I was saying. But John Smith countered, 'No, we've got clubs all over the north – it wouldn't work. Different idea though, the football hooligan and I quite like it. Seven out of ten.'

Lonnie Donegan, who was born in Scotland, was raging. He turned to John Smith and said, 'You don't understand him? I'm from Glasgow and I've gone all over the world and people haven't had a problem understanding me. We've got to sit in Glasgow and listen to Brummie or Cockney comics with their accents and we understand them.

'If you listen properly, you'll understand him. Ten out of ten – I haven't laughed so much for a long time.'

Then it's George Elrick's turn. He says, 'Andy Cameron is a typical Scottish comic – they get themselves a character. I've known a lot of Scottish comics like Harry Gordon, from Aberdeen, who take on a character like a gamekeeper. Andy has taken an up-to-date character. All you read about in football is the hooliganism and Andy's character is one of the likeable football hooligans. It was terrific and I really enjoyed it – nine out of ten.

I might have only been runner-up on the night, but I was quite happy with the way it went. The exposure on national television also meant that along with my profile going up, I was able to put my fee up as well. The clubs could put on their posters, 'Andy Cameron – straight from the hit TV show *New Faces*.'

It was more of the same after that until the big break on Sydney Devine's show. Then it was bigger clubs, theatres and the odd spot on television. I didn't just do well in the west of Scotland. I would be away from home for a week at a time, maybe doing a week's worth of shows in the Dundee area with gigs in the many clubs they had up there at the time. I'd get maybe ten gigs in the one week and since the clubs were booming, the money was good and I never seemed to have any problem filling a club when I was performing.

The oil boom in the north-east was on its way and I would fly up to Sullom Voe to the big oil terminal there and do shows for the hundreds of men working and living in camps. The guys loved comedians like Hector Nicol, Clem Dane and myself, but they hated singers. All they wanted was a good comic who would give them a good laugh.

These guys worked hard and played hard – they could drink for Scotland. When a vocalist was on they would pile all their empty beer cans into a pyramid on the table. If they really didn't like the vocalist who was on they would give each other a signal and knock all the cans down at the one time. The poor singer would be in the middle of a number and hundreds of cans would come crashing down at the one time, making a noise like the building was collapsing round them.

Yes, things were good and I was working all the time. If I was doing a one-off gig I always drove home no matter where the show was. I always had this thing about wanting to get home to my own house and my own bed. If you come off stage and have had a good night you're on a high. There's no way you're going to get to sleep until you come back down, so you may as well use all that adrenalin that's keeping you awake to drive home, even if you don't arrive there until 2 a.m. If you'd stayed in a hotel you wouldn't get to sleep until 1 a.m. You'd get up, have your breakfast and not start heading for home until 10 a.m. By the time you are home that's half your day gone. Coming home every night after gigs meant I had most of the day at home and saw plenty of Jennifer growing up.

I was working with some really big names in Scottish show business, but none more so than Andy Stewart, who was a real hero of mine and the consummate professional. There was an incident which really epitomised this, and I have never seen anything like it since. I was on the bill with Andy in Arbroath and my spot ended the first half. Then I was due to come back on, do a few gags and introduce Andy for the rest of the show. Just as I was about to start the second half, I noticed Andy sitting in the wings bent double in pain. He was as white as a sheet and holding his stomach. I said we should get an ambulance because he was obviously seriously ill, but he was having none of it and was determined to go on that stage.

I offered to do the second half for him, but there was no persuading him. So I went on stage, told a gag or two and said, 'Ladies and gentlemen, the man you have all come to see . . . Andy Stewart.' I exited stage left; he came on stage right.

He went right into, 'Come in, come in, it's nice to see you . . .' and I couldn't believe it was the same guy. It was like someone had swapped the Andy Stewart I saw at the side of the stage for the Andy Stewart who was out there performing. He had colour in his cheeks, he was swinging the kilt and the sparkle was there.

He walked off the stage after a 55-minute performance and collapsed before he was carted off to hospital. He had a stomach operation the next day. I could not believe the change that man had effected and it proved to me he was a show-business legend. It also proved that I was not a show-business person in that mould.

If it had been me, I'd have been saying, 'Get me an ambulance – I'm not well. I'm off to the hospital.'

We moved to another house in 1977 and again we spent a lot of money doing it up. I had got one of the guys I played football with, John McTear – not the same guy who compèred Bella's parties in an American accent – to build a magnificent Cumberland slate fireplace. I thought it was the business and looked great in the lounge.

The house was in Clarkston Road, opposite the synagogue and backed on to Williamwood Golf Club. The first time Bella came to the house I thought she would be impressed with the fireplace. But she came in and said, 'My, look at the height of the ceilings.' She walked by the fireplace to the window, looked out and said, 'You're handy for that Stakis place across the road.' She had seen the entrance to the synagogue with the menorah seven-branch candelabra sign on the front and thought it was a Stakis hotel.

If I thought I was doing well at this point, a chance remark from fellow comedian Clem Dane one night put me on the road to even bigger and better things. He said, 'Why don't you write a song to finish your football act?'

Chapter 10

MARCHING WITH ALLY'S ARMY

THE LOUNGE BAR WAS PACKED WITH CELEBRATING SCOTS FOOTBALL FANS who had just seen their team qualify for the World Cup finals in Argentina. An hour or two earlier, Scotland had defeated Wales 2–0 with goals from captain Don Masson and Kenny Dalglish in the qualifying match at Anfield.

Scotland manager Ally McLeod had captured the imagination of a nation and we all thought World Cup glory was just around the corner. The atmosphere was tremendous and there was as much beer flowing that night in the Holiday Inn, Liverpool, as there was water in the River Mersey.

The fans were packed into the lounge like sardines and the noise was incredible. It looked to me as if half of Scotland was there. The Big Yin, Billy Connolly, is still in his bevvy period and standing at the bar knocking 'em back with the rest of us. I'm at the other end of the bar when Scots DJ Tom Ferrie calls me over and introduces me to Billy.

'You've got a song for the World Cup, Andy,' says Tom.

'Aye, "Ally's Tartan Army", it's called,' I replied.

'How does it go?' asks The Big Yin. So I let him hear the tune with a few dee-dee-dees and Billy says he reckons it's a catchy wee tune and I should definitely put it out as a record. And when I sing him the line, 'England cannae dae it 'cos they didnae qualify,' he says that's the hook line everybody will go for.

At that point, Watt Nicol – who had a hypnotism act and called himself The Man – comes over and says, 'See that football song of yours, Andy. Going to get up and let the lads hear it?'

Watt tries to get some order over the din and he's shouting for people to be quiet. 'Gentlemen, we've got a song here to take us to the World Cup,' he says. 'This is Andy Cameron.'

Since I'd been doing the clubs for a few years, a lot of the guys there that night knew me. I stood on a chair and told a few football gags for about ten minutes. By this time, everyone had gathered round the chair I was standing on and I was getting a laugh from the crowd. After a few gags, I said, 'Shhhsh, shhhsh. Watt was telling you about this new football song – well, here it is . . . We're on the march with Ally's Army, we're going to the Argentine.' I didn't have a mike, but still belted out the song and the crowd loved it. Everyone was clapping along and afterwards, when I had finished, they were saying I should bring it out as a record.

So, with the encouragement of the Tartan Army foot-soldiers and The Big Yin himself, how could I not release 'Ally's Tartan Army' as a record?

Soon after the night that Clem Dane had suggested I write a football song to finish my act, I'd started thinking about what tune I could use and what the lyrics could be about. This was in the summer of 1977 and World Cup football fever was starting to grip Scotland as we began to come closer and closer to qualifying for Argentina. I decided I would write the song about Scotland's World Cup bid, but I still had to come up with a good tune.

Over the many years of supporting Rangers, I had stood on the terraces and sang a song called, 'Who's That Team They Call The Rangers?', which I thought was a great tune. So I decided to use that melody, which I believed was a traditional tune.

Next, I had to come up with some lyrics and the first part of the song that came into my head was the words for the chorus. Over a few days, I managed to write the rest of the song in my head and soon the basis of it was there. The version I sang in the Holiday Inn in Liverpool wasn't what eventually came out on the record because in the course of recording the song, changes were made to the lyrics.

Enthused by the reaction of the fans when I sang the song, as soon as I got back to Scotland I called Clem Dane and we began to plan the recording of 'Ally's Tartan Army'. Clem knew a sound engineer at Radio Clyde called Pete Shipton, so we booked the studio at Radio Clyde, which was in the Anderston Centre, just off Argyle Street, in Glasgow.

I arrived there at two in the afternoon, ready to commit the tune to tape. As we recorded it, though, we kept coming up with different and better ideas for the lyrics. There were bits of paper lying all over the place as we changed this bit and then that bit until we eventually got what we reckoned were the best lyrics. I wrote most of the lyrics and I was credited for this on the record sleeve.

A drummer called Harry Barry was playing on the record and he suggested using a glockenspiel on the song. I had never heard of a glockenspiel, but it worked well with ideas like this being thrown in at the last minute as the song was recorded.

Clem knew a very talented young songwriter from Lanarkshire called Peter Nardini, who was very clever with lyrics and had written some catchy songs. We decided to put one of his songs, 'I Want to Be a Punk Rocker', on the B-side. We were in the studio for 12 hours solid, having drunk gallons of tea and coffee and munched our way through a mountain of carry-out pizzas. It took us half an hour to record 'I Want to Be a Punk Rocker' and eleven and a half hours to record 'Ally's Tartan Army' because of the changes we were making as we went along.

'I Want to Be a Punk Rocker' is such a brilliant song that, in hindsight, I should have kept it for a follow-up single instead of putting it on the B-side. 'Ally's Tartan Army' was strong enough to sell the record on its own and we could have put any daft football song on the flip-side. Over the years, as many people have come up to me and mentioned 'I Want to Be a Punk Rocker' as 'Ally's Tartan Army'.

I was absolutely shattered by the end of the recording session and, to be honest, it got to the stage late on when I could have seen the whole project far enough. I thought to myself, 'All this trouble and I might not sell any records.' But Clem took a tape of the song to Gus MacDonald and Isobel Waugh, who had just launched a record company in Glasgow called Klub Records. As soon as they heard 'Ally's Tartan Army', they knew they had a hit on their hands. Klub had 5,000 copies of the single pressed as a first run to see just how well the sales went.

In the weeks before the record was released, I finished my act by singing 'Ally's Tartan Army' and everybody was raving about it and telling me I should record it and put it out as a single. 'It's out next week,' I must have said hundreds of times. I even managed to get a few gags out of the record. 'It's selling like hot cakes,' I would say. 'Three for a shilling.' Another one was, 'It's been in the shops that long the hole in the middle has healed up.'

When the record was released in January 1978 I started selling it round the clubs and, sure enough, it did go like the proverbial hot cakes. My daughter Ellen turned record sales executive and traipsed after me at gigs selling them. We could easily sell 100 records a night and after a month we had sold 2,000 of them. By this time, Gus MacDonald at Klub had been down to London and managed to get a national distribution deal for 'Ally's Tartan Army'. This made all the difference as the record was now in all the big record stores and shops like Woolworth's and W.H. Smith, in England. It had taken us into another league and the record flew out of the shops as it started to get airplay on Radio Clyde. Although 'Ally's Tartan Army' has a wee go at their football team, the English really liked 'I Want to Be a Punk Rocker' and they were buying the record for the B-side.

Richard Park – who went on to become hugely successful in radio and the music industry as well as being head teacher in *Fame Academy* – was a DJ at Clyde at the time. He would announce, 'This is a record by Scottish comedian Andy Cameron and it could be Scotland's official World Cup song.' As it turned out, Rod Stewart did the official song – 'Ole Ola'.

Just as it seemed nothing would be able to stop us, the bombshell dropped. The music publishing and record company giant EMI contacted Klub records, saying we had breached their copyright on the melody to the song. I claimed it was a traditional piece of music and that, therefore, no one had copyright. But EMI wasn't for budging and they were adamant they had the publishing rights for that piece of music. They took us the whole road and we ended up in court being sued for breach of copyright. Soon after the court case started, we realised we couldn't afford to pay for lawyers in what could have been a lengthy legal battle. So we had to give up and give EMI the publishing royalties.

The record was becoming so popular, people were stopping me in the street asking where they could buy the single because it had sold out in their local record store. The record was obviously selling well in Scotland on the back of all the hype about the World Cup and it even got to number one in the Radio Clyde charts. I was delighted, but in reality, since I was very well known in the west of Scotland and the record was selling well in my heartland, it wasn't that surprising.

By this time, Scots songwriter and music publisher Bill Martin was involved and was promoting the song among the heavyweights of the national music industry. And then the phone call came.

I had been doing a gig in Aberdeen one Saturday night in March and had arrived back home at two o'clock in the morning. I made myself a cup of tea to wind down after the long journey home before I headed for my bed. I was looking forward to a lie in since it was Sunday morning and I fell asleep as soon as my head hit the pillow. I was awoken by the sound of the phone ringing on the bedside table and I looked at the clock – it was just after 6 a.m. My first thoughts about getting a phone call this early in the morning is that somebody I knew had died. I picked up the phone and heard a voice: 'Andy, it's Pete Shipton here. Guess what? You're on *Top of the Pops* on Thursday.'

'F**k off, Pete,' I said and put the phone down. He called back a couple of minutes later and managed to persuade me it wasn't a wind-up and, sure enough, I had been booked to perform 'Ally's Tartan Army' on *Top of the Pops* – the most influential music show on British television.

I couldn't get back to sleep and Norma had woken by this time and asked me what the phone calls were about. I told her there was nothing to worry about, she should get back to sleep and I would tell her later. When Norma got up I was already pacing up and down, my head spinning about all the things I had to do before my spot on *Top of the Pops* was recorded. Although the show went out on a Thursday night, it was recorded live on a Wednesday.

Later in the morning, I called my father and told him I'd be coming to London the following Wednesday. He asked me why I was coming down south and when I told him I was going to appear on *Top of the Pops* he was flabbergasted. 'That football record you told me about when I met you at the Scotland game in Liverpool last year?' he asked.

'That's the one,' I said. 'It has obviously hit the national charts and you'll see me on the telly next Thursday night. In fact, you, Stuart and Ian can come to the studios with me on the Wednesday to see it being recorded.'

It didn't really hit me until the Tuesday night, as I was getting ready to fly down to London the following morning. I was pinching myself thinking this couldn't be happening to me. I'm a Scottish comedian with a daft wee football song – what on earth was I doing on *Top of the Pops*?

I sat in my house and wondered if I could really pull it off. It was recorded live. What if I forgot the words? What if I make a complete arse of myself and let everybody down? It was a real whirlwind time, but these moments of doubt don't last long as the next wee shot of adrenalin gets you going. I knew the record was doing well in Scotland, but never in my wildest dreams did I think it was going to be in the national charts.

So, there we were, the 'Ally's Tartan Army' team trooping off the plane at Heathrow, piling into my dad's and Stuart's and Ian's taxis – they drove black Hackney cabs for a living – heading for the BBC Studios in London. We arrived at the BBC Television Centre and when I got past security and into the big round building all those famous people from television were walking by me. I kept saying to Peter de Rance, Clem Dane, Pete Shipton and Bill Martin, 'Did you see who that was? He nodded to me on the way by. He was on the telly last week.'

After I had met the show's production staff, the rehearsals began and they went on all day. I'd been given a group of four backing singers to do the harmonies and one of the singers was a Scot – Danny Street, from Stirling. I'd heard a lot about Danny Street: he was in big demand as a session singer as he had such a fantastic voice. I was in awe of Danny, he was that good, and he was brilliant with me. 'Great song, wee man. Get right in there and give it to them,' he said to me. He was a great source of encouragement.

We went through the rehearsals and my head was full of instructions about where to stand and what cameras to look into. Even the floor manager came up to me and said his parents were Scottish. 'Don't worry that it's not a pop song – it's a football song. The England World Cup squad did a football song in 1970. It's different and it's great,' he said. I got a lot of support from the studio staff.

I had told my dad and Stuart and Ian that we had arranged passes for them to be in the studio audience and to get backstage and they arrived just after 5 p.m. Danny Street joined our wee group for a cup of tea before the recording began. 'I can't believe this is happening,' says Danny. 'A Scottish boy starring on *Top of the Pops*.'

'Danny,' I replied. 'This Scottish boy can't believe someone like Danny Street is a backing singer for me. I've got a voice like a foghorn.'

'Not at all,' Danny adds. 'You've got the right voice for the song and you'll be great. And tomorrow you'll sell another 10,000 records. That's what an appearance on *Top of the Pops* does for you.'

I had all the gear on: the Scotland jersey, the tammy on my head and a tartan banner round my shoulders. Not exactly the normal attire of a pop star, but I was ready and waiting to go on stage. And that's when I thought my dad was going to throttle punk singer, Billy Idol, of Generation X.

Billy Idol was on *Top of the Pops* after my spot and he ambled up behind us. He's about 6 ft 4 in., wearing platform shoes and the *Oor Wullie* haircut. Now, if I think he looks weird, you can imagine what he thinks of me.

'Who the f**k are you?' he sneers.

And before I can get a word in, my dad's in Billy Idol's face saying, 'Who the f**k are you talking to? That's my boy.'

Stuart intervenes and calms everything down and quickly the tension is released and we're all having a laugh. I'm standing there thinking, 'I'm 38 and my dad's wanting to fight a punk rocker, giving it the "that's my boy" line. My dad's about 4 ft 11 in. and if he really wanted to have a go at Billy Idol, he'd have to stand on a chair.'

I get the signal and move into position. As soon as I step onto that stage the adrenalin rush sweeps away all the nerves. In my head, I'm not in the *Top of the Pops* studio, I'm in the Blantyre Miners Club or Lochore Welfare getting steamed right in, giving it my all. The kids in the audience have been given tartan scarves and they're waving them above their heads, although they probably can't understand a word of what I'm singing.

I was on near the end of the show and after I'd finished singing 'Ally's Tartan Army' I had to stay on that stage until all the acts were finished. When the show was over there was a bit of chaos as the kids in the audience rushed over to their idols looking for autographs.

Elkie Brooks was on the show that night and one girl couldn't get her autograph. Instead, she turned to me and asked me to sign the back of her *Top of the Pops* invitation card. I asked her name and wrote, 'To Denise, Andy Cameron loves you', and added a couple of kisses. When I handed it to her she said, 'And who are you anyway?' My dad saw this and asked what the girl had said and I told him she just wanted to know when my next record was out!

Everyone thought the performance had gone down well, so we headed off to the BBC Club for a wee celebratory refreshment or two. The first guy I saw when I walked in was Danny Street, and I handed him a fiver to get the backing singers a drink. About two weeks later, I got a letter signed by all the session singers congratulating me for my performance on *Top of the Pops* and saying they were delighted to see the record doing so well.

According to Danny, no one had ever bought them a drink as a thank you for being their backing singers. I didn't do it for effect, though. It's something I did in every club I was in – you buy the band a drink and it's just something you do. I thought the singers did a great job and made me sound good. In fact, having Danny Street as my backing singer was almost as much of a thrill as being on *Top of the Pops* itself.

That night, everyone else went off to their hotel, but I stayed with my dad and Doris, my stepmum. We went to the pub and my dad had his usual bottles of brown ale and we talked about football.

There was a bit of banter with his English pals in the pub who kept telling me Scotland had no chance in Argentina. 'Well, we've a better chance than you, because you lot aren't going,' I told them.

The next day, my dad drove me to the airport and I flew back into Glasgow. There was no question of me just basking in the glory because I had a gig that night at Lochore Welfare, in Fife. I arrived at the club about 7.20 p.m., just before *Top of the Pops* was due to start. There weren't many people hanging around the club's main hall and I wondered where everybody was.

One of the committee men pointed me in the direction of the television room and said, 'They're all in there waiting to see you on *Top of the Pops*.' The room was mobbed and quite dark, so I was able to slip in at the back and nobody noticed I was there watching along with them. I hadn't seen any playback of my performance at the BBC studios so this was the first time for me as well. 'Ally's Tartan Army' came on and when it was finished everybody burst into a round of applause. As they filed out the door I could hear them saying, 'The wee man was brilliant . . . he made Scotland proud.' That's all I had been worried about, not letting anyone down, and I was glad I hadn't.

When I went on stage that night I could have read out the telephone directory and got a laugh. As usual, I finished the show with 'Ally's Tartan Army' and they were clapping and cheering. I did 'I Want to Be a Punk Rocker' as an encore and then they're shouting, 'Sing "Ally's Tartan Army" again,' so off I went: 'We're on the march with Ally's Army . . .'

The following day, Norma told me the story of what had happened when my daughter, Jennifer, saw me singing 'Ally's Tartan Army' on *Top of the Pops*. Jennifer was about 18 months old and she was sitting on her potty when the programme came on. When I started singing, she was looking at the television and saying 'Daddy'. When I finished and the camera cut to someone else, Jennifer got up off her potty and looked round the back of the television to see where I'd gone. That was the pinnacle of 'Ally's Tartan Army' for me: my wee lassie seeing me on telly and looking at the back of the TV set thinking, 'Where's daddy got to?'

The sequel to this story is that years later, Jennifer, Elliott and

Spencer were sitting in the house watching Terry Wogan on *Auntie's Bloomers* and what should come on but me singing 'Ally's Tartan Army' on *Top of the Pops*. You should have heard them: 'Oh no, we've got to go to school tomorrow – what a slagging we'll get.' I hadn't realised they didn't know about the *Top of the Pops* appearance. I had assumed they did and it was never spoken about after all that time. Ever since then, when any of them go on about their favourite pop stars, I remind them that their dad was a pop star as well.

In the run-up to the World Cup, I introduced the Scotland team to the fans at Hampden. About 10,000 fans turned out to see their heroes walk onto the pitch to take their applause. I was wearing a tartan jacket and one by one introduced the team and the coaching staff to the crowd. Beforehand, while waiting in the tunnel to go on while a technician was fixing me up with a radio mike, I'd looked round and realised who I was standing with. They were the heroes of Scottish football – Alan Rough, Danny McGrain, Willie Johnston, Lou Macari and Derek Johnstone. I was like a 38-year-old schoolboy.

I had a perm at the time and as I introduced Alan Rough, he came onto the park and shouted to me, 'Who did that to your head?' My reply was, 'Obviously the same barber who did the same to you.'

Last out onto the park was the manager, Ally McLeod, who was met with a huge roar. I introduced him with the words, 'Ladies and gentlemen. We're all on the march with Ally's Army – will you welcome the one and only Ally McLeod.'

Ally loved the record and later he told me he thought the song gave the country a real boost. He said the record had just as much to do with the euphoria created over Scotland going to the World Cup than anything he had said or did. By the time the World Cup came round in June 1978, we had sold 360,000 copies of 'Ally's Tartan Army' and we got to No. 6 in the national charts in the week of 4 March.

As a follow-up, I recorded a live album of gags and football songs for Klub Records which was supposed to capitalise on the success of the single. It was recorded in the Orchard Park Hotel in Glasgow and was called *Andy's Tartan Album*. But we had no inkling of the disaster that was about to befall the nation – and my recording career – within a matter of days.

On Saturday, 3 June, Peru beat Scotland 3–1. We were playing minnows Iran the following Wednesday, though, and everyone thought Scotland would easily win that game. On the Monday before that game, I was playing the BNC Club in Bathgate and everyone was in a party mood with the gags going well, me telling them how we were going to play Iran off the park and giving a rousing rendition of 'Ally's Tartan Army' to end the show as usual.

On the Wednesday night, I was booked to do a show in the upstairs function room of the Tartan Arms pub in Bannockburn, which is run by a lovely guy called John McHugh. I was beginning to have my doubts about how easy it would be for Scotland to beat Iran and I phoned John and suggested I do my act before the game came on television in case it all went pear-shaped.

John said, 'Don't be daft. We'll beat Iran and when you come on the audience will be in great form and ready for you.'

I even offered to do my hour before the game and if Scotland did win, I'd come back on and do another set. But John was having none of it and insisted I was to have a bite to eat at the buffet he was putting on and watch the game with him. Foolishly, I agreed.

Scotland had a disastrous 1–1 draw with Iran and the atmosphere was horrific. It was so bad I almost suggested to John that he should cancel the gig, but I went on. I was still wearing the daft football gear, but trying to do anything but football gags and I was getting no reaction from the crowd.

Eventually, one guy shouted from the audience, 'Andy, do us a favour – f**k off!'

I tried out the old shout-out-a-subject-and-I'll-tell-a-gag-about-it routine, but I still wasn't making any inroads. Another guy shouts to me, 'See if you start that "Ally's Tartan Army", I'll throw you out the f*****g window!' I don't think he was kidding, either. I had only done about 15 minutes when I decided enough was enough and told the audience that was it – the show's over. I said, 'I'm sorry, but I don't think anyone is in the mood for laughing tonight.' And at that, I got a round of applause. One woman came up to me as I walked off stage and said, 'At least you went up there. You had no chance tonight.'

I went downstairs to the bar and warned John McHugh not even to think about offering me the money for the gig. He admitted he was wrong and that I should have gone on before the game. You could say that was the night 'Ally's Tartan Army' were in retreat, although in the weeks ahead there were still a few clubs where the audiences wanted to hear the song.

After Scotland's World Cup exit, Ally McLeod's star waned back home, and so did sales of 'Ally's Tartan Army'. Within days, there was a guy in Dundee selling copies of the song for a penny and giving you the loan of a hammer to break it. The football debacle also put paid to any hope of success with *Andy's Tartan Album* and although it was released, the sales flopped and thousands were dumped in a skip. If there are any left they'll have been made into ashtrays and flowerpots by now.

But by then, 'Ally's Tartan Army' had given my career a huge boost and because of that record I started doing pantomimes, had my own radio show and wrote a newspaper column for the paper I used to deliver – the *Evening Times*, in Glasgow.

I did a lot of things in the next 15 years that would never have happened if it hadn't been for 'Ally's Tartan Army'. I couldn't believe what I got out of that one record. There's no doubt it was a tremendous springboard for my career in the entertainment business. It was like the *Opportunity Knocks* appearance that I never got. This time, opportunity knocked, the door opened and I walked right in.

The final word on 'Ally's Tartan Army' and the Argentina fiasco has to go to a Glasgow man who saw me coming out of Lewis's, in Argyle Street, later that summer and asked, 'How did Derek Johnstone no' get a game for Scotland in Argentina?'

'How would I know?' I said.

'Well, you did that bloody record, didn't you!'

Chapter 11

I'M GOING RADIO RENTAL!

IT'S A LIVE, OUTSIDE RADIO BROADCAST AND HUNDREDS OF PEOPLE ARE crowded round me outside the Beach Ballroom in Aberdeen. I see a wee boy with a Rangers top on and I push through the bodies to ask him a few questions. 'What's your name?' I say to him.

'Colin,' he replies.

'How old are you?'

'Eight.'

'Are you enjoying your holiday?' I ask.

And with a broad Aberdeen accent, the lad says, 'I'm nae on holiday. I'm frae Aberdeen.'

'Well, how come you're a Rangers fan? You should be supporting your local team. Aberdeen has got a great team just now.'

'My dad comes frae Glasgow and he takes me all over the place to see the Rangers.'

'Who's your favourite player?'

'Davie Cooper.'

'Well, you must know something about football – he's a really good player. Nice to speak to you, Colin.'

As I turn away to push through the crowd to speak to someone else, there's a tug at my jacket. It's young Colin again.

'Can I tell a joke on the radio?'

155

I look at the boy's parents, who are standing next to him, and they nod their heads to let me know it's OK.

'All right, Colin,' I say jovially. 'What's your joke?'

He pauses for a second and says, 'What vegetable makes your eyes water?'

'That'll be an onion,' I said.

'No, no, it's a turnip.'

Now, I am genuinely bemused by his answer, so I ask him how a turnip could make your eyes water.

'Have you ever been hit in the balls with a turnip?' replies Colin.

Well, to say the least, I was not prepared for that one, but the crowd just roared with laughter and applauded the boy. There was nothing I could do about it because it was live on the air and there was no delay to catch things that should not have been broadcast. I just stood there with my mouth open while the laughing got louder. I looked at the boy's parents and they were nudging each other saying, 'Oh, he's an awful boy!'

That incident in the summer of 1981, during my long-running radio show, *Andy Cameron's Sunday Joint*, turned out to be one of the most memorable moments of my career. I couldn't believe an eight year old would come out with something like that on the radio. I wouldn't have dared tell Bella a joke like that when I was that age.

But young Colin certainly made an impact on the country with his cheeky wee joke. I had no idea the response to that joke would be so huge. There were stories in the papers about it and for weeks people would be phoning me up saying, 'What about that wee boy and the onion joke – wasn't he just brilliant? By the way, Andy, did you set that up?'

Another guy was on holiday in Spain when the show was broadcast and he phoned me up as soon as he got back home. 'What was that joke a wee boy told on your show last week?' he asked. 'My mother says it was hilarious, but she wouldn't tell me what the boy had said.'

I thought he was at the wind-up and I wouldn't tell him the joke. He phoned me a few days later and said everybody at his work was talking about it and they told him wee Colin's joke. He thought it was brilliant and said the wee guy should do the show instead of me!

Another woman spoke to me and said it was my fault that she dropped an iron on her foot. I asked her why and she said, 'I was listening to that wee boy while I was doing my ironing and when he told the joke about the onion I laughed so much I dropped the iron on my foot.' Even 23 years after Colin told his onion joke, people still mention it to me.

And I most certainly did not set the boy up to tell the joke. I wouldn't dare risk losing my show on BBC Radio Scotland. As it happened, there never was any comeback from the bosses at the BBC, and anyway, they couldn't have dreamed up a way to get as much publicity for the programme in a month of Sundays.

That was my first live outside broadcast and it was arranged at the last minute. Originally, the show was to be broadcast from inside the Beach Ballroom starting at 11 a.m. All the crew arrived at 9 a.m. and the sun was splitting the skies – a wonderful day.

The show's producer Phil Whittaker – I called him the Yorkshire Pudding because he's from Bradford – asked me if I fancied doing the show from the park area outside the Beach Ballroom. I said OK, but had no idea how they were going to carry this off. Before I knew it, the technicians had backed the big BBC lorry onto the grass and they were hauling out all manner of equipment. The back of the wagon was to be the stage, but I was to wander around the crowd interviewing people.

I had never done anything like this before and I was shaking like a leaf. Phil saw what I was like and reassured me, 'You know you are good with the punters – just go round and talk to them as you would normally do. Just make your way through the crowd talking to folk and when you want us to play a record give a hand signal and watch for my hand signal to cue you to start talking again.'

An hour before the show was due to start, the place was packed with people who had turned up to hear it. I had a mike in my hand and one of the technicians followed me around with a pack on his back and a second mike to pick up what the people I was interviewing were saying. It was exhilarating doing this for the first time and a great learning experience for me.

The chance to have my own radio show came after the success of 'Ally's Tartan Army' and *Andy Cameron's Sunday Joint* – between 11 a.m. and 1 p.m. – was first broadcast in November 1978. That year, the BBC's radio output was being drastically overhauled and, for the want of a better word, was being modernised. Radio Scotland was born.

I had a phone call from a BBC producer called Ben Lyons, who asked me if I would be interested in coming to speak to him about me doing a radio show. I met him in the BBC canteen, in Queen Margaret Drive – they call it a staff restaurant, but to me it was the works canteen – and he told me the show would have a 13-week run.

Ben was a lovely man and had been with the BBC since it had been run by gas and the newsreaders had to wear dinner suits. He had all the high standards you would expect of someone who had been with the BBC for many years, but wasn't averse to modern ideas, so long as they were good ideas.

Ben told me the idea for my show was to play records and have me tell a few gags in between. This is how we played it for the first couple of shows and it was a disaster. I was telling gags, but not getting any response to them because there was no audience in front of me. Well, of course you don't get a response because it's not like a club where you can see and hear people laughing – on radio, you're talking to people you can't see or hear.

There was also the culture shock of me coming on to the very pukka BBC and speaking on air with a broad Glasgow accent and me, well, just being me. I don't think Ben Lyons' secretary, Jean McKinnon, was too happy about the way the radio station was becoming populist and having me as a presenter. I could hear her saying to Ben, 'He can't say that.' And Ben replying, 'Leave him alone, Jean. That's where his popularity comes from. The audience is full of Andy Camerons. They know what they are getting and they like it.'

But after the first few weeks I was ready to chuck it and so was the BBC. The format of the show just wasn't working. Then Jean, of all people, came up with a brilliant idea. She pulled me aside and said, 'I've seen you with people, you can talk to people and get them to talk to you. And when it comes to kids, you can speak to them on their level. Why don't you get the kids to phone in and tell a joke instead of you telling gags?'

I thought it was a great idea and we decided to go for it. We began promoting the kids' joke phone-in on the show a few weeks before we tried it. On the Sunday, we began with three girls manning the phones, thinking that would be enough to handle the calls coming in. The show started at 11 a.m., we opened the phone line after the first record and by 11.20 a.m. the phone lines were jammed and the three girls couldn't cope with all the calls. We finished up having to put 12 people on the phones every Sunday to deal with the hundreds of calls we would get.

Most of the jokes you would have heard before and were typical kids' jokes. Why did the hedgehog cross the road? To see his flat mate. But when a youngster came on the show to tell a joke I made sure they felt it was the first time I had heard it. I would laugh out loud when they delivered the punch line. Sometimes, I would put on a made-up laugh, but more often than not it was a genuine laugh. No matter what, I was going to make sure that wee boy or girl would enjoy their moment of fame on the radio.

After a few years, the BBC put out a joke book with the best of the jokes the youngsters had told on the show. I think you can still buy it at the BBC – you get it from under the counter and it comes wrapped in plain brown paper! The programme hadn't just blossomed, it had exploded, after Jean McKinnon came up with the idea of having kids phone in with a joke.

I also had some great times doing the outside broadcasts from places all over Scotland like Stornoway, Dundee, Skye, Aberdeen, the Borders, Stranraer, the Shetlands – we were taking the show to the people and we would go anywhere during the summer. We even did a show from the Isle of Man. The day we broadcast from Belfast was out of this world. I had the comedian Frank Carson on as guest and he just took over the whole show. Frank was in great form. He was hilarious and I couldn't get a word in edgeways.

On one occasion, that brilliant comedian Jasper Carrot pulled off a great wind-up when I was interviewing him. He was playing in a Variety Club golf tournament at Carnoustie along with Jimmy

Tarbuck, Bruce Forsyth and Ronnie Corbett. During my interview with Jasper Carrot – which was live on air – he said, 'You know this is the highlight of my career being on your radio programme. I've admired you from afar for a long, long time and I've got to say thanks for having me on your show. What did you say your name was?'

Stitched up good and proper.

I also recorded shows when I visited Hong Kong and Canada and talked to all the ex-pats and all the chat was about plain bread and square sausages. We would broadcast what I had recorded when I got back to Scotland.

I had a great day in Aberchirder, in Aberdeenshire – or as the locals call it, Foggieloan – when I was asked to open a local flower show there. It was a big deal this flower show because they had people like Diana Dors and Stratford Johns doing the honours in previous years. We decided to combine the opening and the *Sunday Joint* programme. We recorded the radio show on the Saturday and broadcast it the following day. We did all the usual stuff and had kids telling jokes and me interviewing the organisers of the flower show.

I had to interview the guy who won the biggest leek prize and it's not easy describing a giant leek on radio, I can tell you. So I asked him to tell the listeners how big it was and how he'd managed to grow a leek that size. He started talking away in the Doric and after he finished I said, 'I don't know if the people listening understood that, but I haven't a clue what you just said.' At that, his wife came over and apologised, saying, 'I've been married to him for 46 years and sometimes I can't even understand him.'

Later that day, I had been asked to pay a visit to a local old folk's home, meet the residents and sign a few autographs. I was happy to oblige. All the old folk were in a big lounge and they had laid on tea and scones. I was chatting away to everybody and things were going fine until I saw an old man sitting, looking out of the window. I went over and said hello to him and asked why he was sitting alone and not talking to anyone.

'I'm not talking to you,' he said.

'Why is that?' I asked.

'I like to read the papers on a Sunday and I can't get peace for you rabbiting away on that radio these women have on.'

'But I'm only on for a couple of hours,' I said.

'Aye, you might well be only on for a couple of hours, but this lot talk about you for the rest of the afternoon. Did you hear this wean tell that joke? And did you hear what that wean said? If I want some peace and quiet I've got to go to a room at the other end of the building and there's never any heating on there. I'm always bloody freezing.'

He gave me a real doing that day and when the matron tried to stop him I told her just to leave him alone. 'You might think you're good,' he says. 'But I think you're s***e!' I loved it. The old man was brilliant – what a blast he gave me.

I might have loved talking to that old man, but I was raging with a letter someone sent to the producer of the show. When I was talking to the kids on air I would always ask the girls to blow me a kiss down the phone and it became a bit of a feature of the programme me trying to persuade them to give me a kiss and telling them it would make their boyfriends jealous.

Terry Anderson was producer at the time and he showed me this letter which read, 'Dear Sir, I object most strongly to Andy Cameron asking children of five years of age for a kiss. Doesn't he know these children are very vulnerable?'

I was angry that someone would think I would do anything that would harm the kids. I wanted to write a reply to the writer and when I was told there was no address I was even more angry. I don't mind constructive criticism, but when people do write in to criticise they should have the courage of their convictions to put their address on the letter.

Andy Cameron's Sunday Joint was only supposed to last those initial 13 weeks, but it went on for an amazing 15 years. I loved it, and the punters loved it. A generation of youngsters grew up with the show and over the years I've had dozens of adults coming up to me and saying that their dad used to go for a run in the car on a Sunday and the family would listen to *Andy Cameron's Sunday Joint* on the car radio.

After a few years of presenting the *Sunday Joint*, I was given a Saturday show as well. This was broadcast between 10 a.m. and noon and this time the kids were invited to phone in and sing or play a musical instrument. We had youngsters playing everything from the organ, to the trumpet and the recorder.

One wee lad from Partick called in and said he wanted to play the accordion. He was live on air and explained how he had been playing the accordion for 18 months, he practised every day and went to lessons on a Thursday night.

'That's great,' I said. 'What tune are you going to play for us today?'

'I'm going to play "The Sash",' he says.

'No, you can't do that,' I said. 'You can't play "The Sash" on this programme. You'll need to play something else.'

He says, 'I'll play "Scotland the Brave". But you'll have to wait a minute.'

There's a pause and I assume the boy is getting his accordion ready. I hear 'Scotland the Brave' being played and it's absolutely brilliant. The wee lad wins the prize for the best performance of the show and we send him a goody bag.

The following Saturday afternoon, I'm opening the new Radio Rentals television shop in Drumchapel. I'm standing on a chair telling a few gags and I do the honours, cut the ribbon, sign a few autographs and everything is fine. I'm in the back shop having a cup of tea and one of the assistants says that she was listening to the Saturday show the previous week and she knows the wee boy who plays the accordion. Apparently, he stayed up the stairs from this woman.

'Imagine him wanting to play "The Sash" on the radio,' I said.

'We're Catholics,' she said. 'They're in one of these Orange accordion bands, but they're a really nice family.'

'The boy can certainly play the accordion,' I said. 'He played "Scotland the Brave".'

'No, he didn't,' she said. 'He can only play "The Sash". It was his mother who played "Scotland the Brave". She's a really talented musician – plays the piano as well. All that kafuffle while he was "getting ready" – that was the mother putting the accordion on.'

Even after years of doing the *Sunday Joint*, I never did learn the lesson to watch out for wee boys telling naughty jokes. While Colin's onion joke was during my first outside broadcast, a young lad told an even worse gag on my last outside broadcast. In fact, he had the very last word on the show and there was an outcry among the mandarins at the BBC because they accused me of deliberately setting it up.

The *Sunday Joint* outside broadcast was in Arbroath and there was a big crowd there. Everything went well and I was preparing for the handover to the newsreader Ian Aldridge at 1 p.m. We were always warned to finish our broadcast a few seconds before the hour so they could add the pips. It was a real crime if you crashed the pips, so I was always careful not to. There were about 45 seconds left of the broadcast and I was going to use these seconds to thank everybody for turning out and mention the producer's name. As I was about to start, a wee boy gave me a tug and said, 'I want to tell a joke.'

'What's your name?'

'Andrew.'

'What age are you?

'I'm five.'

'Right, you'll have to be quick, we're running out of time,' I said.

The boy starts, 'How many animals can you get in a pair of tights?'

'I don't know.'

'A pussy and as many hares as you like . . .'

'Beep, beep, beep, beep. This is the Radio Scotland news with Ian Aldridge.'

I could not believe it. As soon as he finished the punch line the beeps started and the broadcast went straight into the news. I couldn't say another word.

Because it was the final outside broadcast they thought I had deliberately set it up and I got memos from all over the Queen Margaret Drive headquarters of the BBC. But there was no way I could have timed it that the boy would finish his joke immediately before the pips.

The other time I was caught live on air with a naughty joke was when a wee boy from Ballingry in Fife asked, 'How do you make a snooker table laugh?'

'I don't know,' I said.

'You put your hand in its pockets and tickle its balls.'

Caught out again!

One of Scotland's top female comedians was first heard telling a joke on the *Sunday Joint* and I didn't find out about it until years later. I was speaking at a dinner in Dundee with Karen Dunbar who did *Chewing the Fat* and now has her own show on television. I was telling her how I thought the characters she does were brilliant when she said she got her first big break on the Andy Cameron *Sunday Joint*. 'Aye, right,' I said. 'You're at the wind-up.'

But she went on to tell me that when she was a wee girl she came along to an outside broadcast in Ayr and told a joke on air. She was due to win an Andy Cameron joke book as a prize, but I was having a bit of fun with her saying she wasn't getting the book because she told me she supported Celtic.

Karen also said that after all the banter, I gave her the prize and a 50 pence piece, telling her to get some sweets with the money. This jogged my memory and I remembered this wee girl with short hair being very confident and chatty. Who would have guessed telling a joke on the *Sunday Joint* would have launched that gallus wee lassie into the world of entertainment?

This period of my working life was also the time when I'd managed to get my own column in the *Evening Times* newspaper. I really enjoyed doing that column, which started in March 1979 and lasted nine years. It was called 'Please Yersel''. We got the name after the *Evening Times* editor Charlie Wilson and I were discussing what we should call it. I said, 'Och, whatever – just please yourself.' And he said, 'That's it. That's what we'll call it – Please Yersel'.'

When Charlie Wilson approached me about writing a weekly column I was a bit hesitant because I knew I couldn't write like a professional journalist. But he told me to write the way I spoke and that was what appeared in the paper. I had an old typewriter in the house and I managed to persuade Norma to type out the column as I dictated it to her. That didn't last long, so I reverted to writing it out in longhand. Eventually, I got a new typewriter and soldiered on doing the two-fingered symphony until I became more proficient.

I would write about anything and everything that came into my head. If I was ever stuck for an idea, I would go into a drawer and look out some old photographs and write about the old days and all the characters from Rutherglen in the 1940s, '50s and '60s. I would give all my pals from the old days nicknames in the column. George Dunn was 'The Quiet Man' because he was just that; Roy McGregor was 'Dapper Dan' because he wore out shop windows looking at himself, and my cousin, Campbell Gordon, who could eat for Scotland, was called 'The Guzzler'.

I still get a laugh thinking back to the stories I wrote in 'Please Yersel''. Another stalwart of the 189th BB – we were known as the Paratroopers – who got a mention was Sammy Mauchlan, who unfortunately had protruding front teeth. Sammy and Tom Smith – he of Radio Moscow fame – were having an argument and Tom said to him, 'See you – you could eat an orange through a tennis racket.'

I would also visit places in and around Glasgow and do stories about the people there. I visited the Govan Shipyard one day and I was talking to the trade union leader Jimmy Airlie. I was recalling a guy who used to come on stage and sing Al Jolson songs at the Rolls Royce Club when I was compère there in the early days. He worked in the yards and his name was Jimmy McCrindle, but everyone knew him as 'The Pig'. I made the mistake of asking why he was called The Pig and Jimmy Airlie pointed at Jimmy McCrindle and said, 'Are you blind? He's the ugliest man in the world.'

I heard some great stories about Jimmy McCrindle. During the workers' occupation of the UCS (Upper Clyde Shipbuilders) yard, there had been a big meeting in the Lyceum cinema in Glasgow, which was supposed to have been addressed by some MPs. The TV cameras were there for the meeting, but the MPs' plane from London was late. The 3,000-odd guys at the meeting were becoming a bit restless and someone suggested putting Jimmy McCrindle up on stage to give the lads a few songs. So up he went and gave it laldy in front of all these guys and the Scottish media.

Another shipyard trade union leader, Sammy Gilmore, was showing me round the shipyard and he told me that Jimmy McCrindle was working away when one of the gaffers pulled him up and asked, 'Is that whisky I smell on your breath?'

And Jimmy replied, 'It f*****g better be or that licensed grocer's getting a doing.'

The making of the column were Russell Kyle, who was the *Evening Times* features editor, and the assistant features editor Stevie Henderson. They were both Celtic supporters and I was a Bluenose, so you can imagine the banter that went on when I came into the *Evening Times* offices every week. I started naming them in my column, calling them 'The Bishop' and 'The Cardinal' and I had a fabulous time working with these two guys.

My pal Andy Bain – who lost a leg in the war and is a great Rangers fan – regularly appeared in the column. I described him as the 'World's Number One, One-Legged Cigar Tapper' – well, he was great at always cadging a cigar off me – and told stories about his life and the things he would get up to. Andy Bain's stories were so incredible, people thought he couldn't possibly exist in real life. Andy was at a sportswriters' dinner I was speaking at and another friend of mine, BBC sports presenter Dougie Donnelly, came over to the table. I said, 'Dougie, this is Andy Bain. I don't think you've met him before.'

'Andy Bain – the guy from your column?' asked Dougie. 'There really is an Andy Bain? I thought you made him up!'

Another night, Andy was with me at a do in the Orchard Park Hotel and a woman came up to me and started giving me a hard time. 'You're well out of order giving that poor guy Andy Bain so much stick in your newspaper column,' she said.

Andy said, 'It's OK, we've been pals for 30-odd years – it's all a bit of a wind-up.'

'But you didn't need to say he only had the one leg,' she replied.

Andy told her to come round the other side of the table and he put his artificial leg out and said, 'Give that a tap.'

When she tapped it and realised that he really did have an artificial leg, she lifted the tablecloth up and said, 'Aye, but you've got your own foot.' It was the sort of moment where everyone burst out laughing at the same time.

The 'Please Yersel'' column appeared every Friday and I had to get the copy in by the Thursday. I would say I was in the middle of the most productive period of my career and the *Evening Times* column played a big part in my life then.

While the *Andy Cameron's Sunday Joint* radio show gave me a huge amount of enjoyment and happiness I was absolutely shattered when the BBC decided to drop the programme. I was never technically brilliant working the desk, as they say, but I've no doubts the public loved the show and how I put it across. Near the end, as the winds of change were about to blow through the BBC, I was given a new producer, Robert Noakes, who was better known at the time as the folk singer Rab Noakes. He tried to change the show's format a wee bit. He tried to make me more like a traditional BBC presenter instead of just being myself and I think that was wrong. I had been given carte blanche to do the show in my own style and that's what had made it work.

Not long after that, the winds of change became a hurricane and a host of well-known and well-loved BBC radio presenters – including me – were dumped off the air. It came at a time when John Boyle had taken over at BBC Scotland and he wanted a major change in the types of programmes BBC Scotland were broadcasting. The BBC was rife with rumours and, from the way people were talking, I soon had an inkling I would be for the chop. Along with me heading out the door were presenters Art Sutter, Gerry Ford, Tom Ferrie and the late Jimmy Mack. We weren't the kind of thing they were now looking for.

One of the *Sunday Joint's* former producers, Ken Mutch, said he didn't think they would take the show off the air because it was so popular. I wish his prediction had come true. The bad news came in a memo telling me about changes at Radio Scotland – new horizons and all that. The bottom line was that they were not going to renew my contract.

Art Sutter – who is a very good musician and has his own band – took his departure really bad and at the end of his last show played the Neil Sedaka song 'Our Last Song Together' on the studio piano. He was in tears and his voice was breaking up as he said goodbye to the listeners. But the biggest protest from the public was the axing of country singer and presenter Gerry Ford. He had a huge following and I wasn't surprised at the backlash. Country music was having a resurgence and he played some really good music on his show.

On my last show, I decided there wouldn't be any tears and I did a normal programme until the last few minutes. I was introducing the final record and I told the listeners, 'The last 15 years have been the happiest of my life. I've thoroughly enjoyed doing the show. Thanks to everybody who has phoned in and told us all a joke – some of you are probably married now. And it's also thanks to the wee boy who told the onion joke.

'It's been great and there is only one record I can leave you with, so if you see me in the street always say hello – so all the best to everyone.'

I went straight into playing the Alexander Morrison version of 'Goodbye' – a song from the light opera, *At The White Horse Inn*. We had timed it that as soon as it finished we were straight into the beeps – perfect. It was probably the most professional thing I ever did on the show and that's how I said farewell to the *Andy Cameron's Sunday Joint* radio show. I thought it was a great way to go out and say cheerio.

I thought to myself that the listeners will be sitting in their homes thinking that they'll miss the show for a while, but there you are – life goes on; it wasn't that big a deal for them. For me, though, when it sank in that there wasn't going to be an *Andy Cameron's Sunday Joint* any more, I felt sick. I tried to convince myself that I'd had a good innings, 15 years is a long time, more things to do with my time and all that nonsense. I even made a joke in my act that I had written to John Boyle at the BBC asking for the *Sunday Joint* to be brought back and I got a three word reply: 'No, you can't.' The punch line to the gag was that you'd think a man like him would know how to spell 'can't'. I would laugh along with that gag, but deep down it was a real blow and I was hurting.

About four weeks after the show stopped, I did write a letter to

John Boyle basically saying, 'Please can I have my radio show back? I really miss it and judging from what I've been hearing from the public, they miss it as well.' I got one of those official replies about not having plans to rethink the schedules. I didn't realise how much losing the show would affect me, because six months later I would have done anything to get back on the radio and I would go into wee pockets of depression. Maybe depression is too strong a word because depression is a serious thing, but I would certainly feel very sad.

I would be driving along the road listening to the radio and a record would come on or somebody would say something and it would remind me of how much I missed doing the show. I used to think I was hurt, but it wasn't a personal thing because the BBC got rid of a lot of presenters. For me, doing the *Sunday Joint* wasn't like presenting a radio show – it was like visiting friends every week. Every Sunday, I would stop at the doughnut shop in Clarence Drive on my way to the BBC and buy a box of doughnuts. Somebody would make the coffee and everyone in the studio would have one. I would tell the listeners I'm going to play a long record because I've got a doughnut to eat.

I even had my own wee jingle, which was written by guitarist Ronnie Christie. It was just a few seconds long and it went, 'Andy Cameron on the radio . . . nice to know that you've got a friend.' We'd play it maybe half a dozen times on every show. People have come up to me and said they listened to the show every week and felt that I was their pal. For me, that showed what we were doing worked and we brought something good and worthwhile into their lives. You can't be doing much wrong if you can do that.

Fortunately, for the last three years I have been back on the radio with much the same format as the *Sunday Joint*. I have my own show on Clyde 2 on a Sunday between noon and 2 p.m. It's great and we're still getting the kids to phone in telling their jokes. There's also the bonus of having the Internet, because that means we've got listeners from all over the world and they e-mail the show every week.

I started broadcasting on Radio Clyde after I'd been winding up the station's boss Paul Cooney. Any time I would meet him at dinners, I would tell him it was time they had somebody decent on his radio station – and that somebody decent would have to be me. Months later, Paul phoned me and asked me to come into the station for a chat. We talked about what format my show would be and he asked if I thought the jokes were necessary. I told him that the show wouldn't work without the kids coming on and telling their jokes.

It's just like old times and I get the same reaction from people as I did all those years ago. The show is just as successful too, because it's marvellous when you get a kid on with a great personality. And I make sure I know what joke they're going to tell before they get anywhere near broadcasting it to the world!

Radio has always played a big part in my life. When I was growing up, radio was just as important to us youngsters as television is to today's kids. Nowadays, everyone has been turned into a peeping Tom watching all those reality shows like *Big Brother* and looking in on other people's lives. When we listened to the radio, it made us use our imagination. Before I was old enough and allowed to go to the café for a Dig Deep, I would run home from the Life Boys to listen to *Dick Barton Special Agent* on the radio. I would be sitting listening to the adventures of Dick Barton and I would be transported to another life of excitement, danger and derring-do. Another favourite of mine was *Valentine Dyall – The Man in Black*.

Comedy was great on the radio during the late '40s and the '50s. There was Stanley Baxter with his catchphrase, 'If you want me thingmy, ring me.' None of us had phones, but everyone at school would go around saying this to their pals. I first heard other great Scottish comedians like Jimmy Logan and Ricky Fulton on the radio. And one of the best radio comics I ever heard was Ted Ray, and *Round the Horn* was a great programme as well.

Everybody listened to *The McFlannels*. They were like *The Broons*, only on radio. Another lovely memory I have is after getting home from Farie Street School sitting eating a bowl of soup Bella had made me and listening to *Workers' Playtime*.

My first memories of a radio was the one in Bella's house which was an accumulator set attached to a 12-volt battery in a wee box at the back. I would take the battery to Paton's electrical shop to have it recharged. But when we got electricity in the tenement, my Uncle Jim bought a radiogram and this was like a piece of furniture, which took pride of place in the room. This also meant that Uncle Jim would buy records and I could listen to people like country singers Hank Williams, Kitty Wells and Patsy Cline. He also bought Scottish country dance records by Jimmy Shand and Will Starr.

Talking about Will Starr, I heard a great story about him from Jimmy Logan. Will liked his bevvy and he was in a summer show at The Metropole, in Glasgow. He would always be disappearing to the pub and people would be looking for him. Jack Short – Jimmy Logan's father – had this idea that he would ask Will to bring his accordion up to his office shortly before the show started. When Will arrived, old Jack chastised him about his drinking habits and told him to put on the accordion, and he padlocked the strap around Will's back so he couldn't take it off and go to the pub.

This worked for six or seven nights until Will did his disappearing act again and was nowhere to be found. Jack Short asked the wardrobe mistress if she had seen Will and she said he was away to the pub. 'What, he's away to the pub? But he's got his accordion strapped on,' says Jack.

To which the wardrobe mistress replied, 'Aye, but he came in and asked me for the biggest coat I could find.' Will put the big coat on to hide the accordion!

I owe a lot to radio because, as well as entertaining and informing me ever since I was a youngster, it has helped in my career in show business. I have made a lot of good friends out of working in radio. There have been decent people who have helped me along and I hope I have been able to help others as well.

I love both working on the radio and listening to it. Every minute of being a presenter has been a joy. I love the people who have called the show saying they were from Rutherglen and did I remember their mum and dad or granny and grandpa, along with the callers who remind me of great times as a teenager, the Boys Brigade or going to BB camp in Macduff.

Throughout my life, radio has been a great turn on for me – if you'll forgive the pun!

Chapter 12

LOOK OUT, HE'S BEHIND YOU!

I HELD MY HANDS UP TO SHIELD MY FACE AS SCORES OF CARAMEL WAFERS rained onto the stage. The biscuits were bouncing all over the place and all I'd done was to announce that a group of ladies were in from the Tunnocks biscuit factory. It was my third panto at the Pavilion in Glasgow and I had no idea that four rows of the audience would decide to launch a salvo of caramel wafers at me.

That started a tradition and, for years after, any time a party of girls from the Tunnocks factory in Uddingston, Lanarkshire, were at a panto I was appearing at, they would throw biscuits at me on stage. Mind you, the backstage crew didn't mind because the first time it happened they picked up 84 biscuits and that kept them going for quite a while during their tea-breaks.

I did my first panto in 1979 – *A Wish for Jamie* – at the Pavilion and it was the start of a long and happy association with that wonderful form of entertainment which enthrals young and old alike. In that first panto, I played the dame Auntie Jeanie and the singer Peter Morrison played Jamie.

It was his first panto as well and both of us were taken by the hand and shown the secrets of a successful pantomime by the likes of producer Jamie Phillips, director Dougie Squires and the rest of the cast.

Since that first performance when I trooped onto the stage

173

wearing enormous and outrageous dresses, I've appeared in more than a dozen pantos – such as *Cinderella*, *Mother Goose*, *Dick Whittington* and *Snow White and the Seven Dwarfs* – and I've loved every minute.

My favourite panto character to play is Buttons, in *Cinderella*. He's great fun to do and everybody in the theatre loves him and you get the biggest cheers. My favourite panto performance, though, has to be that first one I did – *A Wish for Jamie* – because it was a new experience for me and I learned such a lot about that form of entertainment from it.

Although you are acting a part you are allowed to be yourself and put your own character into the performance. Before I started on *A Wish for Jamie*, I heard veteran Scots entertainer Johnny Beattie on a radio interview. He said the secret of playing a panto dame is that you have to let the audience know you are a man dressed up as a woman and never let them think you really are a woman.

An actor called Ray Jeffries was appearing in that first *A Wish for Jamie* with me. One of the scenes in the first act had Ray and me coming on stage dressed as the Scots singing sisters, Fran and Anna. We were in fishnet tights, high heels and mini kilts. Fran and Anna were a big name at the time and although the critics treated them as figures of fun, they could entertain and got plenty of work.

Ray and I would each walk on from either side of the stage and the band would be playing while the audience roared with laughter. Once the noise died down, we would start singing, 'Blaw, blaw, ma kilt's awa . . .' and that would get more laughter. The idea of us coming on dressed as Fran and Anna worked really well and we used it every night.

One night, the curtain was ready to go up and the stage manager, Laurie Kelly, rushed over to me and said, 'You're not going to believe this, but Fran and Anna are in tonight – ten rows back in the stalls.' I didn't know if we should do the Fran and Anna walk on because I didn't want to offend them. But Laurie said we should go for it, it will be priceless. So we came on and got the usual good reaction, only this time Fran and Anna stood up and took the applause. We're on the stage with the daft gear on and they're out of their seats taking a bow, waving to the audience and milking all the applause.

When I appeared in that first pantomime there was a lot of what is known as corpsing – doing or saying something to put your fellow actors off and have them in fits of laughter. Peter Morrison was the easiest person in the world to corpse and I had him in fits of laughter one night just off stage so the audience wouldn't see us.

The dress I wore at the end of the first act was bright yellow and shaped like a table with plastic plates and cutlery sewn on to it. One night, I sent someone across the road from the Pavilion to get a bag of chips and I laid the chips out on the table of my costume. Peter's waiting to go on stage and I turn to him and say, 'Do you want a chip?' It took him all his time to compose himself and get on the stage.

On the last night of the run I got him again. This time, when Ray Jeffries and I appeared dressed as Fran and Anna, we walked on puffing on huge King Edward cigars. Peter had to walk off the stage and come back on when he had composed himself.

The following year, I played Buttons and the very experienced performer Anne Fields was in the cast as well. When I was a teenager, I used to walk her sister, Sally Logan, home from Rutherglen Academy. Her family had Logan's Dairy in Rutherglen and we were pals. She later went into show business as a singer with Joe Gordon.

Anne gave me a good piece of advice and that is not to get caught up in the corpsing until the last night. It's a tradition that on the last night of a panto the actors have a bit of a laugh and people who know this deliberately come to the theatre to see what is going to happen between the cast.

Anne told me that after New Year, when the corpsing is most likely to happen and there's a temptation to play to your pals, there are still a lot of old folks or handicapped clubs coming to see the panto. 'Remember this,' she said. 'You might be doing the panto for the 84th time, but there are people in the audience who are seeing it for the first time.'

Another piece of advice she gave me was that I shouldn't play the dame in a pantomime. She had seen me the year before and said I was being restricted by having to wear the outlandish costumes as a dame. 'With trousers on you can run about the stage and be yourself,' she said. 'OK, you're playing Buttons, but you are still Andy Cameron and that is who people come to see.' As soon as she said it I knew she was right and I've rarely played a dame since.

One of the things I always made sure happened in any panto I was in was that any groups who were in the audience should get a mention from the stage. I would give the Boys Brigade party a mention, as well as the Union of Catholic Mothers. I would do a gag that if any of the UCM aren't mothers yet, they could come backstage and we'll see what we can do for them.

One night during a Pavilion panto there were boys from about half a dozen BB companies in the audience and I mentioned that some of the happiest days of my life were spent with the 189th in Rutherglen. I started belting out the old BB hymn, 'Will your Anchor Hold?', and I ended up doing the whole song. I got a great round of applause and after the show Laurie Kelly said I should do that every night. I didn't sing it every night, but when there was a BB company in I would sing it and I always got a roar from the audience.

The Pavilion stage has a slight incline towards the front and one year I was Jack in *Jack and the Beanstalk* and my mammy was played by Dean Park. Part of the set was a house and at one point in the show the two of us were upstairs in the house. The stagehands hadn't put the wedges in properly and the house started rolling towards the front of the stage. The only thing I could think of saying was, 'Mammy, you didn't tell me we were moving house!' It was an ad-lib and it got a good laugh.

I don't do pantos any more because a few years ago, when I was 60, I was playing Buttons and I ran onto the stage shouting, 'Hi boys and girls – I'm Buttons. Say hi to Buttons.'

'Hi, Buttons,' the kids shouted.

My next line was, 'Has anyone seen Cinderella? I really love her.' I'm looking at the first four rows and the kids are looking at me as if to say, 'Are you some sort of paedophile? She's about 16 and you're old enough to be her grandfather.' You can only get away with the age difference for so long and the kids aren't daft.

Pantos are all about the kids enjoying themselves and some of the kids can give you a real laugh when you get them up on stage. I was doing a panto one year when I did the usual stuff about needing two volunteers and there were several school parties in the theatre. There was a mad rush to the front and a couple of ushers picked a boy and a girl. By coincidence, a brother and sister were picked and the wee girl was a bit shy, but the older brother was giving it, 'How are you doin', Andy?' and giving the thumbs up to his pals in the audience.

'What's your name, son?' I said.

'Steven.'

'What age are you?'

'Eight.'

'This'll be your sister, so what's her name?'

'Patricia.'

'Hello, Patricia. And what age are you?'

'I'm six,' the wee girl says.

At that, the bold boy interrupts and says into the mike: 'Is she f**k. She's only five. She's no' six until next Tuesday.'

You've never seen teachers moving so quick to get down the front and get him off the stage.

One of the years I did panto in the Gaiety Theatre in Ayr and – I almost did myself a serious injury. I was Buttons in *Cinderella* again and there was a 12- to 15-minute period when I wasn't on stage. I would normally go to my dressing-room and get changed for my next scene and spend some time watching a portable television I had brought in. On this particular night, I got so engrossed watching what was on the television that I never got changed, and when I got the three-minute call it was a rush to get ready and back on stage in time. I had to run to get on without missing my cue and when I got there, I couldn't stop and I kept going and fell into the orchestra pit. I landed on top of Gordon Wilson, the drummer, and all you could hear was crash, bang, wallop. The audience loved it and the place was in an uproar. When I got back on stage, I said that was the nearest we'd got to a tune out of the drums all season. I hurt my back in the fall and there were bruises all over my body. The things you do to get a laugh in panto.

I've always loved the theatre, even when I was young and Bella would take me to the Glasgow Empire to see the great variety shows. I remember hearing Lena Martell singing with big bands at the Barrowland using her real name Helen Thompson and who would have guessed I would be performing on the same bill in her shows during the '80s? I also did shows at the King's Theatre in Glasgow with Jimmy Logan and particularly enjoyed two seasons of performing in King's High with Allan Stewart in the early '90s.

Although people will probably recognise me as a comic, I have tried my hand at serious acting on the stage. In 1987, I appeared in the Sam Cree play, *Wedding Fever*, with Una McLean and directed by Jimmy Logan. I got reasonable reviews from my performance at the King's in Glasgow. The *Glasgow Herald* said at the time: 'It's a likeable performance, full of Cameron's own personality and, I suspect, ad-libs.' A lot of people think that comedy acting isn't serious, but it is, and I got some great experience from doing *Wedding Fever*.

That experience certainly helped when, in 1993, I got the lead part in a really serious play called *The Guid Sodjer Schweik*. This is an anti-war play by Scots playwright Carl MacDougall, which he adapted from the novel *The Good Soldier Schweik* by Jaroslav Hasek, and was produced by the Borderline Theatre Company. I played Schweik, who has been certified by military doctors as an imbecile, but who signs up with the army anyway, and in his ramblings he reveals a deeper understanding about the futility of war than most.

The play – which also featured Phil McCall, Laurie Ventry and Billy Riddoch – toured all over Scotland, including four weeks at the Edinburgh Festival. It was a major departure from what I was previously known for – a stand-up comic with a cheery smile and a gag always at the ready.

I was delighted not only at how I managed to adapt myself to playing a serious and demanding role, but also for the rest of the cast as we won an award for the best adaptation and new play at the Edinburgh Festival. Obviously, I was hoping to make an impression on the serious actors and make that leap from comedy to serious theatre. You could have given me a million pounds, but that wouldn't have made me feel as good as some of the compliments I received during the play's run.

During our stint at the Edinburgh Festival, we performed in Moray House Theatre and I heard an American woman leaving the theatre saying she didn't understand much of the broad Scots dialect in the adaptation but, 'That guy who played Schweik – I've read the book and he's Schweik.'

The other remark which boosted my confidence no end was when Laurie Ventry pulled me aside after a performance and said, 'You're a f*****g actor. That was brilliant tonight.'

I learned so much from these fantastic actors who were earning a fraction of what I could earn doing stand-up comedy. I have nothing but admiration for these guys. I've never taken acting lessons, but I've had the best teachers you can get from working with the good actors I've been privileged to share a stage with.

But not everyone appreciated my performance as a serious actor. One of my pals, Alan Munro, walked out of *Schweik* after 20 minutes, wondering when Andy Cameron was coming on. Someone said that's him playing the daft soldier and he said that's not the Andy Cameron I came to see, so he went and had a pint.

There's a scene at the end when Schweik is surrounded by all his dead comrades and he makes an emotional speech about the war and the death of his fellow soldiers. After one of the performances, when Norma and a lot of our friends came to see the play, we all met up in the Ho Wong restaurant in Glasgow for a meal. We were sitting chatting and I noticed that Norma's mascara had been running. I asked her what was wrong and she said the last scene had made her cry. Norma has never been a pat on the back type of person, but those few words about my performance were better than a million pats on the back.

Theatre is definitely very fulfilling for an entertainer, but if you want to reach a bigger audience nationally then you've got to get yourself on television. In 1984, Clarke Tait, at Scottish Television, offered me my own eight-week TV show, which was a mixture of sketches, stand-up and musical guest artists. Naturally, I jumped at the chance, and *It's Andy Cameron* was born.

I had never been so well dressed for a show. A real toff in top hat and tails, silk scarf, silver-topped cane – I was a real Burlington Bertie. The show brought in great viewing figures in the autumn of 1984. On my last episode of the first (and what was unfortunately to be the last) series, I was determined to go out with a bang, singing 'New York, New York'.

I was belting it out when suddenly the audience in the studio started pelting me with rotten fruit and the cameras were still rolling. I couldn't believe this was happening until I saw all the crew laughing their heads off. The producers had supplied the audience with the rotten fruit and told them to throw it at me as I was doing my big finishing number. But I was determined to finish the song – after all, I had suffered eight weeks of constant interruptions at the end of each programme – so, undaunted, I carried on singing as the apples and tomatoes and other assorted fruit bounced off me. Then the crew put on Celtic jerseys and threw sludge all over me until I was a complete mess.

That wasn't the end of the pranks they had planned to play on me. All through the series I had a private running joke with all the girls on the show. I would tell them that I knew when they broke wind whenever they were wearing tights because their ankles would puff out. All very non-PC, but they thought it was a great laugh.

However, they got their own back when I was in my dressing-room wearing only my underpants trying to get the gunge off myself. The door burst open and a cameraman came in followed by four of the girls wearing basques, stockings and suspenders. They were all over me as I tried to preserve my modesty and the cameraman was filming the lot. No doubt, there will be a tape of this incident somewhere in the vaults of Scottish Television. To spare my blushes, all I can say is that I hope it stays there.

The rotten fruit finale was a superb way to end the series. The show's director, Jim McCann, was looking for a running theme for all eight shows of the series and I suggested that at the end of each show I would try to sing a song and be constantly interrupted until we ran out of time and the credits rolled. He thought it was a great idea and each week there was a different interruption.

Scots actress and comedienne Dorothy Paul had been working in the wardrobe at Scottish Television at the time and she got the part of a cleaning lady who would come and sweep up just after I started singing. Dorothy – who was famous for her appearances in *The One O'Clock Gang* many years before – had faded out of performing and it may well have been that show that got her back in the way of things. Then there was a basketball player who bounced his ball around me as I tried in vain to complete my song. Another interruption came from Scots entertainer, Allan Stewart, who came out of the audience dressed as Auntie May and continually butted in as I tried to sing 'New York, New York'. Allan is a fantastic performer and I worked with him several times over the years.

After the final show, there was a party and Clarke Tait was telling everyone what a great start we had made in the series and there was another series planned for the following March. Tragically, he dropped dead the next day in his office after suffering an aneurysm. That was it. Sandy Ross took over and he was a bit more of the politically correct type and I never got a second series. It was a shame, because I thought we could have built on that first series, made some changes and improvements, and turned it into a very successful TV show.

Before the success of the Scottish Television's *It's Andy Cameron*, I had one abortive attempt at launching myself as a television star with my own show. I did a pilot programme for the BBC in 1979 called *The Andy Cameron Show*. We recorded the pilot and it was broadcast as a one-off, but the critics didn't fancy it. And neither did the bosses at the Beeb because they never followed it up with a series. Needless to say, I was very disappointed at the time, but I just had to accept it wasn't going to happen this time round.

However, almost ten years later, the BBC came back and offered me a show called *Andy Cameron Live*. It was a *Parkinson*-type show with me interviewing people like Bill Treacher, who played Arthur Fowler on *EastEnders*, and the film actress Stephanie Beecham. At the beginning of each show, I did a stand-up routine telling gags about what had been in the news that week. I enjoyed doing it, but the series never got another run and I wasn't sure myself if I was good enough to carry off the chat show format.

I did several series of a television programme made by Grampian in the late '80s called *Shammy Dab*, which means the cat's pyjamas. It was a celebrity quiz show and I was one of the team captains, while well-known north-east of Scotland comedian George Duffus was the other. Dougie Donnelly was the quizmaster asking questions about Scottish names, places and nostalgia.

At the start, we had mainly Scottish personalities on the teams, but in the later shows they would bring up celebrities from down south. Philip Schofield was on my team in one show, which was recorded in a small studio in Aberdeen and the audience, which consisted of mainly farmers' wives from Buckie, were sitting only a few feet away. One of the women in the front row of the audience was sitting with her legs open and you could see her wearing a good, old-fashioned pair of bloomers. I nudged Philip Schofield and whispered, 'Don't look now, but the woman third from the right in the front row is giving you a flash.' Of course, he couldn't help but look at her and he went into a fit of laughter and couldn't say a word.

He asked to be excused to go for a glass of water and got a hold of the floor manager telling him he would have to move the woman with the bloomers or else he wouldn't be able to do the show for laughing. The floor manager handled it with great aplomb. He addressed the audience, telling them that he'd just got word from the gallery that everyone was sitting in the same seats as they had been during a different show's recording previously that day, and they'd have to be moved around.

A year or so later, I was appearing on *The Telephone Game*, which was recorded in London and hosted by Philip Schofield and Emma Forbes, Nanette Newman's daughter. When we got on the set I said to Philip, 'Is it OK to start laughing if I see someone in the front row with their legs open?' He had a right good laugh at the memory of that day at Grampian and he made me tell the story to Emma Forbes.

Shammy Dab was a smashing wee programme, but when Scottish Television took it on their schedules, the critics panned it, although they loved it in the north-east.

I thought I had become a sex symbol when I got a spot on national television in the *Live From Her Majesty's* show, which was hosted by Jimmy Tarbuck in 1982. I flew down to London and my stepbrother Stuart met me at the airport and we drove to the rehearsals at the theatre in his taxi.

As I stepped out of the cab I saw about a dozen young girls screaming and running towards me. I said to myself that I must be more popular with the ladies than I thought, until they ran right past me heading towards Shakin' Stevens, who was getting out of a car further down the road.

Getting on Tarby's show was a big deal for me and another major step in my career. I was dressed in a dinner suit and was wearing dark tinted glasses which, all these years later, looks like I was wearing two LPs over my eyes. I was very nervous, but I got plenty of laughs. Petula Clark was top of the bill and after the show she came over, took my hand and said she thought I was super. It was a very nice touch and very gracious of her. After all, she was a big singing star and I was just a wee guy from Rutherglen trying my best to build my career.

I must have impressed them doing that show, because in 1986 I was asked to do a guest appearance on the *Tarby and Friends* television show. I decided to wear a double-breasted, coloured-check jacket for this appearance, thinking that it was the height of fashion – which, I assure you, it was in 1986. But when I got to the studio and bounced onto the stage the director told me I'd have to take the jacket off because the rather loud check was causing a technical problem on the television screens. I didn't have time to buy a new jacket, so I had to wear the suit that I had on travelling down to London. So much for looking the part in my fancy jacket. Well, I did look the part – of an insurance salesman.

I also got my first straight acting part on television in October of that year playing the editor of a national newspaper in an episode of *Taggart*. I only had six lines and I could have phoned them in, but it was great working with Mark McManus and having another new experience of working in a television drama – especially one as popular as *Taggart*.

I told the director Hal Duncan that I wanted to play the part of the newspaper editor differently. He asked what I meant and I told him that I would play the part sober, because most journalists I know like a good bevvy. Everyone had a good laugh at that. The scenes were filmed in the offices of the *Glasgow Herald*, as the paper was known then.

The storyline was that Taggart doesn't want me to run a particular story and he comes into the newspaper office to argue the point. I tell him, 'I've got to run this story.' He replies, 'You cannae run this story, we don't want them to know we're on to them.' 'Well, you've got 24 hours,' I reply. 'Do it before tomorrow because it's going in the next edition.' Then I walk away with the parting shot, 'If you don't mind, I'm a busy man.'

We did a couple of rehearsals of the scene and then went for a take. Fortunately, I must have been OK at it because that one take was all that was needed.

I was managing to get guest spots on television programmes like Sydney Devine's show on Scottish Television, and game shows like *Funny You Should Say That*, *Battle of the Comics* and a celebrity version of *Wheel of Fortune*. Television took a bit of getting used to for me because, although there was often a live audience in the studio, you have to force yourself to ignore them and play to the camera because that's how you are going to reach the audience of millions at home.

In 1992, Irish singer Daniel O'Donnell was becoming a real star not only in his homeland but in the UK as well. I featured in one of his videos as compère when it was filmed before a live audience in Aberdeen. I would do a few jokes before introducing Daniel and the first night there were 12 nuns from a local convent sitting at a table near the front of the audience.

I was a bit concerned my gags might be a bit too risqué for them, but I was told everything would be fine as the nuns could take a joke as well as anyone else. To be on the safe side, I kept apologising to the nuns after every second joke just in case I was offending them. But everything was fine and I was going down well during the filming, which was done over four nights' performances.

On the final night, I was left speechless in the middle of my act. I had noticed there was a nun sitting at a table down the front and, since nothing untoward had happened on the first night with a dozen nuns in the audience, I didn't pay too much attention to her. I was well into my stride when the nun got up out her chair, stepped onto the stage and started stripping off her habit. I couldn't believe my eyes. A nun had come onto the stage and was taking off her clothes in front of me. How am I going to handle this, was the question racing through my mind.

But the penny dropped when the nun dropped her habit to the floor to reveal she was wearing a Rangers top, stockings and suspenders. I knew then it was a wind-up and I later discovered the man behind it was Eamonn Leahy, who was one of the guys running Ritz Records – Daniel O'Donnell's record label. He had hired a stripper to go on stage to give me a shock. Everyone thought it was a hoot and even I, for once, was glad that I was the victim of a wind-up and a real nun wasn't stripping off in front of me.

I enjoy working on television as it's a very different form of entertainment from doing clubs or theatres and requires different skills. I was thrilled in 1984 to be presented with Scotland's TV Personality of the Year award by the *Daily Record* and the following year I won the Television and Radio Industries Club of Scotland Radio Personality of the Year award. I might never lift the Scottish Cup as captain of Rangers, but these two will sit fine in my trophy cabinet – if I had one, that is!

Chapter 13

I'LL TAKE THE HIGH ROAD

IT WAS WITH NO LITTLE TREPIDATION THAT I STOOD OUTSIDE THE DOOR OF THE green room in the Scottish Television studios at Cowcaddens, in Glasgow. When I opened that door I would be walking into a whole new experience in the entertainment world and mixing with performers who were seasoned in their profession and me, a newcomer with little or no experience of what I was about to take on.

It was my first day working on the highly popular TV soap *High Road* and I was terrified. Clutching a bag containing my script I paused and took a couple of deep breaths before opening the door. Inside the room, I put my bag down on the floor and looked around at the assembled actors whose faces I recognised from the programme and said: 'Hi, I'm Andy Cameron.'

Jackie Farrell, who played Jocky McDonald in the soap, was right at my back and he introduced me to everyone and offered me a cup of tea. I'd known Jackie for several years and he made sure I was made to feel welcome. He showed me where the cast rehearsed and asked, 'Do you know your words?'

'I know every word,' I told him. 'But I'm not sure if I know how to portray them.'

'Well, that's what we're here for,' says Jackie. 'If you get it wrong first time, don't worry about it. We'll stop and rehearse it again until it's right.'

Getting a part in *High Road* was a major step in my television career as an actor, instead of doing a stand-up comedy routine. Sydney Devine had given me a big break in the theatre, the 'Ally's Tartan Army' record had given me national exposure and my show on Radio Scotland had further increased my profile throughout Scotland. Now I was about to find out if I could repeat the process as a TV actor.

I met John Temple – the *High Road* producer at the time – when he came along to see the panto I was performing in at the Pavilion in Glasgow in 1994. My agent, Peter de Rance, introduced me to him and we were having a drink in the bar of the theatre after the show when I mentioned that I wouldn't mind auditioning for a part in *High Road*. He said I wouldn't need to audition, that he'd get a character written into the show who would last about six weeks. I said I didn't want a short-term thing, that I would commit myself to the programme and I would prefer a part which could be developed.

John told me to come to his office at Scottish Television the following week and when I sat down across the desk from him he threw me a script, which had this new character Chic Cherry arriving in Glendarroch. 'I like that name,' I said. 'I think it suits the type of character I could play.'

John replied, 'That's right, Andy – Chic Cherry's a chancer.' I hope he was just referring to the character I was to play in *High Road*!

I had watched *High Road* on television and thought it was great that a soap opera was being made in Scotland. There were some great characters built up in the show over the years – characters like Effie and Mrs Mack. All of that appealed to me, even though I knew that TV acting would involve a steep learning curve for me. Give me a noisy, smoky social club, a packed theatre or even a stand-up routine on television and I could handle that no problem. This was different. On television, you've only got to reach as far as the camera a few feet away, whereas in a theatre you've got to project yourself and reach all the way to the furthest seat in the circle for your performance to work.

I was told all of this before I started filming *High Road* and advised against overacting. My problem was that I was so intent on getting this right, I was going too slow and overacting the underacting. However, with the patience and help of both the cast and crew of *High Road*, I soon got the hang of it, became very relaxed about the performances and eventually no one could see the joins. I enjoyed everything about the process of putting together the programme – the rehearsals, the recording of the scenes and mixing with people who had been actors all their lives.

The other actors were especially good with me and were very protective. They would do lines with me and stop in the middle of rehearsal and suggest I do something like get up and get a glass of water to make everything seem more natural. It was certainly a tricky time at the start because some television critics were very negative and destructive, saying my performances were like watching furniture act. I have never objected to criticism, so long as it's constructive. If a critic writes that Andy Cameron's obviously new to this game and he's got a lot to learn, or if he or she even suggests that I should take acting lessons – that's fine by me because I can accept that. But I was never one for criticism for criticism's sake, being negative just to get a headline or for trying to be clever with a few fancy phrases in a newspaper review.

I was in about a dozen of the next 18 episodes, although I wasn't that hard pushed, and as time went on I fitted in well with the way they operated. Although I found it tough at the start, it was like any new job, and it just took me a while to get used to the routine of the place and their different ways of doing things.

One of the *High Road* writers was Anne Downie, whom I had worked with in pantomime, and she was a great teacher. I would pick her up in the morning and take her into the studios. On the way there, she would go over my scenes with me, speaking the other parts and making sure I had everything spot on. The car journey would be 15 to 20 minutes, but it was a great way to have the script fresh in your mind for rehearsals.

I also learned it was important to have someone feed you the other lines because, although you have created a part for yourself, you can never do it yourself – you need other people. Acting is about reacting to other people and one of the first lessons I learned on *High Road* was the importance of listening. It's a natural and obvious thing when you think about it, because that's what happens in real life and you're trying to recreate real life in a studio or out on location. If you go to acting school you will be taught all that, but I was coming into this learning process in my mid-50s and had to pick these things up as I went along. I enjoyed the thrill of learning something new.

The hardest part for me was looking into the eyes of another actor and believing I was Chic Cherry and they were the character they were playing. Once you do it a few times it becomes second nature to you and you do become the person you're playing.

I put a lot of effort into making a good job of acting in *High Road*. I would be driving along the road with the kids in the car going over my lines and they would ask me whom I was talking to.

When I first joined the cast of *High Road*, I wasn't aware of any dissent from the other actors about me being there without having a lot of experience as a straight actor. I put my cards on the table right away. I didn't make a speech, but I let it be known that I recognised I wasn't an actor, I was relying on them to help me out and they weren't to be shy about telling me when I was doing something wrong.

The cast were really good to me, and I had worked with a few of them before, either in theatre shows or on the television shows I appeared in as a stand-up or doing comedy sketches. Eileen McCallum, who played Isabel Blair, is one of the finest actresses I have ever seen. She could be Isabel Blair in her wee shop in Glendarroch one day and the next she could be doing Shakespearean theatre. They were all really good professionals and it was a joy to work with them.

Everyone in the cast got on well with each other. Of course, like in any place, people have off days and might get a bit grumpy, but in general the green room was a jovial place to be. I would always tell them gags and because they were actors they would tut and say, 'Now that's not very politically correct, is it?' But I would tell another joke and say here's another one you won't like. Eileen McCallum used to laugh at all the dirty jokes I would tell.

Actress Briony McRoberts, who played Sam Hagen, was terrific.

She was English, very well spoken and a real 'actor, dahling' and all that sort of stuff. But she liked a right good carry on and if we were ever out at a dinner or a charity do, she'd be up dancing with everyone.

Although we all got on well with each other, we weren't best pals with everyone. Sometimes, you just didn't have anything in common with the other actors in real life. A strange thing I noticed was that Jackie Farrell and Mary Riggans, who played his wife Effie, didn't talk to each other a lot in the green room because they didn't have a lot in common. But on screen when they were playing their parts, you would have thought they were married in real life, they were that good.

There was a storyline that my wife turns up in Glendarroch. She was played by actress Libby McArthur, who's now in *River City* as Gina Rossi. When she walked into the green room I said; 'Are you Libby?'

'Yes,' she said.

'Right, come here and give me a cuddle. I mean, you're my wife and I haven't even cuddled you yet,' I told her.

We got on great and there was one scene where she had to slap me and I wanted it to look authentic. I told her that in rehearsals she should just pretend to slap me, but for the take, she was to hit me for real and make sure she didn't miss.

'Just you whack me,' I said. And when she said she wasn't sure about hitting me I assured her that it would make the scene all the more realistic. Well, she hit me all right, and it made me stagger for a few seconds and my ears were buzzing. One of the crew came over to me and asked if I was OK, because it looked as if Libby had given me a sore one. 'It's OK,' I replied. 'I told Libby to hit me, but could you speak into my other ear because this one is still buzzing after being slapped.'

I was fine after ten minutes and as far as I'm concerned it was well worth the pain. I might not be an experienced actor, but I'm a viewer and I hate to see actors pretending to hit one another when you can see they have missed by a mile. When you hear the crack on the soundtrack of the punch 'landing', you think it must be static electricity you're hearing.

About a month after I started on *High Road*, I was sitting in the green room with Richard Greenwood, who played Eric Ross-Gifford, the Glendarroch hotelier, and I asked if they ever have any nights out.

'What do you mean?' he asked.

'A wee night out for everyone on the programme. We could go to a restaurant one night for a meal, a few drinks and a good laugh with each other,' I explained.

'Nobody's ever suggested that,' he told me.

So I decided to organise a Ho Wong night at the well-known Glasgow Chinese restaurant, went round everyone to see when they would be available and got the *High Road* works night out off the ground. About 16 of us from the show came along and everyone had a great time and it became a regular event. These nights out are great for camaraderie and helping us to work together better. It's a bit like a football team, because if you go out together you build a team spirit. That's the benefit of having nights out like that, but initially I just thought we should be pals and have ourselves a good time.

After several months of working on *High Road*, Richard pulled me aside and told me that I was like a breath of fresh air for the programme. I said, 'No, no. I'm just doing my wee bit.'

But he insisted, 'You're doing well. You've not acted on television before and it takes a wee bit of getting used to. But in that green room everybody talks to each other now, nobody ever saw anyone else outside the studio until you started organising the nights out.'

I really appreciated these words from Richard as he's such a genuine guy. After *High Road* he bought a derelict house in the Highlands between Inverness and Ullapool, did it up and built a recording studio. He now earns his living doing voiceovers. They send the script up to him and he records it and sends it digitally back down the line.

When we were doing *High Road* we would be working two three-month slots every year – March, April and May, then October, November, December, filming three episodes a week. My first involvement in an episode would be in the location shooting which took place on a Thursday and a Friday. You rehearsed the scene on location a few times and then went for a take.

On a Saturday, we were at Scottish Television rehearsing the scenes, which were to be shot in the studio, and on the Monday morning you had a run through with the help of a script to remind you of what was going on. In the afternoon, you had what was called the producer's run, which was done without a script. There were no cameras in the studio when you were doing the producer's run, but you had to be aware where the cameras were going to be when they recorded the scene for real. So they would use a coat stand in the place where the cameras were going to be. It may seem strange, but you soon got used to the idea that the coat stand was actually a camera.

On the Tuesday and Wednesday, we would film the studio scenes and the following day we would be back on location at Luss, on Loch Lomondside, for the start of the next cycle. There was a spell for three or four months when I was in almost every episode so I'd be working six days a week and it was hard work, but I loved it.

My favourite part of the filming was at Luss doing the location shooting. I think it's more natural than being in a pretend lounge bar, which is a set built in a studio. If we were filming at the quay in Luss there would be tourists turning up to watch you. I enjoyed that and it was good to see their reaction after a scene.

The storylines for my Chic Cherry character were very good and he was always getting into scrapes – some of his making and some not. Chic – taxi driver, garage owner and general handyman – just couldn't handle success. When things were going well he was King of the World, but it would pretty soon fall to pieces round about him. He was that kind of character and I know so many people like him who promise so much but never achieve it.

I think there's a bit of Andy Cameron in Chic Cherry because people who were at school with me and knew me when I was growing up say that they recognise me in some of the mannerisms Chic Cherry has. I loved getting into the character and I still get people coming up to me and saying, 'I'm still waiting for that taxi,' and, 'Hey, are you going to come round and finish off my kitchen?'

That's exactly what would be happening in Glendarroch.

Once I was in a pub when this guy came up to me and started giving me a hard time about charging a pensioner too much money for some electrical work and I had no idea what he was talking about. 'By the way, you're right out of order,' he said. 'Taking £5 off that old pensioner to fix her light – that was a liberty. A wee bit of flex and a plug and you charge her a fiver.'

'What are you talking about?' I said.

'That Mrs Mack,' he answered. It never occurred to me he would be talking about something that happened in *High Road*, and that's when I realised that some people are really into the programme. They know it's not for real, but in some way they still treat it like real life. Other people have come up to me and said, 'See that Lafferty, it's time you gave him a right good kick in the backside. He's always up to no good and needs sorting out.'

Simon Weir, who plays Lafferty, and I got on like a house on fire and we would have a great time trying to make each other laugh during rehearsals. He would pull a face during a scene I would be doing and try to make me lose concentration. Once, when we were filming a scene, I come into the bar of the hotel in Glendarroch and ask, 'Has anyone seen Lafferty?'

'No.'

'Well, when you see him, tell him I'm looking for him.'

At that point, Lafferty – who ran the garage with me in Glendarroch – and the young boy Dominic, who is being led astray by him, walk in, and I say, 'You leave that boy alone, he doesn't need your influence. Anyway, get back to the garage, we've got an engine to take out.'

At that, I leave the bar and Lafferty and Dominic are supposed to follow me outside. When I walk through the door and out of camera shot I turn round and drop my trousers and when Simon comes out the door he sees me and doesn't dare start laughing because the camera is still on him.

There was a lot of good banter between the guys who were Celtic fans and me, the diehard Rangers supporter. I would see Simon at Parkhead for Old Firm games and I would wind him up by rushing over to him and doing all the luvvy bit and hugging him. There was a great chemistry between us off camera, which I think helped during filming.

In 1998, when Celtic won the Scottish Premier League and stopped Rangers getting ten titles in a row, I knew I would be getting pelters from the Celtic fans among the cast and crew. So I decided I would get it over with and pull a stunt that would have them speechless. I wasn't in the week after Celtic won the league, but I knew all the Celtic supporters were in on the Monday – guys like Simon Weir, Derek Lord, who played Davie Sneddon, Alan McHugh, who played PC Tony Piacentini, Garry Hollywood, who played Dominic, and head cameraman Jack McNair.

I parked my car in the garage instead of the normal parking place so they wouldn't know I was at the studios. I had bought six cans of Guinness and I taped a miniature of whisky to each can and carried them in a Safeway bag into a disused kitchen next to the rehearsal room. I had tipped off the director what I had planned and he agreed I could interrupt the run-through.

They started a scene and suddenly I burst into the room in the middle of it singing, 'Hail, Hail, the Celts are here', and handed each of them a can of Guinness with the miniature of whisky. I said well done on your team winning the league and walked out. They were speechless and the next time they saw me they came into the dressing-room and gave me a hug and said I had taken it really well. To be fair to them, any time Rangers beat Celtic they would stand me a pint of Guinness.

Just over six years after I joined *High Road* I got a feeling of déjà vu. Just like when my Radio Scotland show was dropped, rumours started spreading about Scottish Television not doing another series of *High Road*, as there was no money for the soap's production. The rumours were further fuelled when we were told that, instead of doing two sets of three months filming, we were to work right through the summer months of June, July and August to get as many episodes filmed as possible.

We were told we would be back the following year, but that never transpired. I think Scottish Television helped kill off *High Road* when they started dropping the programme to make way for other one-off shows and we lost the continuity. It was such a shame, and not just for us – it was supposed to be the Queen Mother's favourite soap.

Three years after filming stopped, they were still showing the odd episode and they've now sold *High Road* to Australian television. Early in 2004, I got a text from former Rangers manager Walter Smith who was in Australia on holiday. 'I can't get away from you,' he wrote. 'I'm sitting here having a beer and you have just come on in *High Road*.'

I did a text back asking him to record it, as I wanted to hear what I was like with an Aussie accent.

I'm glad I took the *High Road* because it was another high point in my career and I enjoyed it immensely.

Chapter 14

FOLLOW, FOLLOWING RANGERS

'COME ON THE CARAMEL WAFERS, THAT'S THE GAME, CLEAR YOUR LINES,' shouts the Rangers fan sitting behind me in the stand at Firhill. I turn round and give him a wry smile and wonder to myself what on earth he's talking about. 'Erzi caramel wafers, get right intae him,' he shouts again. I turn round again and say to him, 'OK, I give up, who's the caramel wafers?'

'It's Colin Jackson and Tom Forsyth,' he says.

'What do you call them that for?' I ask.

'Cos they're grey and done,' he replies.

Well, this reference to Gray and Dunn, the company that makes caramel wafers, was one of the funniest lines I've ever heard at a football match and I thought it was brilliant. Colin Jackson was a big, tall centre-half for Rangers whose hair was turning grey, and fellow defender Tom Forsyth – well, he may not have been in the first flushes of youth, but I wouldn't have gone so far as to say he was quite done yet. However, the line was too good not to remember and I decided I would store it away in my head and use it in my act at some point.

I didn't have to wait long. In fact, the next night I was speaking at Sandy Jardine's testimonial dinner. It was the perfect opportunity, since Colin Jackson and Tom Forsyth were sitting at a table only a few feet away from me. So I point them out to the guests: 'A big welcome to the caramel wafers, Jackson and Forsyth – they're grey and done!' What a roar there was and everyone fell about laughing.

A few days later, on the Wednesday, Rangers manager John Greig invited me out to lunch as a thank you for doing the testimonial. Now, for a diehard Rangers fan like me, it's like I've died and woken up in a blue heaven. One of my all-time football heroes is taking me out to lunch, I'm inside Ibrox and Greigy's come out into the foyer and says, 'Away into the dressing-room and have a chat with some of the players. I've got some calls to make and I won't be long.'

As a young lad standing on the terraces, being invited to do this would have seemed an improbable dream. But there I was, on first-name terms with my heroes and strolling down the corridor into the famous home dressing-room at Ibrox. Tom Forsyth comes out the door and almost knocks me over. 'How're you doing, wee man?' he says. 'You were in great form on Sunday night.'

'Thanks very much,' I replied.

I'm just inside the dressing-room door and I hear his footsteps halt and he's heading back towards me. Big Forsyth is standing behind me now and he says, 'Grey and f*****g done, is it?'

He's got me cornered and from inside the dressing-room, the Rangers goalkeeper Peter McCloy stands up with a wicked smile on his face and moves towards me. I look at both of them and I think, 'Oh s**t! I'm for it now.' Sure enough, the two of them grab me, drag me towards the big players' bath, which was full of water after their morning's training, and throw me in.

They're killing themselves laughing at me as I climb out of the bath, water dripping from my suit, shirt and every other piece of clothing I was wearing. Then, in walks Greigy with a giant smirk on his face that says – so you've met Mr Forsyth, have you? I take off all my soaking wet clothes and Greigy gives me a tracksuit to wear while he sends my gear out to an express dry cleaners. 'Right,' says Greigy. 'Are you ready to go to lunch?' So there I was sitting in the Swallow Hotel in Glasgow's Paisley Road West having lunch with Ibrox gaffer John Greig, and me sitting in a Rangers tracksuit.

I have been Rangers daft since I was about five years old. At that tender age, I was taken to one of the biggest games played at Ibrox in the 1940s, when Moscow Dynamo were on a tour of Britain and they played Rangers. I have a vague memory of being on my Uncle Joe's shoulders and what appeared at the time to be millions and millions of people watching the game and my uncles talking about the game a long time after. The precise year was 1945, and the Rangers game was the only match that great Russian team played in Scotland. The result was a 2–2 draw.

It would appear that my Uncle Joe took me to the game without telling Bella and they tried to keep it a secret from her. Years later, I was out with my Uncle Joe and Auntie Marion and I was asking if I really was at that game. He said, 'Take it from me, you were there, but don't ever mention it in front of Bella.'

My first clear memory of seeing Rangers was when I was about seven and I was standing outside Cathkin Park after Rangers had played Third Lanark. The Rangers captain, George Young, came out of the ground proudly wearing the Rangers blazer and walked towards me. I couldn't believe how big he was and I asked him for his autograph. He was standing next to me and it was like talking to the town hall.

'Have you got a bit of paper and a pencil, son?' he asked me. I said no, so he went into his pocket and pulled out a piece of paper and a pen and wrote on it, 'George Young – Glasgow Rangers FC'. I couldn't believe I had George Young's autograph and I kept that bit of paper until I was about 12.

That wasn't the only autograph I got that day. I got Willie Woodburn's and Willie Waddell's as well. When Jock Tiger Shaw came out I said to him, 'Mr Tiger, can I have your autograph?' He laughed and said, 'My name's Jock. Call me Jock.'

I said, 'No, your name's Tiger because that's what people call you.'

He explained that Tiger was his nickname and I just looked on, bemused. When I got home I had to ask my Uncle Jim what a nickname was.

Getting these autographs was the start of my love affair with Rangers. I was really impressed by the players that day. They looked very athletic and smart in their club blazers. Like every young boy, I wanted to emulate my football heroes and when I was kicking the ball around the street I imagined I was playing at Ibrox and scoring the winning goal. I might have been kicking the ball against a wall out the back door, but at the time I could hear the crowd roar as my rocket shot rippled the twine and bulged the onion bag.

I also loved going to Wembley on the Quarry Bar bus. Not only did I get to visit my dad in London every two years, but also I got to the games and saw Rangers players wearing the dark blue of Scotland.

Three or four weeks after coming back from Wembley, you would go to the pictures and the Pathé News would come on and they would show you pictures of the England–Scotland game. I would tell the other boys I was there and they would say: 'Aye, right. How could you get all the way down there?'

Another milestone was the day I got my first Rangers scarf. I was about ten years old and it was the first of many times that I dogged school to watch Rangers. It was a mid-week game at Ibrox and the kick-off was 3 p.m. My Uncle Joe took a half-day off work to go to the game, which was a Scottish Cup replay against Raith Rovers.

The day before, he pulled me aside and said he would come to the school and pick me up because he was taking me somewhere. He wouldn't say where it was and he warned me not to mention it to Bella. Sure enough, Uncle Joe turned up at Farie Street Primary, told them I had a doctor's appointment and the teacher let me out of class. I asked Uncle Joe where we were going and when he said to see Rangers I thought, 'Brilliant!'

We got on a train to Glasgow Central and then another train to White City, which is no longer there as it's part of the M8 motorway. Just as we were pulling into the station, my Uncle Joe pulled his scarf out of his pocket and put it round my neck. I can still feel the elation after all those years as I walked from the station to Ibrox wearing my Rangers scarf, surrounded by all those men wearing bunnets and smoking Woodbines after they had managed to wangle a pass out from their shipyard or factory.

Uncle Joe sat me up on a stanchion on the terracing and it was a marvellous feeling. Somebody would swear and there would be a chorus of, 'Haw you, a bit of order – there's a wean here.'

At other games my Uncle Joe would take me to, it would get very crowded where he was standing and I couldn't see. So I would be passed down the front over people's heads until I reached the wall where I would sit. The youngsters there would sit on the wall with their legs hanging over trackside. Every so often, a policemen would come along and tell you to put your legs on the other side. We would wait until he had walked further round the track and we would sit on the wall with our legs trackside again. Other policemen wouldn't bother you, but when the first policemen came back round again, it was another order to move.

Of course, I would watch teams like Clyde, Third Lanark and Queen's Park, but that was all in the name of being a young business entrepreneur. That was when we were collecting the empty beer bottles from the terracing on a Saturday afternoon.

We used to tell the joke as youngsters that there's an Old Firm game and the crowd at the back are throwing empty beer bottles, which did happen from time to time. Anyway, there's a guy down the front on his knees with his hands covering his head and the guy next to him says, 'Get up. It's just like being in the war, if your name's on the bullet it will get you.'

'That's what I'm worried about,' the first guy says. 'My name's McEwan!'

All the men in my family were football daft, but they didn't all support Rangers. My Uncle Jim was a Clyde man, although if Clyde were playing away from home he would go with some of his pals to see Rangers. Uncle Joe, of course, was a regular at Ibrox and he was the uncle who would normally take me to the games. My Uncle Alec started off as a Clyde supporter, but when he married my Auntie Lizzie, with the influence of her brothers he went to watch Celtic. His daughter and my cousin, Kay, is a season ticket holder at Parkhead and his son, Jim, is also a Celtic fan although he now works in London. Jim, Kay and I have great banter between us because of the Old Firm rivalry and that's OK because that's all it is – a bit of banter.

Even at a young age, I was Rangers daft and if any of my uncles would start winding me up about Rangers getting beat, I would head off to the bedroom for a good greet. Come to think of it, I still feel like greetin' the way we play in some games nowadays!

When I joined the BB and started playing for the football team, the games were on a Saturday afternoon and I never got to as many Rangers matches as I would have liked. But there were always the mid-week afternoon games and the fantastic atmosphere of the evening games when they introduced floodlights in the mid-'50s.

When I was in secondary school, I played truant to see both Rangers and Scotland play. When the Hungarians came to Hampden in 1953 some schools had taken tickets for the schoolboys' enclosure and would organise for the boys to go to the games. But not Rutherglen Academy, so I had to make my own arrangements and skip lessons that afternoon. I managed to get into the schoolboys' enclosure and I suppose that's almost the same as being in class.

I made up all sorts of stories to get away from school, but if Bella had ever caught me she would have marched me back to the school and sat outside to make sure I didn't make my escape again. And when I got home she would have given me a right doing into the bargain.

Bella only found out about me dogging school years later when I worked on the buses. One day, my Aunt Sarah was in at Bella's when I arrived and she said, 'We were just talking the other day about how you used to stay off school to go to football matches.' My cousin Campbell Gordon must have said something to her about it. Bella said, 'No, that can't be right, he never dodged school in his life.' She was none too happy when I admitted that I had.

As I got older, I joined the Rutherglen East Rangers Supporters Club and travelled to away games on the supporters' bus. I would take my turn on the organising committee and I just loved the camaraderie of it all – turning up every Saturday and having a few beers and a laugh with your pals.

The first time I went to an away game on a supporters' bus was with the Hutchestown Rangers Supporters Club. I was about 15 and was working in Weirs when one of the guys in there asked if I wanted to go to see Rangers play Hearts at Tynecastle. Of course, I jumped at the chance.

I was just a young boy and I sat at the back of the bus with all the other younger lads. Although I was working, I got a lift over the turnstile and headed down to the front of the terracing. That was the day I actually got to touch the jersey of Rangers legend Don Kitchenbrand. He had been running down the wing and crossed the ball, which was put out for a corner by one of the Hearts defenders. But Kitchenbrand's momentum carried him across the track and into the crowd. I was excited about having actually touched a Rangers player, never mind the fact that Rangers won 4–1 that day.

I've never hidden the fact that I am a Rangers fan – I love Rangers – and I'll be a Rangers fan when I die. But that doesn't mean I can't see and recognise the skills and qualities of players from other teams and that includes Celtic. The day I can't say to a pal of mine who is a Celtic fan that Jimmy Johnstone, Bobby Murdoch or Henrik Larsson were fabulous players, I'll chuck it.

Sure, you want to see your team win and in an Old Firm match I'm desperate for Rangers to beat Celtic, because they are our greatest rivals. And if you do win you've got the bragging rights with all your pals who support Celtic. Of course, if you get beat, it works the other way and you have to take pelters off them.

I love Rangers and I love to see them winning. In the past few years, Celtic have had great runs in Europe and I've been happy for all my pals who are Celtic supporters and there are plenty of them. At the same time, to use that old football cliché, I've been sick as a parrot about it because that's even more glory for Celtic and not for my team. However much I appreciate the pleasure my pals have been getting, I still want to see Rangers knock Celtic off the back pages because we're the ones winning big games in Europe.

But let me say here and now, there is no place in football for sectarianism. Sure, when I was younger I stood on the terracing singing 'The Sash' and about being up to my knees in Fenian blood. But it's just a phase and you should grow out of it and it's the same with the songs the Celtic fans sing. You don't really mean what you are singing. Of course you don't want to be up to your knees in Fenian blood, it's just one of those things you sang when you were young and daft. It should wear off when you grow up. And just because you don't sing these songs, it doesn't make you any less of a Rangers or Celtic supporter.

I discussed this with the former Celtic player and manager Tommy Burns one night and he agreed with me that supporters of both sides sing the sectarian songs, but they don't really mean what they are singing.

I stopped singing these songs after I married May, who was a Catholic. I'm not proud that I stood on the terracing and sang sectarian songs in the first place, but I grew up and realised it was wrong. My oldest daughter, Ellen, is Rangers daft and she heard plenty of Rangers songs in the house, but never any of the sectarian stuff.

I do lots of Celtic charity events and for years I have either performed or done the auction at the Cardinal's Ball, in Glasgow. I can't stand other Rangers fans who say I shouldn't be doing these things and telling me I should f**k off to Parkhead with the rest of my pals. My message to them has always been, 'Get a life!' I realise that my strongly held belief that religion should have nothing to do with football has not met with universal acclaim, particularly among a certain section of Rangers supporters.

I caused a bit of a furore when I stood up at one Rangers annual meeting being held in the Mitchell Theatre, in Glasgow, and suggested they should sign Catholic players – although some sections of the press blew the row right out of proportion. Some of the papers said I was jostled and manhandled, but that never happened. Jock Wallace had not long come back to Rangers as manager for the second time and I stood up at the AGM and asked why Jock had been fourth choice. I told the directors, 'You went for Alex Ferguson and he knocked us back. Jim McLean knocked us back and John Lyle, the manager of West Ham, wouldn't come either.

'Why did these people knock us back? Was it because they were told they could only sign players of a certain persuasion and who had gone to certain schools? We've got to come into the twentieth century and sign the best players whatever their religion.'

That sparked off some shouts from the less enlightened of the shareholders who didn't like what they were hearing. After the AGM ended, I was having a coffee outside the hall when someone came up, ignored me and said to the guy I was talking to: 'It's terrible when one of your own lets you down.'

I looked him in the eye and said, 'If you've got something to say to me, say it. Otherwise shut your mouth, you bigoted b*****d.' The guy backed down at that and they were the only angry words I spoke that day.

Shortly after that, the Rangers chairman John Paton came up to me and said he didn't disagree with what I said, but he thought it was the wrong time.

The incident made the papers and the following Saturday I was at Tannadice with my daughter to see Rangers play Dundee United and there was some verbal abuse thrown my way from a few Rangers fans. But that never changed my view that Rangers' unwillingness to sign a Catholic hindered the club and it was a stupid rule.

You should sign players for their ability, not because of their religion. John Greig told me that when he was manager he would have gladly signed a Catholic, but he didn't want to be the first. Nowadays, Rangers do sign Catholics, or players of any religion and you've got to hand it to David Murray and Graeme Souness for that.

I would say that 99 per cent of Rangers supporters were happy with the likes of Maurice Johnston and Lorenzo Amoruso and the other players who happen to be Catholics that Rangers have signed. I certainly was because Rangers should be signing the best football players and where they go on a Sunday is nobody's business.

Maurice Johnston's signing for Rangers sent shock waves round Scottish football and it was a good thing. It showed Rangers were leaving behind the sectarian policy of not signing Catholics, but the media tended to concentrate on the negative side, trying to stir up controversy even more. I got calls from journalists asking me if the signing would stop me going to watch Rangers. It would take a lot more than Rangers signing a Catholic to stop me from seeing my team, that's for sure.

Maurice Johnston gave Rangers two great years and I've spoken to coaches and managers who have worked with him over the years and no one has a bad word to say about him. He was very conscientious and a very good player. I got a real good laugh on the morning Maurice Johnston was paraded by Graeme Souness to the media. I was going to present a cheque to a school for handicapped kids, in Glasgow. I was driving to the school and I heard on the radio that Rangers had signed Maurice Johnston. I was as shocked as everyone else at the news.

When I got to the school, the wee janitor was waiting for me and he said, 'That's some news from Ibrox. I'm a Celtic fan and the first thing that came into my head was that Maurice Johnston will have to get a room in Salman Rushdie's house.' I thought that was brilliant and I couldn't stop laughing.

While he played for Rangers, Maurice Johnston took some abuse from a few supporters, but in general I think he was accepted by Rangers supporters – especially when he scored a goal.

There are people who believe that Rangers are a Protestant club and they are entitled to believe that if they want. But I would say that's not right. The majority of Rangers fans may be Protestant, but that doesn't make it a Protestant club.

The other thing that really annoys me about some Rangers fans is that they give the Nazi salute and sing 'Rule Britannia'. Now, I'm British and I'm proud to be British, but before I'm British, I'm Scottish. Rule Britannia is not a British song, it's an English Tory song and as for the Nazi salute – we've all got relatives who died in the Second World War fighting the Nazis. I worry that this kind of behaviour has become more common and Rangers have got to do something about it.

On a more general note, one of the unfortunate things I've encountered in my years as a Rangers supporter and a football fan is the animosity which has grown between fans. Take the situation between Aberdeen and Rangers just now. We used to go to Aberdeen for away games and the locals would welcome us with open arms. After the game, we would go to a few pubs and have a great time, not only among ourselves but with Aberdeen fans as well. But all the carry on after Rangers' midfielder Ian Durrant was injured by Neil Simpson's tackle changed all that. Now you are herded out of the place as quickly as possible by the police so there is no fighting between the two sets of supporters. Not being able to have a pint with the Aberdeen fans after a game and talk about the match with them certainly takes something away from travelling to watch your team.

One of the worst defeats I witnessed as a Rangers fan was getting beat 7–1 by Celtic, at Hampden, in 1957. I was standing on the terracing with two minutes to go and my pals were saying, 'Right, c'mon, let's go. I can't stand any more of this.' I was encouraging them to stay on, saying we can fight back. Nothing like blind optimism. When we got back to Rutherglen, the Celtic fans were singing, 'Seven–one, seven–one, seven–one,' and one of my pals said out the corner of his mouth, 'Don't let them see it annoys you.' I replied, 'Tell them we're looking so sick because we had a bad pie at half-time.'

My favourite Rangers player of all time was Jimmy Miller, who signed for Rangers from Dunfermline in 1959. The first time I saw him play he was like a wee warrior. In fact, his nickname was the Old Warhorse. This incident sums up just how much I idolised Jimmy Miller. I introduced my daughter Ellen to Jimmy about five years ago when she was with me at Ibrox one time, and she said to him, 'Mr Miller, when I was about four, I wanted to be you.' When she was that age, I used to come home with a wee glow and go on about Jimmy Miller being the greatest Rangers player ever. What I liked about Jimmy Miller was that as a centre-forward he would get kicked round the park by some real tough centre-halfs, but he never complained to the referee. He just remembered the opposing player's number and took his own retribution later in the game.

My other Rangers heroes were Ritchie, Shearer, Caldow, Greig, McKinnon, Baxter, Henderson, McMillan, Brand and Wilson. I thought Billy Ritchie was a very athletic goalkeeper and Bobby Shearer was a bit of a hard case letting any forward know he was there. Eric Caldow was a more cultured player and although he tackled his weight he was a great passer of the ball. Although he was small he was a great full-back and that was in the days of two full-backs, three half-backs and five forwards. John Greig was outstanding at right-half and didn't take any prisoners either. And centre-half Ronnie McKinnon always had his shorts pulled high up his legs and, although there weren't sunbeds on every street corner in those days, he always seemed to have a great tan. He was very good in the air and quick for a big guy. But the man that made that Rangers team tick was Jim Baxter. What a cultured left foot he had, strolling about the park, and all the Rangers fans just loved him. Willie Henderson on the right wing was like one of those dolls you can't knock over. Every time a full-back would put a heavy tackle in, he would bounce back up. Willie was very quick, but I think even he would admit that the service he got from Ian McMillan helped make him the great player he was. Ian McMillan was known as the Wee Prime Minister and he only trained two or three nights a week because he was part-time. He worked on a Saturday morning and would come to Ibrox from his work. When he got the ball, it was instantly under control and there would be a precision pass inside the full-back and that would be Willie Henderson's cue to get off his mark. If you think footballers nowadays play for penalties, you should have seen Davie Wilson. If you tripped him in the centre circle he would do three double pikes and a somersault and land in the penalty box.

I was so into all these players when I was a teenager that I remember thinking that MB bars were named after Jimmy Miller and Ralph Brand – that's how naive I was.

I've got quite a few favourite Rangers games, and apart from winning the European Cup-Winners' Cup in Barcelona in 1972, one other match in particular sticks out in my mind. That was against Eindhoven, in the European Cup in November 1978 after a 0–0 draw at Ibrox. It wasn't long after they had introduced the away goals count double rule, but still the general opinion was that Rangers wouldn't get a scoring draw, never mind beat Eindhoven on their home ground.

I was at the game and we got off to the worst possible start with

Eindhoven scoring in 23 seconds. It was 1–0 at half-time and I was in the gents when this wee Rangers fan came in with so many metal badges on his scarf, if he'd walked by a magnet shop he'd have got pulled in. The heads were a bit down after losing an early goal, but this wee guy just said, 'Lucky b******s! They started before we were ready.' The place was full of Rangers fans and we all erupted in laughter.

In the second half, we equalised and then Eindhoven went 2–1 up, before we equalised again. There wasn't long to go when Tommy McLean shoved a lovely ball through to Bobby Russell, who made a great run to take the pass and as their goalie came rushing out he sweetly placed it under him and into the net. We won the match 3–2 and got through to the quarter-finals.

The first of my two favourite Rangers goals is one that Paul Gascoigne scored against Hibs at Ibrox when he beat about 28 players – including some of his own team – and slipped it into the corner of the net. But that was also the day that humour went out of football. When the referee dropped his yellow card, Paul Gascoigne picked it up and for a laugh pretended he was giving referee Dougie Smith a caution. The ref obviously had a humour bypass because when he got the card back he booked Gascoigne for showing him the yellow card. It was ridiculous. Gascoigne didn't undermine the ref's authority, he was just having a laugh and entertaining the crowd. The ref should have taken it in good part and had a smile himself. And when you compare how other referees handle football matches, it makes that booking all the more galling.

My other favourite goal is Davie Cooper's blockbuster free kick against Aberdeen in the League Cup final at Hampden. Davie Cooper ran up to the ball and just hammered it into the net – what a scorcher.

Years later, I was doing a turn for the Scotland squad up at Gleneagles and was sitting at a table with Davie Cooper, Ian Durrant, Roy Aitken and Jim Leighton, who was the Aberdeen goalkeeper that day at Hampden. We were talking about great goals and I mentioned Davie's goal in the League Cup final. Jim Leighton chimes in, 'I actually got a hand to the ball in that shot.'

And Davie Cooper replied, 'Aye, on the way out!' A sad loss is Davie Cooper – he was a magnificent player.

One of the best referees I have ever witnessed is Big Tom Wharton. Those of you of a certain age will remember Tom as a giant of a referee – he was 6 ft 4 in. and a big, big man who commanded the respect of players on the park. I regularly have lunch with Tom and he told me of one Old Firm game he refereed in which he gave a penalty to Celtic. John Greig races after him and says, 'That was never a penalty. For f***'s sake ref, never a penalty.' Big Tom looks Greigy in the eye and says, 'If you read the *Sunday Post* tomorrow, you will see that it was indeed a penalty.' Not another word was said.

Another incident involving Tom Wharton in an Old Firm game was when he ordered off Celtic's Jimmy Johnstone. Tom had ordered the winger off in the previous Old Firm encounter and Jinky had been booked earlier in the match for having a kick at Totty Beck. When Jinky committed another bad foul he knew he was for an ordering off and an early bath. Big Tom called him over and when he asked Jinky for his name the wee man replied, 'Roy Rogers.'

'Well, Mr Rogers,' says Tom, 'when you go up the tunnel you'll find Trigger waiting for you in the dressing-room!'

Ally McCoist also tells a great story of an incident when Rangers were playing Hearts at Ibrox and Brian McGinley was refereeing. A couple of days before the game, Brian McGinley had been stopped by police and charged with drink-driving and, of course, it was all over the papers the following day. During the game, Ian Ferguson had shot for goal and the ball came off Gary McKay for what should have been a corner, but Brian gave a goalkick.

Ian Ferguson chased Brian McGinley all the way back to the centre circle shouting, 'That was a corner, it came off McKay. Are you blind or something – that was a corner.'

At that point, McCoist pulled Ferguson away and said, 'Leave him alone. If he can't see a big white motor with a blue light on top what chance has he got of seeing a corner?' Brian McGinley just laughed along with the rest of the players and the situation was diffused. That's how you handle players and get their respect.

When I was younger and went to Ibrox, I always stood on the terracing in front of Stairway 13 between the Rangers end and The Shed – which in those days was called The Derry – opposite the main stand. And had fate not intervened, I might have been one of those who perished in the Ibrox disaster on 2 January 1971.

It was a terrible, terrible tragedy the day 66 people were killed in the crush at Stairway 13 and if I hadn't been given tickets for another part of the ground, I would have been right on the spot heading down the steep stairs where the disaster happened at the end of the traditional New Year's Rangers–Celtic game. Although I always stood on the terracing I thought it would be good to watch the game from the comfort of a seat in the stand for a change. I had been to the stand a few times and had enjoyed it.

I was going to the game with a pal called Jimmy Roberts and I offered him the other ticket, but he said he would rather go to his usual spot on the terracing. So I took my tickets, sold one to a supporter outside the ground and took my seat in the stand.

As everybody knows, Jimmy Johnstone scored for Celtic to put them 1–0 in the lead and in the dying seconds, Colin Stein equalised. As the celebrating Rangers fans headed down the steep incline of Stairway 13, it is believed that one fan stumbled on the stairway, causing a crush which buckled the metal barriers and ended with 66 people dead and many more injured.

I hadn't a clue what had happened after I left the match and headed to the Viking Bar in King Street, Rutherglen. I was sitting in the pub and at about half past six someone came in and announced something terrible had happened at Ibrox. None of us knew what he was talking about and we turned on the black and white television in the bar to see the news that the death toll at that point had risen to 33. All you could hear was people saying, 'For f***'s sake – I can't believe it,' as they watched the news, hardly able to take in the enormity of what had happened.

When I heard the disaster had happened on Stairway 13, my first thoughts were for Jimmy Roberts because I knew he would have been standing there and used that stairway to get out of the ground. Terrible thoughts raced round my head that Jimmy had died and I wished I had made him take my spare ticket for the stand. I immediately left the pub and got a taxi to the Gorbals where Jimmy came from. Although the Granite City pub was a real Celtic bar, Jimmy was a local and sometimes had a pint in there where everybody knew him.

It was like walking into a cowboy saloon at high noon. I pushed my way into this pub full of Celtic fans staring at me because I was still wearing my Rangers tie. I kept squeezing past people looking for Jimmy and eventually someone said, 'What the f**k are you doing in here?'

'I'm looking for Jimmy Roberts,' I said.

'What do you want him for?' someone asked.

'I just want to make sure he's all right,' I said. 'There's been a disaster at Ibrox and dozens of folk have died.' They obviously hadn't heard about it and at first, they didn't believe me, but I assured them it had happened. Suddenly, I felt a tremendous sense of relief inside me when one of the guys in the pub said, 'Jimmy was in about an hour ago. He's away down to the bowling club.'

I then headed for the Hutchestown Bowling Club just to make sure Jimmy was alive and well. 'How did you get out?' I asked Jimmy. He told me he decided to stand with his brother in a different part of the terracing and watch the game with him. After the match, they got out through a different exit and he missed the disaster.

I had worked beside one of the 66 people who died that day – Wullie Shaw. He worked with me on the buses and that was how he always spelled his name on his bus lines. Not Willie or William, but Wullie.

In normal circumstances, I would have been standing in front of Stairway 13 and I would have been among the mass of bodies making their way down the stairs at the end of the game. I always stay to the end of games, so I would have been in the usual rush to get out and down the stairs. I might have been one of the poor souls who died that day – and I just count my blessings that I wasn't and it's thanks to that spare couple of tickets to the stand.

I have heard people who were there talking about the scenes. They were stumbling over dead bodies unable to stop the downward momentum of the crowd from above them, seeing guys dying in front of them. It must have been horrific – undoubtedly, the saddest moment in the history of Rangers.

Over the years, as I became better known as a comedian, I have been asked to perform at many Rangers functions and player testimonials and it's been a fantastic honour. One of the best nights I remember was at John Greig's testimonial in 1977, and I'm not talking about my stand-up routine at the dinner, I'm talking about my performance on the park.

Rangers were playing a Scotland Select at Ibrox and there were 65,000 people there for Greigy's testimonial match. The Scotland team had been held up in the traffic and the kick-off had been delayed. There were tens of thousands of fans in the stadium waiting for the game to start and Willie Waddell asked me to go out onto the park with a microphone and entertain the crowd.

There's a Caribbean steel band playing and the fans are giving them pelters. I take my Rangers tammy off and put it on the head of one of the steel band members. 'You're a Rangers fan, now,' I said into the mike.

'Yes,' he replied. 'I'm a Rangers fan.' And the crowd just roared their approval. I walked back to the main stand side and told them that the game was going to be delayed for 15 minutes and it had nothing to do with the traffic outside. 'It's Lou Macari,' I said. 'He's going round to check the ice cream vans to make sure they're making enough money.'

The Scotland team eventually came out for a warm-up and Alan Rough was in goal. The previous Wednesday, he had flapped at a couple of balls and let two soft goals in when he was playing for Partick Thistle against Aberdeen. So I shouted him over and said I was going to show the crowd how he was waving to his father in the stand during the game last week. I got away with murder that night, but the fans loved it and cheered every joke I made. Not only did that make me happy, but Rangers won 5–0 as well.

Another great occasion for me was when I was able to wear the Rangers strip and kick a ball around Hampden Park. It was the semi-final of the Scottish Cup and I was entertaining the fans. I had a deerstalker hat on and trainers, but still managed to score the winning goal for Rangers that night. I wish.

I've had fantastic enjoyment following Rangers at home and abroad over the years and I hope there are plenty more big games in the future. I've had great fun follow, following the Gers, either going on a supporters' bus and standing on the terraces or hob-nobbing it in hospitality suites. But there's one story that has me splitting my sides laughing every time I think about it. It happened in the early '60s when I was travelling all over Scotland in supporters' buses to see Rangers. When we would go to an away game we would have a night on the town after the match. Sometimes, the supporters' bus wouldn't get back to Glasgow until the early hours of the morning.

We were up in Dundee and we had adjourned to the Arctic Bar and a group of four of us were sitting at a table. Four girls were sitting close to us and we began chatting them up. One of our group – we'll call him Billy – was getting on really well with one of the girls whose name was Theresa and we were invited back to her house for a party. When he found out her name was Theresa, he said, 'Just my luck. The one I fancy is a Tim.' But it didn't stop him trying to get her into bed.

We were in the flat and you could hardly see the walls for holy pictures. I've got one of the girls on my knee and the other guys are chatting to the other girls. Billy is now getting on famously with the lovely Theresa and is checking her tonsils with his tongue. After a while, they disappear into her bedroom and there are knowing looks all round.

Suddenly, we hear shouting: 'Ya bastard! Ya f*****g bastard!' We all ran through to the bedroom thinking that either Billy was hitting Theresa or she was getting ladled into him.

'What's happened?' we ask Billy, who's holding his head in his hands. And when he explained, we couldn't talk for laughing.

Billy was going like the clappers with Theresa on the bed and a holy picture fell off the wall and hit him on the head!

Two hours after we'd left the pub we were in the hospital casualty department waiting on Billy to get stitches in his head from being hit with the holy picture. The hospital staff wanted to call the police because they thought he had been in a fight and didn't believe us when we told them what happened. Eventually, they let Billy out with a huge bandage around his head. Maybe that was a wee message that we should practise true ecumenicalism all the time and not just when we fancy a bird called Theresa.

Rangers also played a big part in my second daughter Marion's wedding, because she was married in the Blue Room at Ibrox. So there we were at the top of the marble staircase in the Blue Room and John Greig, who had organised this for me, made a wee speech welcoming everyone to Ibrox and saying he was delighted my daughter had chosen Ibrox as a place to get married.

There was nothing like that when my first daughter Ellen got hitched. As far as I knew, she was in Thailand for a holiday, but then I got a phone call from her saying, 'Don't know if I'm married or just had an MOT. I'm looking at a marriage certificate and it's all in Thai.' Ellen and Dennis had been living together for 12 years and they decided they would avoid all the hassle and just get married on the beach in Thailand three years ago.

I now work for Rangers as match-day compère at Ibrox, wandering around the park, giving the fans the latest team news and leading the singing before the game starts. At the beginning of season 2004–05, I was asked to write a new Rangers song for the club, which was a great honour for me. It's called 'Loyal and True' and I wrote new lyrics to the tune of the Boys Brigade hymn, 'Will Your Anchor Hold?'. I've always thought this would make a great Rangers song with new lyrics put to the melody and I wrote the words in a way that – hopefully – can't be changed to include a sectarian element. I hope the fans will adopt it and make it part of their repertoire.

Rangers have been very good to me over the years. I used to work for the club interviewing present and ex-players in the hospitality lounges in the main stand. I got to meet some great punters, the players who pulled on the royal blue shirts of Rangers and some of my heroes of bygone years. Oh, and I got to see my favourite football team play as well!

A few years ago, I would be asked from time to time to go onto the park at Ibrox before a game and give the supporters a few gags. It went down well with the home fans, but on one occasion an Aberdeen supporter took umbrage.

It was in April 1999, when the Dons visited Ibrox for a game that would have a bearing on where the League title went. I was in the centre circle singing away when a 19-year-old Aberdeen fan ran on to the pitch and raced towards me. I had no idea he was on the park and one of the girls forking the park shouted, 'Andy, look behind you.' I thought she was at the wind up.

When I did turn round, this guy was still running and had almost reached me. He was about a foot away from me when he froze. I wasn't frightened and just laughed. Within seconds, he was being carted off by police and stewards.

The worst of it was when I got back into my seat in the stand the guy sitting behind me said, 'It's all right, Andy, he's not an Aberdeen fan – he's a music critic.'

Chapter 15

HAIL, HAIL, ANDY CAMERON'S HERE

THE CARDINAL WALKED ONTO THE FLOOR TO RESOUNDING APPLAUSE. WHEN the noise died down, he took the mike and thanked everyone for their efforts in raising thousands of pounds for charity. He had just about finished his speech when he took his red skullcap off and put it on my head.

The crowd roared with laughter at the sight of a diehard Rangers supporter like me standing there with Cardinal Thomas Winning's hat on. I was loving every minute of it, and so was Cardinal Winning and the audience as well.

'There's photographers coming out the walls,' I said. 'That's my season ticket at Ibrox out the window.'

Cardinal Winning turned to me and said, 'See how much you can get in the auction for that.' So I kept it on my head and started asking for bids. Eventually, a guy called Martin Hughes, who bid £5,600, bought the Cardinal's red hat.

I had been doing the auction at the fund-raising Cardinal's Ball – before that it was called the Archbishop's Ball – for years. This particular event when I auctioned the red hat was held not long after Archbishop Winning (who is now, sadly, deceased) had been made a cardinal in December 1994. I got on really well with the Cardinal and we really hit it off the first time I performed at his annual ball. I was standing in the middle of the

217

floor doing my stuff when the Cardinal came into the room and walked over to me.

I was wearing an outrageous suit which had been specially made up for me at the tailor's. It was blue material on one side and green on the other. Cardinal Winning said to me, 'Where on earth did you get that suit?'

And I replied, 'You're no' that well dressed yourself. Is that not a frock you're wearing?' He laughed at the gag and from then on we were good friends.

The money raised at the Cardinal's Ball goes to charities all over west central Scotland and it's a great night with both Celtic and Rangers supporters going along. I must have done about 14 of these balls either in cabaret or doing the auction.

The year we auctioned the Cardinal's hat, everyone involved in organising the event was taken out to dinner and Norma and I were invited along. These dinners are great fun and during the evening I said to Cardinal Winning, 'Well, you did it. We got £5,600 for your hat. How are you going to follow that next year?'

'How about if I get you one of the Pope's hats?' he replied.

'No way,' I said.

'Not a problem,' says the Cardinal. 'He wears one every day and if we want one for charity he'll bless it and we can have it.'

Sure enough, the following year, one of the auction items was the Pope's white skullcap and it came in a glass case on a plinth. The bidding started and very soon it became apparent there were two guys willing to go the whole road to get their hands on the Pope's hat all the way from the Vatican. The two were John Maguire, who runs car dealerships, and Michael Docherty, whose company digs the trenches for cable phones and television. Eventually, Michael Docherty won the bidding war and got the Pope's hat for an amazing £26,000.

What a round of applause Michael got when he bid that amount of money. All that money for a hat just shows how special it was. After he was presented with the hat, I told Michael, 'Twenty-six grand is no' bad for a working bunnet with no skip. If you had given it to me a week ago, I could have had RFC embroidered on it and we would have raised an even bigger fortune auctioning it.'

I've always enjoyed doing the Cardinal's Ball and even if I was doing a show the same night, they would hold the auction back until I could get there. I always got a good response to the auction. There might be about 20-odd items up for auction. Some of them would have holy significance, while a few would be Celtic and Rangers packages.

I would wind up the guys in the audience I knew were Rangers fans. 'I know why you're bidding for this,' I would tell them. 'You've got a new dartboard in the house.' Everyone would have a good laugh at all this sort of nonsense.

I also had Cardinal Winning playing football at Ibrox wearing a Rangers scarf, although I have to admit when I was playing keepy-up with him on the park I was wearing a Celtic scarf at the time! The occasion was the filming of a piece against sectarianism and we were showing that although people may support Rangers or Celtic, there's no reason why they can't be pals at the same time.

Willie Waddell was manager of Rangers back then and he came down the tunnel to see us and to welcome Thomas Winning to Ibrox. Willie invited us both up to his office for a cup of tea and the three of us chatted away for an hour.

Some of the money raised at the Cardinal's Ball is given to my favourite charity, St Vincent's School for the Deafblind, in Tollcross, Glasgow. I've nothing but admiration for the work they do at that school and I've had many hours of pleasure with the teachers and pupils there. The spirit and enthusiasm of the children – all of whom have either a hearing or seeing disability, or both – is a lesson to us all.

I was at a dinner one night when a guest who had heard me talking about St Vincent's approached me and said his son was at the school. 'We're not Catholics,' he said. 'But they're doing a terrific job helping my boy and all the other kids at the school.' He told me that the kids who are blind at the school always listen to the *Andy Cameron's Sunday Joint* radio programme and could I organise it for a few of them to come into the studio while the programme is being broadcast. I was more than happy to do this and one Sunday half-a-dozen kids came into the BBC.

I mentioned on air that we had kids from St Vincent's in and I had a wee boy beside me who was blind and was going to introduce the next record. His name was Bobby Etherson and I said to him, 'Give me your hand, this is the button you're going to press after you tell the listeners what the record is.'

Now, I can't remember what record it was that we played, but let's say it was Bobby Darin's 'Mac The Knife'. Young Bobby was brilliant. He even changed his voice as he announced to the nation: 'This is Bobby Darin singing "Mac The Knife".' He pressed the button and the record started. Perfect timing.

Bobby was all excited and said, 'Did I do that? Did I do that?'

'You certainly did and you were brilliant,' I told him.

Having these kids in the studio that day certainly put a lump in my throat and every time I went to the school after that, wee Bobby would run up to me saying, 'Andy, Andy, how're you doing?' I watched that lad grow up until he left the school. A few years later, I asked the headmistress how Bobby was doing and sadly she told me that he'd got into drugs and died of an overdose. That was such a tragedy and I could have cried the day she told me that.

Another pupil from St Vincent's whom I used to see regularly was Joseph Sheridan. Joseph is deaf, but was a really bright boy when he was at St Vincent's and a great advert for the school. He's grown up, married now and his wife – who is also deaf – signs for the deaf on Tyne Tees Television. When he was younger, Joseph worked in the paper shop I would go to on a Sunday as I made my way to the BBC for the *Sunday Joint* radio show. He was a Celtic fan and if Rangers had got beat the day before, he would be at the counter waiting for me to arrive to give me pelters. If, on the other hand, Celtic got beat, he would stay in the back shop so I couldn't wind him up. I've a lot of time for Joseph and all the staff and pupils at St Vincent's. Anyone who works with handicapped kids is brilliant, as far as I am concerned.

I've always got on well with Celtic players – past and present – and officials at the club. Both Celtic and Rangers management have been great with me over the years and I'll always be grateful for that. In fact, the legendary Celtic doorman, Bill Peacock, was one of my biggest fans. Bill was a stickler for stopping people getting through the main doors of Parkhead if they didn't have a ticket – even the famous faces of football would have to wait outside until a ticket was hurriedly passed to them. It was easier getting into the Masons than Parkhead when Bill was on the door. But I never had any trouble getting into Celtic Park.

The great Jock Stein used to wind me up and say I was the only person who could get into Parkhead without a ticket. When I asked him why he thought that, he said, 'That Bill Peacock, he thinks you're brilliant.' Big Bill would stand guard at the main door with a they-shall-not-pass look on his face. In the late '60s, Celtic had ten players in the Scottish League team which played the League of Ireland at Parkhead. The Scotland team bus rolled up into the car park outside the ground and the players headed for the main entrance.

The Celtic captain at the time, Billy McNeill, went to step through the door and Big Bill asked him for his ticket to get in. 'I'm playing tonight,' said Billy.

'I know,' Bill replied. 'Players have got tickets.'

'But it's me,' says Billy.

'I know it's you, Mr McNeill. But you're not getting in the door without a ticket,' says Bill, as officials quickly got a ticket to the Celtic captain so he could get in and play for Scotland.

On another occasion, Sir Matt Busby, the Manchester United manager, came to Parkhead. 'Good evening, Mr Busby. Can I have your ticket?' asked Bill.

'I haven't got a ticket, Mr Stein knows I'm coming,' said Sir Matt.

'Well, he should have left you a ticket,' replied Bill, who must have been feeling generous because he told Sir Matt to wait outside and he would see if there was a ticket left for him.

Big Bill was well known for stopping people at the door and not letting them in. But I turned up once without a ticket and he told me not to worry, he would go and get me a ticket right away. A minute later, it's, 'There you are, Mr Cameron. Enjoy the game.' He was brilliant with me.

I always got on well with Jock Stein, who was a man who called a spade a spade. He was also a growler, but if you growled back at him he would respect you for it. We used to have some great banter when we would meet up at dinners and football functions.

'I saw you shaking hands and giving the Masonic grip to that guy,' Jock would say to me. 'The two of you were at it for an hour and a half.'

'If that's the case, Jock,' I would reply, 'he's obviously seen me shaking hands with you because the two of you are in the same lodge.'

Big Jock was a giant of a man both in physical and football terms. He knew everything about football, but the players would say he was as tight as two coats of paint – he was a nightmare to get money out of if they wanted more money in their contract.

I've known Billy McNeill since the days I delivered bread for Sunblest to Bellshill and I would visit his pub there after I had finished my run. Billy's mum Nellie ran the pub for him and she ran it with a rod of iron. It was a great man's pub – a quarter-gill shop as we used to call them before the days of metrication. It was also a great pub for dominoes and after my delivery run was finished I would take a loaf and some cakes into the pub for Nellie. While she was making sandwiches and tea, I would do my square up with the day's money and then I would have my tea with Nellie and play dominoes for a couple of hours. Nellie was just like her son Billy because she hated getting beat – even at dominoes!

Nellie was a real character and we became great pals winding each other up about Rangers and Celtic. One day, I was visiting Billy McNeill's dad, Jimmy, who was recovering at home from a heart attack. It was a beautiful sunny day and as I walked up the path of their house the windows were open and I could hear the vacuum cleaner going. Nellie looked out the window and saw me waving to her. The vacuum cleaner was turned off and I could hear her shouting to Jimmy, 'Here's Andy Cameron up to see you. Quick, turn the holy pictures to face the wall.' What a woman.

Another great pal of mine is Lisbon Lion Bobby Lennox. He was a superb footballer and quite a funny guy as well. He's always got a big grin on his face and likes a good laugh. And, like me, Bobby could talk about football for hours. I think that's why we gelled so much, because we both love comedy and football and we play golf together. We always talk about the young football players coming through and who is likely to make it to the big time.

Bobby stays down the Ayrshire coast and one day I phoned him. His wife Catherine answered and, although I hadn't met her at the time, she must have recognised my voice. I heard her shouting, 'Bobby, it's thingmy off the telly for you!' When I eventually met her I introduced myself as thingmy off the telly and she was full of apologies. She didn't need to be because I thought it was a great laugh. Every time I meet her I say, 'Hello, I'm thingmy off the telly,' and she gets embarrassed.

I had a great laugh with another Lisbon Lion, Jimmy Johnstone, when we were making a Rangers Gold video. The scene is a hairdresser's and I'm sitting in the chair getting what's left of my hair cut. The hairdresser asks me how I think Rangers will get on this season and I answer, 'I think they'll win the treble, the Champions League and the Grand National.' The next thing you hear on the video is a voice: 'Aye, that'll be right!' The camera pans round to the seat next to me and Jimmy Johnstone is sitting there with a huge grin on his face.

Another great occasion involving Celtic at a Rangers event was at a dinner to celebrate Rangers being the first team to win 50 League titles. The tributes included video footage on a giant screen of people congratulating the club for this achievement. After a steady stream of diehard Rangers fans appearing on the screen, next up was Brian Quinn, the chairman of Celtic. There were 900 people there and you could hear some of them growling, 'What the f**k's he doing sending a message to us?'

Brian's first words were, 'Hello, hello . . . oh, I wish I hadn't said that.' The whole room just erupted in laughter. His speech was absolutely brilliant. Brian had a wee bit of fun with the Rangers and Celtic rivalry, but finished up on a serious note congratulating Rangers on a great achievement. When it was over, everyone stood up and applauded. They applauded a video of our greatest rival's chairman – magnificent. That's how the Rangers–Celtic rivalry should be – supporting your team, but being able to appreciate each other's achievements.

It was a great gesture on Brian's part. He took the time to do it, and he was complimentary and very funny with it. That was the big talking point that night – the Celtic chairman's video message to Rangers, and I hope it went some way to relieving the intolerance and bigotry we suffer from in the west of Scotland.

Former Celtic player and manager Tommy Burns is as daft about Celtic as I am about Rangers, but we get on really well. I did Tommy's testimonial dinner for him, but that's not the only thing we have in common. We both love singer Bobby Darin and I've given him CDs of singers he's never heard of before.

Tommy's a great singer himself and is never shy to get up with a mike and give the company a song or two. His favourite is 'Mac The Knife'. Last Christmas, Tommy and I were at a pal's do in L'Ariosto's Italian restaurant, in Glasgow, and at the end of the night we were having a sing-song. The keyboard player who had been performing in the restaurant that night was backing us. He happened to have played in a band that used to back me in the clubs. I asked him if he knew any Bobby Darin numbers and he said 'Mac The Knife'. Now, Norma hates that song so I suggested the song 'Beyond the Sea'. So, while everyone is waiting for the taxis to come, Tommy Burns and I are on stage giving it laldy singing 'Beyond the Sea'. Who would have thought there were two Bobby Darins in Glasgow?

I've performed at Celtic dinners, Rangers dinners, testimonials for players both sides of the Old Firm and for players from other clubs as well. In fact, put a plate and a knife and fork down in front of me and I'll do your dinner for you – no matter what colour of football strip your team wears.

Everyone knows I'm Rangers daft, but I've always been well received and appreciated at these dinners because of my willingness to do someone a turn. Another reason I do well at Celtic functions is that, straight away, I declare that I'm a Rangers fan and if Rangers aren't doing well I'll make a few jokes about them and myself. From the very beginning, I knew there was no way I was going to do the 'I'm a Partick Thistle fan' routine and pretend I wasn't a Bluenose. It wouldn't take people long to suss me out if I'd tried that one.

I've always been a Rangers fan and I don't hide that fact. I support Rangers in a balanced way, which means I'm not blind to the other good teams and players that you see at Ibrox or on the television.

I've got two ambitions concerning Rangers. In 1957, Celtic beat us 7–1 and I would like to see Rangers wipe that out with an 8–1 victory over Celtic. My second ambition is to see Rangers win the Champions League before I die. Now, it's very likely I'll have sprouted wings and be in my own blue heaven before that happens. I do a gag about a wee pal of mine who was saving up to go abroad to watch Rangers win the European Cup, but he died a millionaire.

I love all these daft jokes which I tell against Rangers and Celtic. My view is that if you can't take a ribbing, don't give it out. If I was at a Celtic charity dinner and Neil Lennon's boots were up for auction, I would say, 'These boots are authentic, by the way. The blood's still on them.'

And if there was a Celtic football for auction I would say, 'This is the ball Celtic use in training – there's not a mark on it because it's never been kicked.' The fans love all that stuff and they know it's just a bit of fun and there's no malice on my part.

I couldn't go to football if I was a bigot. I can't stand the supporters who are more interested in who is beating their rivals than their own team. They're not really Rangers or Celtic fans – they support anybody who is playing the other side of the Old Firm. I've a pal whose wife is a Celtic supporter and I said to her that she must have been looking forward to the Champions League. She said, 'Yes, I'm looking forward to you lot getting humped.'

'Us getting humped? What about your own team?' I asked.

'I don't care about us,' she replied. 'As long as Rangers get humped.'

I couldn't believe what I was hearing and there are fans like this on both sides of the Old Firm. This woman's got a season ticket and she's telling me she doesn't care how her own team does as long as Rangers get beat. I told her husband he should take the season ticket off her and give it to someone who was really interested in football because she certainly wasn't.

Sure, I would love Rangers to beat Celtic 8–1 in the final of the

Champions League and fulfil my two ambitions in the one night, but that doesn't mean I am going to hate Celtic supporters. Hatred is bigotry and both hatred and bigotry are cancers. It eats away at you and you lose the decency and respect for your fellow man that you should cherish.

Many of my friends are Celtic supporters and even as far back as when I worked with Coca-Cola I would go to the big Celtic European nights with my pal from work, Jimmy McGeachie. I was with Jimmy at Parkhead to see Celtic play Benfica and Tommy Gemmell scored a screamer of a free kick from 25 yards out.

We're standing on the terracing wearing our green Coca-Cola uniforms – well, at least I looked like a Celtic fan that night – when Jimmy turns to me and whispers, 'You'd better jump up and down when we score or I'm telling everybody you're a Hun.' I love all that patter. As it happened, I was up and down like a yo-yo because Celtic won 3–0 and played brilliant football.

Another big game we went to was at Hampden when Celtic played Leeds United. Leeds scored first and Jimmy said, 'Shut your mouth.'

'I never said a word,' I replied.

'I don't want to hear a word out of you,' he said again.

The guy standing behind us said, 'You must be a Bluenose, then. Your pal's just told everybody you're a Bluenose.' Everybody was laughing about it and the guy asked if I had a bet on for Leeds to win. I told him I didn't bet and, in any case, I hoped that Celtic would win and get to another European final. Got away with it again.

I didn't go to all the Celtic European games because the better known I became, the more chance of some Celtic fans giving me a bit of verbal grief. Anyway, nowadays you can see the big games live on television and I take the view that if I go to see Celtic in a big European tie I'm depriving a Celtic fan of the chance to see his or her team on a special night for their club.

I can just hear the shout: 'What are you doing here ya Orange b*****d? My brother-in-law couldn't get a ticket and you're not even a Celtic fan.' I can understand how that could cause anger and frustration because tickets for the big European nights at Parkhead and Ibrox are in great demand.

It's not just some sections of the Celtic support that would give me a hard time for going to Parkhead. There are some Rangers fans who take exception to me watching Celtic. Some of the Rangers fanzines go on about, 'How can you stand amongst these people?' I wonder sometimes what kind of people make all this stuff up.

I was at a Parkhead game once and a guy near me started shouting, 'What are you doing here, Cameron? You're a f*****g bigot.' I told him I'd got a big washing done that morning and I was entitled to go to the football in the afternoon. Another Celtic fan gave the guy a right ear-bashing and told him to shut his mouth since I was there to watch a football match like everybody else.

Another time, I was at Ibrox and a Rangers fan suggested I should be at Parkhead since I was never away from there. Guys like that should take a good look at themselves.

The Celtic supporters I am friendly with enjoy the banter of the Old Firm rivalry just like I do, but that's as far as it goes. We wind each other up, but I would trust some of them with my life. Some of the patter they come away with is excellent. I was on holiday in South Africa when Celtic beat Rangers in the Scottish Cup semi-final in 2004. I got a text from some my pals which read, 'You're gonnae win f**k all. Only kidding, wee man. They're bringing back the Tennent's Sixes.'

Celtic have always been the big rival to Rangers in football – and that's what people should remember – it's football. It doesn't help when the media use words and phrases like 'enemies', 'it's a war' and 'Old Firm battles' when they are talking about a game of football. People die in battles and wars and they are fought with weapons, which can kill and maim. With football we're talking about 22 guys running round a park chasing a white ball and trying to put it between two planks of wood stuck into the ground with a crossbar on top.

Rangers and Celtic fans aren't enemies and they don't fight wars against each other. We're rivals and competitors and one team is trying to beat the other by scoring goals, not launching rockets and grenades at each other to win. The more the media write and broadcast these inflammatory and over-the-top words and phrases, the more people will believe it.

Celtic have a great history and have had great victories. So have Rangers. Now, that's worth talking about, but fighting over it or hating someone because they support the other team is certainly not worth it. I love football because I think it is the greatest game in the world and it's nonsense for people to think they can't say so-and-so is a great player because he plays for the other side of the Old Firm.

There's nothing wrong with supporting your team and wanting them to beat your rivals. I want Rangers to win every game and I want them to beat Celtic, but I don't hate Celtic or Celtic fans and I think that would probably go for the majority of supporters from both sides.

The rivalry between the two sides can be very entertaining and can give you a laugh. Going back a few years, I always appreciated the Celtic fans who made up the parody of the Manfred Mann hit, 'The Mighty Quinn' and had The Jungle singing, 'You ain't seen nothing like the mighty Tims.' When Celtic were on their UEFA Cup run, the Celtic fans brought beach balls to Ibrox and that gave folk a laugh. And when they got beat, Rangers fans replied by wearing police helmets and singing about watching *The Bill* on television. Now all that kind of stuff from both sets of supporters is inventive and it's very clever and that's the way football rivalry should be.

Look at what happened when tragedy struck and Davie Cooper died of an aneurysm when he was only 39. The gates at Ibrox were covered with tributes including many green and white Celtic tops with messages like, 'You'll be sadly missed – a Celtic fan.' It's genuine football fans and good people who would do something like that.

Anyway, I'm not so sure it's as bad as people make out these days. And it's certainly not as bad as it was 50 years ago. If you have a Rangers–Celtic cup final at Hampden, the place will be packed with Rangers fans at one end and Celtic supporters at the other. It's likely everybody will have a relative, pal or workmate sitting at the other side of the ground. There's still the problem of bigotry surrounding the Old Firm, but we've got to break that down and we are making progress. Historically, the Catholic–Protestant/ Celtic–Rangers divide has been used by big business and the establishment to divide and conquer. It's also in the media's interest to have stories about strife and division. It increases circulation and is good business for the newspapers.

I would go along with the theory that the bigotry between Catholics and Protestants keeps the working class divided and is political. Keep the working class at each other's throats and they'll never come together and make a better life for themselves by challenging the establishment. But what has been happening over the last 40 years is that church attendances and membership of the Orange Order have been diminishing dramatically. I believe people are becoming less extreme and more middle of the road, which is a good thing.

My daughter Ellen is probably more Rangers daft than me, and three of her pals at work are Celtic supporters. They couldn't get tickets for the UEFA Cup final in Seville in 2003, so Ellen decided she would have a party at her house and they would watch the game together. Ellen had banners up in her lounge for them coming: stuff like 'Hail, Hail, the Celts are here' and Celtic rosettes. Ellen didn't care if Celtic won or lost. All she was interested in was having a good time and making sure her pals enjoyed themselves and if that meant Celtic winning, that was fine by her. As it happened, Celtic didn't win, but by all accounts the girls had themselves a good party.

Ellen's husband Denis – who is an Everton fan from Liverpool – came over to my house to watch the game. When he arrived he said, 'What's going on in my house just now would never happen back home in Liverpool. If it was Liverpool in the Cup final, I'd be in Blackpool having a donkey ride on the beach just to get away from the television and the game.'

Denis admitted that when he first came to Glasgow he thought the Rangers and Celtic fans would be murdering each other every second weekend. 'The Rangers and Celtic fans are actually better to each other than what goes on between Liverpool and Everton supporters,' he said. 'My father told me that if I ever wanted to bring a Liverpool fan into the house I wasn't to bother, he could wait outside.'

After listening to Denis's story, maybe we're not as bad up here as some folk would make out.

Chapter 16

STARS IN MY EYES

I HATE NAME-DROPPERS, AND I WAS JUST SAYING THAT VERY THING TO HER Majesty the Queen the other day. Only kidding, folks!

I do have a dislike for people who constantly go on about meeting this famous person or that famous person just to show off and pretend they're better than the rest of us. However, that's certainly not my motive here, and I hope you'll forgive me if I tell you a few tales about the famous people I've had the privilege to meet.

During my years as an entertainer, I have met several members of the Royal Family, but contrary to what a lot of people might say, I haven't met Queen Victoria – I'm only 64 for goodness' sake!

I appeared in the Scottish Variety Performance in 1983, at the King's Theatre in Glasgow, and afterwards I met Prince Charles and Lady Diana. Jimmy Logan produced the show and Hector Nicol was on the bill. Now, anyone who has heard Hector will know some of his act can be a bit risqué to say the least and everyone was a bit nervous about what he was going to come out with in front of Charles and Di.

But he was brilliant, and not a word or joke was out of place. He dropped all the risqué stuff and still had everyone, including Prince Charles, in stitches. I was standing in the wings and he was so good I had to bite the tabs to stop myself laughing out loud. He was coming away with fantastic one-liners like, 'Never make love on a stretcher because you're liable to get carried away.'

I was watching the reaction of Charles and Di and they were loving it. After the show, when the Royal couple met the performers, Charles said to Hector, 'I wrote down a couple of your gags – they were gems.'

In my act, I had told the joke about the Queen and the Pope at an Old Firm match when, to please the Celtic half of the crowd, the Pope stands up and waves to them. Huge cheer from the Celtic end. The Queen tells the Pope she is most impressed, and asks if one would mind if one does something to get the Rangers end cheering. The Pope says no, so she sticks the head on him.

Because Charles and Di are there I change the characters in the gag to Glasgow's Lord Provost at the time and a great Celtic fan and me. When I met Charles he asked me if I head-butt anybody who disagrees with me. I assured him I don't. In any case, I'm that wee I probably wouldn't reach far enough up to stick the head on anyone.

I also met the Queen when she visited the set of *High Road* and I met Prince Philip when I presented the Duke of Edinburgh Awards. The other Royal I met was Prince Edward when he visited St Pius School in Drumchapel, Glasgow, in 1990. I interviewed him for my *Sunday Joint* radio show on the BBC.

I am pretty middle-of-the-road on most things and although I have always admired the Queen I wouldn't say I was a monarchist. I can see the argument against the monarchy and I would probably agree with the argument, but I think the monarchy works well in this country. Just look at the money and jobs that tourists bring to this country when they come to see the pomp and ceremony that surrounds the Royal Family.

I've known the former Rangers player and now manager of Manchester United, Alex Ferguson – I suppose I should refer to him now as Sir Alex – for many years. He's a Govan boy and despite his reputation for gruffness and having a temper in the dressing-room he can raise a laugh with his sharp wit. I remember I was doing a 20-minute spot at the ceremony where Fergie was being presented with the Freedom of Glasgow award in 1999. The presentation was in the City Chambers and after the speech from the Lord Provost it was Fergie's turn to say a few words. The council member of staff who wears the red jacket and bow tie handed Fergie the mike and everyone held their breath to hear some pearls of wisdom from the great man.

Fergie cleared his throat, held the mike in front of him and burst into song, 'Moon River, wider than a mile . . .' Absolutely brilliant and everyone fell about laughing.

Talking about awards, the following year I was back in the City Chambers to be presented with Glasgow's Loving Cup, which was a great honour for me.

Anyway, back to Fergie. Any time I was in Aberdeen doing shows during Fergie's reign as manager there, I would call into Pittodrie to visit him and his assistant, Archie Knox. He would send me into the dressing-room to wind the players up and the place was full of guys like Alex McLeish, Willie Miller and Gordon Strachan. We would have some great banter and the woman in the kitchen made great soup and stovies, which I would devour with delight.

Fergie and Archie Knox would also have games of heady-tennis in the afternoon and you would think they were playing in the Scottish Cup final the way they went on. Talk about being competitive. One of the times I was up visiting them, Fergie asked me to referee their heady-tennis match. They played first to reach nine is the winner and it was 8–8 when Archie headed the ball over the net and it landed just inside the line. 'That's it,' I said. 'Archie's the winner.'

'No, he's no',' said Fergie. 'That was out. The ball was over the line.'

'It was inside,' I assured him. 'The ball was inside the line.'

'Right, you get tae f**k,' says Fergie, raging that I've called the point to Archie. 'Don't you come back. You're not getting soup or stovies here ever again.'

He almost physically threw me out of Pittodrie that day and I still kid him on about it. I used to phone him up and say, 'Can I come back now?'

Irish comedian Frank Carson is a very good friend and if I could ever get a word in edgeways with him I would tell him that. They say that Irish folk have the blarney. Well, Frank has more than most. That man can talk for Ireland. He'll phone you and once he's started he'll go on for hours. You can put the phone down, make a cup of tea and by the time you lift the receiver again he still won't have a clue you haven't been listening.

Having said that, he does a huge amount of work for charity and once he invited a host of comics over to Ireland to play some clubs and take part in a golf match. At that time, he was trying to raise £35,000 to buy a machine that removes birthmarks from children's faces. In one weekend, we raised £123,000 and had a great time to ourselves into the bargain.

That weekend we had Stan Boardman, Norman Collier, Lee Wilson, Frank and myself doing clubs from both sides of the divide. We were on the private bus we had to take us around and just before we reached the Rialto cinema in Londonderry, Frank stopped the bus and shouted me to the front. 'Get off the bus and stand out there,' he said.

'What for?' I asked.

'So you can tell all your pals back in Glasgow that you've stood on Derry's Walls,' he said.

'You behave yourself,' I told him. 'Folk will think I'm a bigot if you start all that patter.'

By that time, I had abandoned my football hooligan outfit for a football strip that was half Celtic and half Rangers. The crowd that night was mostly Celtic fans, but there were a few Rangers supporters there as well. As soon as I hit the stage with the Rangers–Celtic strip on they were howling with laughter. I said to the audience, 'I've got to find out how many of one side are in and how many of the other. When I point to the Celtic strip all the Celtic fans cheer – you'll notice I don't touch it – and when I caress the Rangers side all the Rangers fans cheer.' It went down a storm and everyone had a great night. I was telling jokes about being on the golf course in Ireland and hitting a tee shot into the trees. I turned to the caddy and say, 'I think I'll hit a provisional.'

And he replies: 'That's not a good idea over here.'

Frank had organised a game of golf for us all at Ballybunion

Golf Club, in County Kerry. All day, I had been slicing my tee shots and there I was at the 16th, with the Atlantic Ocean all the way down the right-hand side of me. If I sliced the shot, I was in real trouble. The wee caddy I was with handed me my driver and said, 'There you are, Mr Cameron. You've got the whole of Ireland on your left – try to f*****g hit it!' What a great line.

Any time Frank comes over to Glasgow we'll meet up for a drink, or a coffee and a chat. That is, as I've said, if I can get a word in edgeways.

Probably in the entertainment world my closest friend is Dougie Donnelly, who presents the sports programmes on the BBC. He is a magnificent professional and spends hours preparing for each broadcast. I remember when he was sent to commentate on the beach volleyball in the Olympics and I was wondering how on earth anyone would know about that. Before he went there, Dougie spent hours watching beach volleyball videos so he would know everything about the game.

A lot of misinformed people say that Dougie is a Rangers man, but I can tell you he is a fanatical Clyde supporter: so much so, he has shares in Clyde. A few years ago, Clyde were playing Rangers in the Scottish Cup and with 20 minutes to go, Clyde were winning 1–0. A few minutes after Clyde scored, they then hit the bar and one of their players missed a sitter. But in the last 12 minutes, Rangers moved up a gear and scored four goals to win 4–1.

I had arranged to meet Dougie in the directors' room after the game and when I saw him I said, 'That was a tight one.'

'F**k off,' Dougie replied. 'You're only in here to gloat.'

I said, 'Don't talk to me like that. I'm just saying it was a tight game.' After that, we just glared at each other.

Dougie, like me, is very competitive and hates to get beat. He was obviously raging that Clyde lost after being one up so close to the end of the game. But the next day we were on the phone to each other having a laugh at our mini boardroom bust-up.

When we play each other at golf, there's no quarter asked or given. I've beaten him a few times and he's beaten me – it's a real ding-dong battle.

All in all, Dougie's a terrific guy and he's the main organiser of the infamous Bad Boys' Lunches. We call it a lunch, but we meet up about 3 p.m., have a few drinks, eat at about 6 p.m. and spend the rest of the night in various hostelries downing Brandy Alexander cocktails and having a chat, or sometimes a heated discussion, telling jokes or just winding each other up.

Those who attend our Bad Boys' Lunches are usually from the football world and the media. Derek Forbes, who plays bass with Simple Minds, and I are the only ones from the entertainment world. The regulars are Derek, ex-Rangers players Ally McCoist and Ian Durrant, Dougie Donnelly, football pundits Gordon Smith and Murdo McLeod, former Rangers manager Walter Smith and his assistant Archie Knox, and journalists Jim Traynor and Crawford Brankin.

The Bad Boys' Lunches take place whenever we can get a group of us together, maybe once every six weeks, and you can have half-a-dozen guys there or sometimes double that amount. We call it the Bad Boys' Lunch because we drink too much, but to be fair we always get taxis home and the only damage done is to each other's egos as everyone slags each other off. Of course, the next morning is never very clever with the hangover.

At the end of one of our lunches, we had retired to a bar for a few refreshments before we all headed home and Derek Forbes said he was going outside for some fresh air. I went out with him to make sure he was OK and he assured me he would be back in. Forty minutes later, there was still no sign of Derek, so Coisty was dispatched to find him. Derek was nowhere to be seen and we assumed he had jumped in a taxi and made his way home to Balfron, between Glasgow and Stirling.

The next morning, Dougie Donnelly phoned me and asked if I'd heard about Derek. I said no and he told me that Derek – having had more than a couple of shandies – decided he would walk the 16 miles home. At a quarter to eight in the morning, Derek had phoned his wife and asked her to come and pick him up as he'd been walking all night and had just reached Strathblane.

I met Hollywood star Robert Duvall when I made my one and only appearance in a film. He was in Scotland researching for his part in the film about a small-time Scottish football team, *A Shot*

At Glory, starring none other than Ally McCoist. I had been asked to lunch with Robert Duvall – or Bob as I call him (did you hear that name hit the floor?) – so he could hear all my football stories. He was desperate to get the atmosphere of Scottish football from the insider's perspective and he must have spoken to dozens of players and ex-players.

We met for lunch in the Glasgow Hilton Hotel and I was telling him all about Andy Bain and his artificial leg and how he had only ever missed a handful of Rangers' matches in his life. I threw in a few of my other gags too, for good measure, and from this conversation, Bob told me that he wanted me in his film, playing myself.

So that's how I ended up in *A Shot At Glory*, standing at a bar, telling two guys a joke. My part lasted about 30 seconds and I was on the set one day from 8 a.m. to 11 p.m. It was great experience and I met Bob a few times during filming. For a guy of 70, it was outstanding how he got involved and immersed himself in the part he was playing – he was a real gentlemen as well.

Now, how about this for a bad deal. I'm spending my night telling gags in a bingo hall in Possil, Glasgow when at the same time, none other than James Bond 007 himself, Sean Connery, is escorting Norma to dinner in a posh hotel.

That's what happened in August 1994 when I was asked to take part in a celebrity pro-am at Prestwick Golf Club for the Malcolm Sargent Cancer Fund for Children, who have a house in the Ayrshire coastal town for children with cancer. The other celebrities playing in the event were Sean Connery, Kenny Dalglish, former Scots rugby international Gordon Brown – who sadly, is no longer with us – snooker players Alan McManus and Stephen Hendry and motor-racing legend Jackie Stewart.

I was delighted to take part in the event, even though I was already booked to do a spot at the bingo hall in Possil the same night. Norma and the kids were also invited to stay overnight at the Marine Hotel, in Troon, so I came down with them on the Saturday afternoon and headed up to Glasgow for the gig at night. As soon as the gig was finished, I headed back down the coast to Troon and met up with everyone again.

While I was getting ready to head for Glasgow, there was a phone call for Norma telling her to be ready for dinner at 7.45 p.m. I kissed her goodbye and the next time I saw Norma she was sitting at dinner beside Sean Connery having a whale of a time. Apparently, there was a knock on her door exactly on 7.45 p.m. and standing there waiting to escort her to dinner was 007.

When I arrived back at the hotel, I sat with everyone and had a great night with a few drinks, listening to Gordon Brown who was on good form with his stories. Sean Connery asked me where I'd been and I had to tell him I was at the bingo in Possil.

On the Sunday, we played the tournament and then went to the Malcolm Sargent House and spent a few hours with the kids. I've met Sean Connery a few times when he's been at Ibrox with David Murray and he's very easy to get on with. 'Sit down here,' he'll say. 'Tell me what's been happening since I've been away.'

Jackie Stewart is another fascinating man. He is so sharp, yet when he speaks he speaks slowly as if he can't quite remember what he's going to say. But he knows exactly what he's going to say and he's made millions in business. In terms of being a sharp cookie, he's the tops, and he's a great ambassador for Scotland.

I don't see as much of Billy Connolly as I would like to, but he is one of the comic geniuses of our age. It's amazing how he can go on a stage with just the basic idea of what he is going to say, but manages to meander all over the place and get howls of laughter talking about anything and everything but the subject he started on. Billy's a victim of the terrible Scots trait of let's build him up and then knock him down.

Norma was eight months pregnant with our Elliott when she met Billy at Alan Rough's testimonial dinner. And I've no doubt it was because she laughed so much at Billy's patter that she gave birth two or three weeks early. Norma was at his table when The Big Yin told this amazing story about the wee woman and her Morphy Richards toaster. Now I can tell it in a few paragraphs, but Billy managed to spin it out for about 15 minutes.

The gist of the story is that Billy is in a pub in London and a wee Glasgow woman comes in and says, 'You're that Billy Connolly guy.'

'That's right,' says Billy. 'So I am.'

'Do you have one of these Morphy Richards toasters?' she asked.

'I've got a toaster,' says Billy. 'But I don't know what kind it is.'

'Well, you be careful if it's a Morphy Richards toaster like mine. It's supposed to pop the toast up, but it doesn't,' she revealed.

The woman continued: 'My man comes in at night with a wee drink in him and he always likes to put a couple of crumpets in the toaster to go with a cup of tea. But they never pop up when they should. In fact, last week he had a bit more drink than usual, and decided to put some jam on the crumpets before putting them in the toaster.

'Of course, they didn't pop up and before long there's a smell of burning coming from them. My daft man thinks he'd better get them out so he stabs a knife into the toaster to get the crumpets out. And see that toaster that never pops up, well, it popped up all right that night. It popped my man right across the f*****g kitchen and against the wall.'

Norma was literally sliding down the seat laughing at Billy and her mascara was running down her cheeks – she was like a Panda. I really think he is a king of comedy.

Chapter 17

THE BEST OF FRIENDS

WE'RE SITTING IN THE HOTEL BAR LAUGHING OUR HEADS OFF WAITING FOR the phone call. Sure enough, the barman calls over to our group: 'Is there a Mr Cameron at this table?'

'That's me,' I said.

'There's a phone call for you, sir.'

I knew fine well there would be a phone call and who it would be from. I strolled over to the bar and put the receiver to my ear. 'Come up here and give me my leg back, ya bastard!' the voice roared down the phone.

I could hardly talk for laughing and I looked over to the table where the lads were sitting and pointed to the phone. 'It's him and he's raging. We better go up to his room.'

It was the culmination of yet another wind-up between our band of Rangers' supporters travelling all over the Continent watching our Ibrox heroes on another European adventure. This time it was the legendary Rangers fan, Andy Bain, who was at the receiving end of a prank – and not before time. He's a real wind-up merchant himself and we've all been on the receiving end. On this occasion, Andy, who's 78 years old now, had gone for a shower and we had put his artificial leg on top of the wardrobe where he couldn't reach it.

I take Andy to watch Rangers, not only all over Scotland, but to

Europe as well and that artificial leg of his has appeared overnight in hotel foyers standing in the middle of the floor with a shoe and sock on the end of it and flowers sticking out the top.

Would you believe that Andy's leg has also got us into car parks at football grounds? A big policeman or a car-park attendant would stop the car and say we can't get in. I would roll the window down and say, 'My friend here only has the one leg. He lost it in the war and if it wasn't for him you would be speaking German.'

It works every time. They just laugh and wave us through asking me if I think I'm some sort of comedian.

Another great Andy Bain story was when we were going to see Rangers play Cologne in 1983 and we had been staying in Amsterdam for a few days sightseeing before getting a bus there. We were heading for Cologne along the autobahn with signposts flashing by when suddenly Andy shouted, 'F**k me! Look at that.'

'What is it?' I asked.

'There's a sign for Gelsenkirchen. That's where I lost my leg during the war,' said Andy. And one of the guys on the other side of the bus asked him, 'Do you want us to stop and look for it?'

I got a great routine for my act out of that trip. It's all about Andy going back to Germany and us trying to get into a club for a few drinks. Rangers got beat 5–0 and we didn't want to go into the centre of Cologne in case there was any trouble between the rival supporters. So we jumped into a taxi and asked the driver to take us to a club. He dropped us off at the Cologne Disabled Ex-servicemen's Social Club.

When we got to the door there was a guy there and we told him we were over from Scotland for the football. He said, 'Nein, nein.' And I said to him that when we left it was only 5–0.

'You are not welcome here,' he says. 'My brother Franz lost his left eye fighting the Black Watch; my other brother lost both legs fighting the HLI [Highland Light Infantry] – his name is Hans – and I lost an arm in a battle with the Argyll and Sutherland Highlanders. So you are not welcome in here.'

At that, Andy tells him, 'Well, just f**k off then. If it wasn't for us, you wouldn't have a social club.'

When I was a wee boy, my Uncle Joe would say he was going to make me as good a Rangers supporter as Andy Bain. You see, in the '50s, Andy was a real hard, hard man and was one of the leaders of the Billy Boys gang at Bridgeton, in Glasgow. He was a great fighter in his early teens and had the nickname Biff Bain. He is Rangers daft, sees football through blue-tinted glasses and has only missed a handful of Rangers games in the past 30 years. Folklore about the Billy Boys and Andy has grown up over the years and sometimes the legend is somewhat of an exaggeration of the truth. Some people say Andy would have hit you just because you were a Celtic supporter, but they couldn't be more wrong.

In fact, his father and his brother were Celtic supporters and his two sons married sisters who are season ticket holders at Parkhead and he loves these two girls. Because I've got a few contacts in football, Andy's always on at me to get tickets for the girls to watch Celtic if they can't get hold of any themselves.

Andy was at a party one night and some of the boys wanted to start singing 'The Sash'. Andy put them out the door – and it wasn't even his house – telling them there were people there who would be offended and there would be no Orange songs being sung that night.

I've known Andy for 30 years, but before I actually met him at a Masonic meeting, my Uncle Joe would tell me stories about him. I've nothing but admiration for Andy's courage and determination to get on with life after a mortar bomb blew off his leg when he was just 18. He's run pubs for years, made a good living and brought up a family. He would stand at Bridgeton Toll and was nicknamed Sticky Bain because he had to use a walking stick.

Andy is terrible for winding up my son Spencer and me on the way back from the football. We would be sitting in the car talking about the game and out of the blue he would turn to Spencer and say, 'I think you're talking a load of crap about your old man. I'm sure he's going to give you money to go out tonight. I mean, look at him. He's happy his team's won and you're saying he's a miserable old bastard and I don't think he's like that at all.' He's brilliant at that kind of stuff.

Andy is a great friend of mine and he's often come with me to shows up north and kept me company on the long drive back home. He's a great character and it's a privilege to be able to call him a friend.

Another Rangers-daft friend of mine – who is now no longer with us – was George Mulholland, who emigrated to Canada. He was a really funny guy with a sharp wit and a rapid riposte to anything you would say to him. He must have got this from his father because he told the story about making a surprise visit to his parents back home after being in Canada for seven years.

He comes into the house and his father's sitting reading the paper. 'Oh, you're home,' says the old man and carries on reading. The mother asks, 'You must be missing things like a good fish supper. Will I get you one for your tea?'

'No, thanks,' says Mulholland. 'But I'd love a glass of tap water. The water over there is terrible.'

He finishes the glass and his mother asks if he enjoyed it. 'It was a bit warm,' he says. And his father looks over the top of the paper and says, 'So would you be if you had just run all the way from Loch Katrine!' It's certainly a case of like father like son with Mulholland.

When my first son, Elliott, was born I phoned Mulholland in Canada to let him know Norma and the baby were fine. 'That's brilliant. You must be delighted,' he says. 'What are you going to call him?'

'Elliott,' I said.

'Hold on a minute, this is a really bad line. It sounded like you said you were calling him Elliott.'

About two-and-a-half years later, Mulholland comes home and I pick him up at Prestwick and drive him to my house in Thorntonhall. In the house he's got Elliott on his knee and Elliott starts crying. 'Don't greet at me,' Mulholland tells him. 'It was him that called you Elliott.'

Mulholland was a larger-than-life character and in the '60s he would regularly spend a fortune flying home on a Friday to see Rangers play on the Saturday and get back to Canada on the Sunday for his job as a welder. It was his predilection for such trips that led to the break-up of his marriage. His wife was giving him a hard time about always flying to Scotland to watch Rangers and he desperately wanted to see Rangers play Celtic in the 1969 Scottish Cup final. So he hatched a plan that involved telling her a few weekends beforehand that he was going fishing with a pal, George McGeachie.

He never actually went fishing – he just stayed in his pal's house drinking beer and watching television. George would come home with his weekend's catch and Mulholland would take a few fish home to the wife and tell her he'd caught them. All this was to set the scene for him disappearing out of the country for the cup final and to make his wife think he was away fishing again.

When the Cup final weekend arrived, Mulholland pretended he was away fishing again, but instead headed for the airport and a flight to Glasgow. When he got back home on the Sunday night the wife was waiting for him. 'Did you catch anything?' she asked.

'I caught two crackers,' he said. And showed her two fish he'd picked up from George McGeachie's house on the way from the airport.

'No, the biggest one you caught was me. My mother saw you on Argyle Street on Saturday morning. You were back in Scotland watching the football again,' she replied.

Mulholland got away with it for the time being, though, when he pointed at the fish and asked her how he could be catching these fish and watching football in Glasgow at the same time. Straight afterwards, he was working on an oil pipeline in Alaska and was away from home all week. When he got back to Toronto on the Friday the wife's suitcases were on the front porch and she was leaving him. She was standing with a Glasgow bus ticket in her hand dated the previous Saturday. 'Did you get a Glasgow bus to the fishing?' she asked him. Mulholland had put the ticket in the top pocket of his jacket and that's where she'd found it. That was it all over and the next thing they're divorced. A few years later, when she's getting remarried, he gets an invitation to the wedding and there are two boxes at the bottom for you to indicate whether or not you're coming to the wedding. Mulholland scored them out and wrote, 'I was at one of your weddings before and didn't fancy it much.' He put the invitation in an envelope and sent it back to her.

On his way back from that fateful Cup final, Mulholland was sitting beside film star Charlton Heston on the plane. He offered Heston a drink and they spent the whole flight chatting away and having a bevvy. As the plane started its descent into Toronto, the actor suggested they meet up where he was staying and continue the session.

Mulholland told him he had to go and see someone before he went home and Heston said, 'If he's a friend of yours, he's welcome to join us.'

'I don't know if he'd do that,' says Mulholland. 'He had a £50 bet on Stephen Boyd to beat you in that chariot race in *Ben Hur*.' I just love characters like Mulholland.

Jim Cullen is a big, big Celtic fan, and he's also one of my closest friends. I met him about 12 years ago at my golf club, Cathkin Braes. We hit it off immediately and we have a great line in Celtic–Rangers banter. I got him tickets to see Celtic play in the UEFA Cup final in Seville a couple of seasons ago and I was delighted to be able to do that because he loves Celtic.

We have a very strong friendship and we play a lot of golf together. Every Tuesday, we play at Cathkin Braes and I'm the token Hun in our group, who are all Celtic fans except me. There's Jim, Davie Riley, big David Johnstone, Eric McDermott, Joe Gillan and Tommy Keiran.

I really look forward to my Tuesday golf outings because the patter and wind-ups between the guys are great. We each put a tenner in a pot before we tee off and the winner takes the money at the end of the round. You never go home with all the cash because back at the clubhouse you buy the drinks from your winnings.

Jim ran The Montrose pub, in Carrick Street, Glasgow, and I've spent many an enjoyable Friday afternoon in there, having a laugh with his customers. I've even helped out serving the meals when the place got busy. I had a running contest with one of his regulars, Bob Pollok, who always tried to catch me out with a joke I hadn't heard before. It started one day when he said he had a joke for me and I said if I knew it I'd interrupt him and finish it. Bob said if he told me a joke I hadn't heard I was to buy him a pint of Guinness.

I agreed as long as any time I could finish the joke he started, he would put money into a charity bottle. We had more than £100 in the bottle before he gave up.

Jim learned the pub trade and his great patter from his father, Jimmy, who used to run the Prince Charlie Bar near Parkhead Cross, in Glasgow. Even when he was dying of cancer, old Jimmy would have a laugh in the face of that terrible disease. For some reason, he had to have his teeth pulled out. I asked him how he was after getting the teeth pulled and he said they had a problem with one of the teeth and the dentist had his foot on his chest for 45 minutes trying to get it out.

'It must have been a long one,' I said.

'Long one?' Jimmy said. 'When they eventually got it out it had a verruca on it.'

Even when Jimmy hadn't got long to go, he was still making wisecracks. His sons, Jim and Bill, were talking to him about what he wanted done to sort out his affairs and old Jimmy told them to check all his jacket pockets because he had money in all of them.

'That'll get a drink for everyone at my funeral,' he told them. 'And I want a decent coffin. I don't want one of those £300 ones because your arse is out of them in a fortnight and by the end of the month you're in the Clyde.'

Jim Cullen and I are great pals and we will always be close.

Another great pal of mine, who sadly is no longer with us, was sportswriter Jim Blair, who was known within newspaper circles as Sundance. He worked at the *Evening Times* and then at the *Daily Record* and was one of the funniest writers I've known. We would spend many a happy hour in what was known as Dick's Bar, in the west end of Argyle Street in Glasgow, talking about football. Sundance always brought an air of joviality to any proceedings.

There was one night Norma and I were having a few – well, more than a few – refreshments with Jim and his wife Carol. We were in their flat, which was the top flat in a tenement, in Garrioch Road, Glasgow. Carol had one of those Paddington Bears standing at the fireplace, but Jim really hated it and he called it Paddington Blair.

We were having a great time laughing and joking when

suddenly Jim got up out of his seat, grabbed Paddington Bear and said, 'It's time for your flying lesson.' He opened a window and threw the bear out and down to the gardens below.

I had a good drink in me and I said, 'Here, that's a right liberty what you've done.' I decided to rescue Paddington and I dashed out the door and ran down the four flights of stairs with Jim at my heels. We were rolling about the bushes as Jim tried to grab Paddington out of my grasp, but eventually I got free and ran up the stairs. When I got back into the house I stood in front of Carol, saluted her and said, 'Paddington is safely returned.'

I woke up the next morning covered in scratches from my wrestling match with Jim in the bushes. It was a Saturday and I was standing outside Ibrox and a taxi driver called Jim Jardine came up to me and said, 'What were you up to last night in a garden at Garrioch Road? I was passing and I saw you rolling about the bushes with a guy at half one in the morning. I was about to jump out the cab and help you, when I saw you running up the close with something tucked under your arm.' He had a right laugh when I told him what had happened.

But that escapade was just typical Jim Blair. We were very close and like me he was a socialist by nature and had a wee fancy for Rangers. Not many people know this, but Jim's ashes are buried behind the goals at the Copeland Road end of Ibrox.

One of my longest and dearest friendships is with George Dunn and his wife Sophie. I started school with George and we're as much friends now as we were then, all those years ago. George – or, as I like to call him, The Quiet Man – was also in the Life Boys and Boys Brigade with me so there's a strong bond between us. I've known Sophie even longer and they are really good friends to me.

I can go to George's and Sophie's house, have a coffee with them and give them all the worries of my world and I know it won't go any further. Being able to get things off my chest is great and they can do the same with me. There's nothing better than phoning up a friend to share a problem with or to share good news and a celebration.

I've a great admiration for George because as a teenager he was able to apply himself to his studies and while I was out playing football or going to the dancing or the ice skating, George was at home studying. He worked really hard to get his Highers and he ended up with a good job as a systems analyst with Rolls-Royce.

George was the guy who described his life as up, work, home, tea, telly and bed and sometimes he would comment on what a great life I had in show business. I've told him that it's not as glamorous as he thinks. I would have gone to a club and sat there at 7 p.m. waiting to go on at 10 p.m. and when the gig was finished have to drive home. Sometimes, the show would go well and you'd be on a high, but other times the audience would be full of the drink and give you a hard time. Then you're driving home wondering if you should chuck it and see if there are any vacancies for bus drivers.

George has got brains and he worked really hard to make good use of them. But the other thing about George is that he's an awful man for getting me to make dedications on the radio for people he knows. I'd be in his house and he'd say he was talking to so-and-so and his mother-in-law is 87, any chance of giving her a wee mention.

I'd say no problem, right, where's the pen and paper and when I was on air I would say, 'Here's another dedication from the George Dunn Agency.'

Maureen Harte – who sang backing vocals on 'Ally's Tartan Army' – was another very good friend of mine and sadly she succumbed to leukaemia and is no longer with us. Harte was her stage name, as her real name was Maureen O'Hara. Her granddad was an old-time entertainer called Willie O'Leary who used to perform round the picture house queues. He would put a breadboard on the ground, spread sand on the top and then dance on top of the breadboard.

Maureen and her husband Ricky Fillingham were part of Willie's concert party and one night old Willie dropped dead on stage at the Columba Club, in Barrhead. Maureen and Ricky decided to go out on their own and they called themselves Cheeky B. A few months later, they were in a social club in Fife when they asked the comic there where he was playing the next night.

'I'm at the Columba Club, in Barrhead,' he said.

'My granddad died there,' says Maureen.

'Well, tell him not to worry,' says the comic. 'I've died there as well – they can be a real tough audience.'

I was in the middle of a family holiday in Jersey when we got the news that Maureen had died. I was distraught and flew back to Glasgow for the funeral. She was a lovely person and a great performer.

Although football is my number one sport, I'm also passionate about golf and that has led to many good friendships over the years. I was a late starter playing golf and didn't pick up a set of clubs until I was 40. I had told a few folk I fancied taking up golf and I was told not to rush into things and head for the golf course only to embarrass myself, but to take a few lessons from a professional. And, by the way, the wee guy at Cathkin Braes is a good teacher.

So, it was off to Cathkin Braes Golf Club in search of the club pro, Stevie Bree. I may not have been hitting the golf ball so well at first, but Stevie and I really hit it off personally right away. My handicap is 12 now and that's down to Stevie, who not only taught me how to hit a ball, but to have the proper attitude to the game as well. He's another Celtic fan and a good source of tickets for the big games if I'm trying to get briefs for people. I see him as often as I can and we go to each other's houses for dinner.

A few years ago, he stood up at a Cathkin Braes prize-giving and said it was great to see Andy Cameron here because he's worked hard and got his handicap down to 18.

'It wasn't easy for him,' said Stevie. 'Because he's the only guy who could write Merry Christmas with his backswing.'

He's another one who thinks he's a right comedian, because when I first went to him for lessons I asked him to tell me one thing, give me the one tip that would change the whole way I was playing and make me better. He said there wasn't any one thing he could tell me and I said there must be.

'OK, then,' says Stevie. 'Take eight inches off the length of your clubs.'

'What good will that do me?' I asked.

'It will make it easier to put them in the bin,' he replied.

In other words, don't ask stupid questions.

About a year after I started taking golf lessons, I was able to repay Stevie for all his help in a small way – I got Frankie Vaughan to sing a song on stage especially for Stevie's mother. Frankie was up in Scotland for some shows and we were talking about golf and I was telling him how I was getting on with my lessons from Stevie. Frankie said he would love a game of golf the next day, although he admitted he wasn't very good. I got a spare set of clubs for Frankie and said I would try to get Stevie to come out on the course with us and give him a few pointers as well.

When I phoned Stevie to ask if I could bring Frankie Vaughan for a round of golf with us he thought I was winding him up. But sure enough, the next day, the three of us were out on the course and no harm to Frankie but he was hopeless. However, by the end of the round, Stevie had Frankie hitting the ball reasonably well.

Stevie's mother, Jess, is a great Frankie Vaughan fan and when we heard this, Frankie and I arranged for her to get tickets to a show we were both doing in Greenock. During his spot, Frankie told the audience he had a very good friend who had him playing the best golf of his life and the next song was for his mother who is in the audience.

Frankie said: 'Jess, this is just for you . . .' And immediately launched into, 'Give me the moonlight, give me the gals . . .'

Stevie still talks about the night Frankie Vaughan sang to his mother at Greenock Town Hall.

I've met many lovely people and made some great friends through golf and none more so than when I joined a bunch of golf fanatics and we called ourselves the Glenmuir Gorillas. The Gorillas were started by Malcolm Boyd, who was the managing director of Glenmuir Ltd – the well-known golf and leisurewear company.

My pal Dougie Donnelly knew Malcolm and told me that he wanted me to do some work for him. We met for lunch and hit it off right away. During the lunch, he mentioned they were thinking about taking a party to the 1978 Ryder Cup tournament at Muirfield Village, in Ohio, and would I like to join them. He didn't need to ask me twice and when we met at the airport to fly out to the States, the

Glenmuir Gorillas were born. There was Dougie Donnelly; Malcolm Boyd, known as The Heid because his head is twice the size of anyone else's; George Turnbull, Bill Frame; Jim Thompson, John McKenzie, known as The Colonel because he looked and acted like he was a colonel in the army, Derek Milne, who was known as Captain Chaos because everything he touched went wrong and turned into a disaster and, finally, myself.

As you can see from the nicknames people had, the Glenmuir Gorillas didn't stand on ceremony and no one was allowed to get too big for their boots. We had a great time, helped in no small measure by the fact that Europe won the Ryder Cup that year.

The following year, the Glenmuir Gorillas were down to four-strong – The Colonel, The Heid, Jim Thompson and myself – when we went to the US Masters in Augusta. But what a time we had with Sandy Lyle winning on the 18th green against Mark Calcavecchia. Sandy had hit his first shot into the bunker, but produced a wonder shot out of the bunker, landing the ball ten feet from the pin then a putt for a birdie to win the tournament.

I had played with Sandy at Haggs Castle golf course in Glasgow in a pro-am and I always take the credit for showing him how best to take a bunker shot and get the ball on the green. Aye, I wish!

By the time the next Masters in Augusta came along in 1989 we were back to our full complement and we even had our own 'Glenmuir Gorillas' embroidered badges on our sweaters. Then came the Ryder Cup in Kiawah Island in 1991, which saw another invasion of the Gorillas.

Although Dougie Donnelly and I were both well known for our television appearances, everyone was an equal in the Gorillas and everyone was treated as such by everyone else. Nobody was allowed to be a star because everybody in the Glenmuir Gorillas was a star.

As well as watching the golf we would fit in as many rounds on American courses as we could, getting up at the crack of dawn to have our breakfast in the clubhouse before heading out on the course.

The first time we went to the Masters I was doing the *Evening*

Times column and they arranged for me to have a press pass which got me into all sorts of places. The guys were talking about buying some souvenirs and since I had already got mine, I said I was going into the clubhouse for a coffee.

'No way they're letting you into the clubhouse,' they said.

'Just watch,' I replied.

At the clubhouse door, there was this huge security guy who had been stopping people from getting in all day. I strolled up, showed my press pass and he opened the door for me. I turned round and waved to the boys, who couldn't believe what they were seeing. Inside, there were big circular tables and I sat down at one. The waiter came over: 'What can I get you, sir?'

'I wouldn't mind a coffee and a doughnut,' I replied.

He brought the coffee and doughnut over and I was browsing through some golf magazines that were lying about when I suddenly I was conscious of someone sitting down at the same table. The waiter came back over to the table and I heard him saying, 'What can I get you this morning, Mr Hogan?'

I nearly dropped my coffee cup. I was sitting across the table from golf legend Ben Hogan, who has seen the look on my face and is laughing at me. I managed to blurt out a 'good morning' and Ben Hogan replied, 'Good morning. How are you? Is this your first visit to the Masters?'

I said, 'Yes. It's an incredible experience.'

He was sitting at the table making a few notes, I presume for some kind of broadcast on radio or television and as he got up to leave a few minutes later he said, 'You have a nice day.'

I couldn't wait to get out and tell the rest of the boys I had spoken to Ben Hogan. Of course, I should have known better because they didn't believe me. 'Ben Hogan? Aye, right, Andy. You might have been talking to one of his golf clubs, but there's no way Ben Hogan's been talking to you.'

Scots golfer and Ryder Cup captain Sam Torrance does some promotional work for Glenmuir and on the Gorillas' trip to the Ryder Cup on Kiawah Island I met Sam's father, Bob. Malcolm The Heid, Bob and I walked round the front nine and Bob suggested we watch the back nine on television in the clubhouse. I didn't think there was any chance of us getting into the clubhouse, but when we got to the door it was, 'Hello, Mr Torrance. How are you? Would you and your friends like to come in?'

The three of us were sitting watching the television when suddenly the doors burst open and a posse of guys with no necks in dark suits marched in. Out of the middle of them came a wee guy whose face looked familiar to me.

'I think I know that guy,' I said to Malcolm.

'So you should,' he replied. 'He's only Dan Quayle, the Vice-President of the United States.'

Dan Quayle – who's a really good golfer and plays off four – and his security entourage sat at the next table to us watching the golf on television. But not even I had the bottle to go up to him and say, 'How's it gaun, wee man? Your man Bill's a bit of a lad, eh?'

I've had some marvellous times with the Glenmuir Gorillas and back in Scotland we'd get together every so often to play in pro-ams. Sadly, both Jim Thompson and Bill Frame are dead now.

And talking about pro-ams, for several years I would organise celebrity pro-am tournaments for the Variety Club of Great Britain and I've had some smashing days playing those events. We've also managed to raise tens of thousands of pounds for charity at the same time.

Good friends are a lifeblood and if you haven't any friends you have nothing. You can have all the money in the world, but the only two things that make a happy life are good health and good friends.

Luckily, I've been blessed with some great friends over the years.

POSTSCRIPT

WELL, FOLKS, THAT'S BEEN MY LIFE SO FAR AND THERE'S NOT MUCH I CAN do about it now!

You can't help where you are born and I believe the rest of your life is mapped out for you – only you just don't know it at the time.

A lot of what happens to you in life is about being in the right or wrong place at the right or wrong time. That can determine whether you end up as a millionaire or a pauper, in all senses of the words.

I believe in fate and, thankfully, I have been in the right place at the right time. And, just as importantly, the right people have been there to guide me down the right road when I might be about to head off down a blind alley.

I was lucky to survive the Blitz and I could easily have perished in that bombed-out building in London in 1941. Thank goodness the authorities were able to trace my father in the middle of the African desert so he could return home to take me back to Scotland instead of me being brought up in a children's home.

And what a stroke of good fortune it was that I had a gran like Bella who couldn't have been a better 'mum', giving me the immense riches of love and affection as I grew up into a man.

And what about that bus strike, which was the reason I ended up giving Norma a lift to work for ten weeks? If it wasn't for that, I

255

wouldn't have had the chance to fall in love with the one person who gave me the ladder of my life. Norma helped me climb that ladder and make something of myself at a time when I was going nowhere. How lucky was that?

I've come to realise that, whatever fate throws at you – good or bad – the most important thing is to make the best of it and to work hard at everything that you do.

I hope you have as much good luck as I've had.

Anyway, wait till you hear this – there was a wee guy from Rutherglen who thought he was a bit of a comedian . . .